Strategic
Management
of Human Resources

A Portfolio Approach

George S. Odiorne

Strategic
Management
of Human Resources

Jossey-Bass Publishers
San Francisco • Washington • London • 1984

STRATEGIC MANAGEMENT OF HUMAN RESOURCES
A Portfolio Approach
   by George S. Odiorne

Copyright © 1984 by: Jossey-Bass Inc., Publishers
                        433 California Street
                        San Francisco, California
                                &
                        Jossey-Bass Limited
                        28 Banner Street
                        London EC1Y 8QE

Library of Congress Cataloging in Publication Data

Odiorne, George S.
   Strategic management of human resources

   Bibliography: p. 317
   Includes index.
   1. Personnel management.   I. Title.
HF5549.0'29   1984   658.3   84-47993
ISBN 0-87589-625-1 (alk. paper)

Manufactured in the United States of America

The paper in this book meets the guidelines for
permanence and durability of the Committee on
Production Guidelines for Book Longevity of the
Council on Library Resources.

JACKET DESIGN BY WILLI BAUM

FIRST EDITION
Code 8424

A joint publication in
The Jossey-Bass Management Series
and
The Jossey-Bass Social
and Behavioral Science Series

Consulting Editors
Human Resources

Leonard Nadler
Zeace Nadler
College Park, Maryland

Preface

Traditionally, management has tended to view labor in terms of supply and demand, with employees considered as short-term expenses to be minimized. In *Strategic Management of Human Resources*, I take the view that employees can be considered as assets, value can be placed on them, and they can be managed much as a portfolio of stocks is managed, to maintain or increase their value to the organization. These ideas are based on human capital theory— a relatively new economic concept.

Over the past fifty years or so, personnel work has come to be considered largely a matter of maintenance: tasks that have to be done but that have little impact. Certainly, it is not usually viewed as central to handling one of the most important investments a company can make: its investment in human capital. This book goes beyond the usual techniques of personnel and employee relations, valuable though they may be, to apply the tools of strategic planning to personnel management. It places in the hands of managers at all levels of organizations—including private business and industry, hospitals, government agencies, and educational institutions—a means of evaluating the human assets of the organization and managing them for the mutual benefit of employers and employees.

The distinction between employees as assets and employees as expenses is a major one that can substantially alter an organization's policies toward people in its employ. Some major changes would take place for the better in human resources or employee relations practices if human capital theory were widely applied. Employee obsolescence can be averted, for one. Turnover and low productivity can be reversed. New corporate "stars" can be identified and nurtured and long-term, steady employees can be motivated to sustain high productivity. These effects have all been produced by organizations using the tenets of human capital theory. Advantages also accrue to employees, who benefit from better management and, in turn, become increasingly valuable to the organization.

Human capital theory stems from research in economics begun under the leadership of Theodore Schultz, winner of the Nobel Memorial Prize in Economics in 1979. While the literature on this topic has grown substantially, to date this body of knowledge has not produced applications for personnel and employee relations. That is the purpose of this book: to translate the economic theory of human capital into strategies for managing people in organizations.

The three chapters in Part One constitute a kind of primer of current research in and applications of the economic theory of human capital. The first chapter defines the term and elaborates the concept of *human capital*. It links the idea of "people as assets" to socioeconomic forces, such as demographics, and describes ways of investing in human capital as well as the benefits to be gained by doing so. In Chapter Two the reader is introduced to portfolio theory—the rationale investors and investment analysts use to manage the financial assets under their control. It explains financial terminology and shows how accounting methods can relate to personnel assessment. Chapter Three shows how to apply portfolio analysis to human capital in the same way strategic financial managers analyze an investor's securities or corporate product-and-market plans. It introduces the four basic categories of the human portfolio: stars, problem employees, workhorses, and deadwood.

Part Two deals primarily with employees in the high-performance categories of the portfolio: workhorses and stars. Chapter Four describes the workhorse category, which includes employees who are high performers with limited growth potential. The importance of these employees to corporate health is discussed along with ways of managing people in this group so that motivation and productivity remain high over years of employment. Implications for management development, career planning, and job enrichment are among the topics discussed.

The next four chapters deal with employees in the star category. Stars are people who are highly productive and who have great growth potential. Managed correctly, stars will develop into top managers whose skills, leadership, and flexibility will help ensure the health and success of the organization. Chapter Five discusses ways of discovering potential stars through management and staff analysis and describes characteristics that may help managers identify stars. Chapter Six tells ways stars can advance; for example, through education and individual perseverance and inventiveness. The promise and the pitfalls of mentoring are also discussed.

The next two chapters deal with star development near and at the top of the corporate ladder. Chapter Seven describes ways managers of managers can help prepare stars for the special kinds of tasks high-level managers must be able to handle. Chapter Eight spells out tactics corporate heads use for coping with the stresses that accompany leadership. The significance of the nonfinancial rewards that accrue to leaders is also discussed.

Part Three deals with the two categories of low-performing employees, termed problem employees (high potential but not performing up to it) and deadwood (little or no growth potential and low performance). Chapters Nine and Ten address steps managers can take to prevent employees from slipping into these categories and ways to get them out if they do, for example, by making sure the employee clearly understands the job, providing training and feedback, and using discipline effectively. Chapter Eleven deals with the forces and events that can make whole industries—and the people who lead them—obsolete. Ways individuals and companies can anticipate and avoid obsolescence, or recover from it if it occurs, are described in Chapter Twelve.

Part Four describes practical application of the human portfolio in strategic planning. Various methods of performance appraisal are detailed in Chapter Thirteen. It also discussed setting goals and performance standards, using management by objectives (MBO) and Behaviorally Anchored Rating Scales (BARS). Writing objectives, specifying commitment to objectives, and measuring and using results are all described in Chapter Fourteen. Chapter Fifteen takes a fresh look at the role of the human resources staff in strategic planning for a corporation. A number of ways of making such a department more effective are suggested, and some of the chief obstacles to achieving a strong human resources strategy are discussed. Chapter Sixteen is a case study showing how portfolio analysis can be applied to managing one organization's human capital.

In too many organizations, the personnel department is relegated to relatively low status, and in hard times, staff in that office may well be let go. Certainly most books written for the typical personnel department about employee relations address primarily functionary techniques and procedures. This lack of recognition for the role of human resources administration may reflect general attitudes toward the handling of employees in our economy. This book takes a new look at the relationship between personnel administration and management and a firm's employees. It tells how to plan strategically so that the firm's investment in the people who work for it will pay off—just as other investments are expected to pay off.

A word is necessary about language and the search for gender-free terms. In writing I have striven to avoid sexist language, and three women readers reviewed the text, specifically to help in this regard. Yet there are passages in which I have had to resort to the generic "he" to avoid problems of repetition and clumsy wording. I take this opportunity to state that whenever masculine pronouns are used for succinctness, they are intended to refer to both males and females. This is especially true in the chapter on stars and senior executives, because, as one reader pointed out, there are still lamentably few women at the very top of organizations—a situation that should and will change in the future.

Acknowledgments

Thanks are expressed to the many who reviewed the manuscript in its original form, including Leonard and Zeace Nadler, consulting editors for Jossey-Bass, and Sidney Sufrin of the University of Massachusetts, who reviewed the human capital economics portfolio materials. A brief but important set of personal comments from the late Fritz Machlup, a pioneer and architect of human capital theory, were of enormous value, both in the substance they contain and in the encouragement they convey.

Appreciation is also noted for the firms who have cooperated in my experiments with the portfolio approach in evaluating their managers, as well as to numerous graduate students and faculty in human resources at the University of Massachusetts who read the original manuscript and gave generously of their experience and professional judgments. The limitations of the final result, however, are solely mine.

Appreciation is also extended to Elaine Fydenkevez and Rosemarie Owen, who typed the manuscript, and to my wife, Janet, for her boundless support during the writing.

St. Petersburg, Florida George S. Odiorne
July 1984

Contents

Part II. Managing High-Performing Employees:
Workhorses and Stars

Part III. Managing Poor Performers: Problem Employees
and Deadwood

Part IV. Implementing Portfolio Management Strategies

Contents

The Author

George S. Odiorne is Harold D. Holder Professor of Management at Eckerd College, St. Petersburg, Florida. Prior to this appointment, from 1974 to 1983, he was professor of management and dean of the School of Business Administration at the University of Massachusetts at Amherst. He served as dean of the College of Business and professor of management at the University of Utah from 1969 to 1974. From 1959 to 1969, he was director of the Bureau of Industrial Relations at the University of Michigan. He has taught management and economics at Rutgers University and also New York University. He received his B.S. degree (1948) in economics from Rutgers University and both his M.B.A. degree (1951) in industrial relations and personnel and his Ph.D. degree (1957) in economics from New York University.

Odiorne has extensive experience in personnel management in private industry, notably with General Mills, Inc., American Management Associations, and American Can Company, and he has served as a consultant to other major American corporations. He is on the board of directors of numerous corporations and civic institutions. He is a member of several professional groups, including the American Economic Association, the Academy of Political Science, the American Society for Training and Development, and the American Society for Personnel Administration.

Odiorne's first book, *How Managers Make Things Happen*, appeared in 1965. It has been translated into fifteen languages and has been published in twenty-five hardcover and fifteen paperback editions. Since then, Odiorne has produced seventeen more books and over two hundred articles, all primarily on the topics of strategic management of human resources and management by objectives. Among his recently published books are *Sales Management by Objectives* (1982), *The Change Registers* (1981), and *Personal Effectiveness* (1980). His articles have appeared in *Harper's* and *Nation's Business* as well as in numerous scholarly journals.

Odiorne is the recipient of numerous special distinctions and awards bestowed by professional societies and universities. Most recently, in 1983, he received the James A. Hamilton Award for best management book of the year from the American College of Hospital Administrators.

Strategic
Management
of Human Resources

A Portfolio Approach

Part One

A New Strategy for Managing Human Resources

The purpose of a great society is to make great persons.   —*Lyman Bryson*

1

---✐---

Viewing Employees as Assets: The Economics of Human Capital

It is always growing weather.   —*Pierre van Passen*

For almost a century it was considered bad form for an employer to regard an employee as an asset. Such a designation seemed to categorize the worker as a slave or some kind of domestic animal; it was viewed as patronizing and perhaps demeaning to workers.

Considering the quality of work life in the last century, it may not have been so unfair to make a comparison between factory workers and domestic beasts of burden. Karl Marx certainly used their comparison often in his "commodity theory of labor," in which he said that capitalists treated workers as commodities rather than as human beings who were made for better things. Early labor unionists in this country likewise viewed dimly the idea of workers being treated as chattels, or objects to be bought and sold.

Coyness about treating employees as assets has diminished in this century, especially in the past twenty-five years. For one thing, highly talented people such as engineers, accountants,

3

scientists, and lawyers seldom feel they are oppressed and aren't usually insulted if they are regarded as assets. For another, when highly paid people are treated as assets, they are very willing to discuss the relationship of their value to the return they gain from their skills. As a result of these new attitudes, there has been a rising interest in treating employees as assets, much like machines, patents, goodwill, or other assets of the organization. Both employers and employees have come to accept frank discussion of their economic value.

Personnel and human resources managers who approve this turn of events might well have applauded the selection of Theodore Schultz for the Nobel Prize in Economics in 1979. His concept of investment in human capital, upon which his award was based, is an important contribution to economics. In his 1961 presidential address to the American Economic Association, Schultz said:

"Although it is obvious that people acquire useful skills and knowledge, it is not obvious that these skills and knowledge are a form of capital, that this capital is a part of a deliberate investment that has grown in Western societies at a faster rate than conventional (nonhuman) capital, and that its growth may well be the most distinctive feature of the economic system."

Since Schultz presented his theory there have been numerous writings emphasizing investment in human capital as a major concept in economics. Still, for the most part it has remained a theory and has made little impact on personnel and human resources programs. In the eighties, however, this investment management concept may grow into one of the most important breakthroughs in personnel administration since 1904, when Hugo Munsterberg set forth the rudiments of using scientific personality assessment in employment decisions.

Conventional wisdom in management as well as in economics has viewed the employee as one of the three factors of production: "land, labor, and capital." In such a paradigm, labor is an expense item, and its contribution to value-added lies in its cost being minimized. This concept has produced the effect of the employee being treated as an *expense* item on the profit and loss statement. The new human capital theory, on the other hand, sees the employee as an asset that should be valued in much the same way that other assets—such as factories, computers, or inventories—are valued. Far from being mere word chopping, this new paradigm has enormous implications for the human use of human beings. It also has major implications for the professional field of personnel and employee relations, because the treatment of human assets and their valuation, acquisition, and disposal call for new rules and strategies.

The Definition of Human Capital

The definition of human capital is not universally agreed upon. Different people use the term in different ways to gain certain advantage or espouse particular interests. However, from a review of current literature in the economics of human capital we can draw some conclusions about the definition of human capital and the way its value is established. Some of these conclusions are presented in Figure 1.

A summary definition might read as follows: *Human capital economics is a system of inputs, processes, outputs, and adjustments which individuals, firms, government agencies, institutions, and societies make toward the increase of potential and performance which the individual human or humans as groups may contribute to society, the economy, specific employers, or themselves.*

1. The *inputs* are the system's raw material: people who are born, immigrate, die, or emigrate. This study is the study of demographics or population.
2. *Processes* include, but are not limited to, education and training at all levels. They might also include factors in informal learning, such as communication skills, learning ability, knowledge of one's environment, and ability to adapt to change and to obstacles.
3. *Outputs* may be measured in employment at various levels in all sorts of fields. Employment produces earnings in the form of wages or other rewards desired by the individual. Output might also be expressed as returns to the investor or in social effects in groups such as a government, a society, a community, or a firm.

Figure 1. Human Capital—A Society's Investment in Itself.

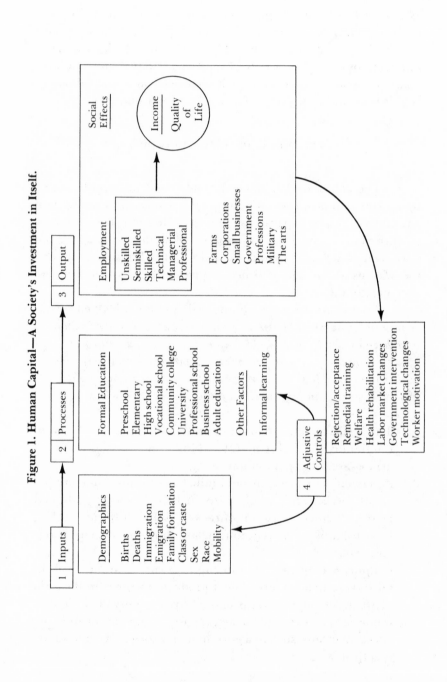

Individuals may have various levels of potential contribution because of past education, experience, or personal qualities. Their actual performance may fulfill all of their potentials or only a very few. The estimation of value-added in the relationship of human input to output is an important element in human capital theory.

4. The final element of the system of human capital is the *adjustive controls* that operate to make the system responsive to change and to maintain its equilibrium. This adjustment is needed because people are sometimes rejected by schools, employers, or society due to personal qualities that apparently limit their ability to work at productive tasks. They may need to be retrained or assisted in some other way. Those who are incapable of such retraining may be supported by welfare programs. If the cause of their rejection is health related, rehabilitation may be indicated. Some people find themselves outside the mainstream of the working world because of labor market changes or technological changes. Such changes may call for some kind of government intervention. Finally, a low level of worker motivation may produce a need for adjustment in the system of human capital by changing managerial practices in personnel and employee relations.

In a way, this book is simply a more detailed explanation of the elements of the system pictured in Figure 1. One great advantage of the systems approach to human capital is that it requires us to start at the beginning, proceed to the middle, go on to the end, make adjustments, and then start over.

The place to begin in understanding human capital is a definition of the system's objectives. Such a definition attempts to relate people in their economic dimension to those personnel and employee relations programs and strategies of employers that are important to their treatment as human beings. The result should be personnel and employee relations systems and practices that not only are more logical but that also help to produce what Norbert Wiener called "The human use of human beings."

The Dual Goals of Human Capital Theory. The concept of "human capital" requires us to tie together two very different ideas. On the one hand, the *human* is the highest level of animal, created some say in God's image, endowed with special qualities of dignity and a unique personality. On the other hand, *capital* is a term from the mundane world of economics, which speaks often in a detached way of value as if it were to be equated with price. It is said that "the language of business is accounting," and the human capital theory purports to define the complex organism called the human in terms of accounting.

Accounting, it has been noted, is shaped around six basic concepts arranged in two groups. *The profit and loss statement* (P&L) contains three of the concepts: income, expenses, and profit-or-loss. The *balance sheet* is a picture of three other concepts: assets, liabilities, and the net worth at the particular instant in time at which these three indicators are measured and recorded. "Human capital" deals with balance sheet estimates of the value or worth of human beings at one instant in time (at year's end, typically).

Can Employees Really Be Treated as Assets? Early efforts to apply accounting principles to human resources in the form of profit and loss or balance sheets seemed to be hung up on certain kinds of professional accounting protocol. Such studies usually tended to focus on the profit and loss aspects of the accounting field. Some firms even prepared parallel P&L statements showing the effects of expenditures in acquisition, training, and development of human resources as being partly expense items and partly investments that should be carried on the asset side of the balance sheet.

Many professors at leading business schools have written extensively and imaginatively on the subject of human resources accounting, including Eric Flamholz who, in 1974, authored a text on the early state of the art; and William Pyle and Lee Brummet as well as Rensis Likert who, in 1972, proposed that measurement of people's attitudes and opinions should be a concrete part of an organization's human resource accounting.

The idea of human resources accounting has not been without its critics, however. Humanists are often shocked by the soullessness of accounting treatments of human beings. At a technical level there are other doubters. Many traditional accountants have noted that since slavery ended, one human cannot acquire title to another;

thus, the ownership of the asset is in doubt. Without ownership and legitimate title in hand, no asset exists. This means that the ordinary conventions of accounting do not always readily accept the treatment of human beings as real assets, except perhaps under the heading of "goodwill." Others have noted that the basis for valuation of human assets is rather soft and that the casting of certain personnel management expenses into the balance sheet is arbitrary and capricious, even when done consistently from case to case.

With due regard to these reservations, let's try to explore systematically the way this portfolio management of humans as assets would look, in the same way an investor views a portfolio of stocks. We begin with step one, the inputs into the system—human beings. This leads us to a study of population, or demographics.

Demographics as the Source of Human Capital

A few years back a large steel company ran a series of "institutional ads" aimed at persuading the readers of certain literary and cultural magazines of the virtues of the free enterprise system. One ad, in bold headlines, made the assertion that "only corporations create wealth; governments and the rest of society consume that wealth."

One reader of the ads, responding to a request for comments, wrote back: "Your claim is a trifle exaggerated. It is not corporations alone that create wealth, even though it is admitted that they often add value to that which they process and sell. God, in the beginning, created wealth and value. The rest of us do our bit to add to value, and some of us consume it."

This might be a suitable theme to bear in mind when we are dealing with human capital, for although the corporation or other employer may handle people as assets, it certainly didn't create them. A number of noncorporate social, cultural, and political influences went into the years of life that transpired for the employee before he or she was hired. Each human thus is valuable from the beginning. The first stage in understanding the human capital system lies in understanding some major forces and principles at work in demographics (population). The importance of demographics in human capital planning and policy cannot be overestimated. It shapes the processes and outputs that follow, including the labor markets, the government, the arts, and ultimately the quality of life. What must we know about demographics if we are to deal intelligently with the policy and strategies of human resources in the world of work?

Effects of Population Growth. In the lobby of the U.S. Department of Commerce Building in Washington, D.C. is a large clock that shows the total population of the United States minute by minute. Each second shows the net addition to the population, now over 230 million. Rapid growth of the population of the world for the past 300 years is the overriding fact that governs all other demographic considerations. World population has grown from 545 million in the year 1650 to more than 6 billion by 1977, and it seems likely to many that population will grow steadily through the middle of the next century. An important cause of this rapid growth was the Industrial Revolution, which had the effect of lowering death rates through provision of more food, better housing, better public health, modern medicine, and similar consequences of higher material income. Large formations of capital, stable money systems, and advances in technology and agriculture have all added to the length of life. Since birth rates remained high in many parts of the world, the result has been a steady rise in the number of people.

Cultural Effects on Birth and Death Rates. The rates of population growth differ as societies pass from agrarian to industrial and ultimately to postindustrial stages. (See Table 1.) When a society moves from a peasant or agrarian stage to an industrial stage, as is occurring in China, India, Brazil, and many other Third World nations today, population explodes during the transition. Once the nation has been fully industrialized, birth rates decline, while death rates remain low. The effect is the slower population growth rates found in European and American societies today. As these nations emerge into a postindustrial stage, the birth rate is likely to settle to a lower rate yet, and population may stabilize or even decline to a zero growth level. Demographic experts tend to agree that this situation exists in some Western nations today and may become common in the next two centuries.

Table 1. The Effect of Stages of Economic Growth on Population Size
and Growth Rates.

	Stages of Economic Growth			
	Agrarian	Transition	Industrial	Postindustrial
Birth rate	High	High	Moderate	Low
Death rate	High	Low	Low	Low
Effect on population size	Stable or falling	Explosive growth	Slow growth	Stable or zero growth

These population differences create tensions between societies
in different stages of development. They also have dire and
immediate effects upon the labor market, for emigration is often
a response to overpopulation. People in developing nations emigrate
to developed lands with higher standards of living, affecting internal
labor markets in both lands.

For example, in the United States and Canada, population
has recently leveled off to a moderate growth rate. At the same
time, in Mexico the population exploded as that nation emerged
from agrarianism and industrialization spread. This led to a
northward movement of population so that in the eighties the rising
level of undocumented aliens within our borders has become a
serious public concern. Thus immigration/emigration, as well as
births and deaths, affects the number of students enrolled in schools
and the number of employees who enter the work force. All these
demographic factors have an overpowering impact on human
capital considerations.

Population and Human Resources in America. In the United
States we have grown from four million inhabitants in 1790 to
180 million in 1960 and 230 million or more today. Much of the
growth prior to 1860 was due to immigration from Europe. Today,
immigration as well as the birth rate have declined. However, other
population influences affect education, the world of work, and
ultimately the quality of life.

The movements of the American people constitute one such
influence. In 1860 only 14 percent of the population lived west
of the Mississippi. Migration westward increased this figure to 37
percent by 1940. During the twenties, agricultural invention and

the rise of industrial jobs in northwestern cities produced a great migration of blacks northward and to the cities. During the seventies there was a steady migration out of the north and industrial east to the south and southwest, toward the "sun belt" states. Many eastern states, such as Massachusetts, had zero population growth during the seventies, and some, such as Maine and Rhode Island, had negative population growth during the same period. The annexation of Hawaii and Alaska accelerated the westward movement even more. Increased immigration from Latin America and the Caribbean area was also mainly to the sun belt states.

Even greater was the urbanization of America as the flight from the farm during this century was completed. Whereas in 1900, 40 percent of Americans lived on farms, by 1968 fewer than 5 percent did so, and the number was declining. Three quarters of a million people left farms each year during the 1960s as small farms were consolidated into larger ones to achieve higher productivity and technological improvements made farm labor less necessary.

Qualitative factors in demographics also produce important impacts on education and employment. Differences in race make a difference, for example, because the relations between the races, discrimination of majorities against minorities, and the cultural coherence of subgroups affect education, living standards, and even the rate of population growth. When discrimination between races and ethnic groups is strong, it lowers the income, housing standards, and stability of family life for those discriminated against. This in turn creates demands for public services and support, rearranges political power, and has numerous other effects on the overall quality of life.

Differences in life span are also an important factor. The average life span is different for different sexes and races. Women live an average of nine years longer than men in our society, which means that through the mechanisms of inheritance, the property of the nation tends to move more and more into the hands of women. Also, morbidity and mortality rates are higher among minorities, which has a bearing on the demand for health services, welfare, aid to dependent children and the like.

As more and more women have moved into the ranks of the employed, the upbringing of children has also changed. This has important effects on education and on family life and values. Changes in values ultimately affect laws and government.

The Future of America's Population. Although forecasts of population are risky, it seems safe to say that America's population will continue to grow during the rest of the century. Predictions of the rate of that growth vary, depending on assumptions about fertility. (See Table 2.) The estimates made in 1965 ranged from a high of 362 million people predicted for the year 2000 down to a low of 291 million. So far, the prediction that produced the lowest estimate (which also predicted a population of 206 million for 1970 and 233 million for 1980) seems to have been the most accurate one.

Even assuming this lower level of growth, what does the expected increase in population suggest for education and the employer of human capital during the remaining decades of this century? Here are some of the most likely predictions.

- Almost 70 million new people will be in the population by the year 2000. They will require schools, teachers, roads, food, fuel, fiber, jobs, recreation, and governmental services.
- Although large masses of unoccupied land remain in America, most people will cluster in urban areas. New urban areas will rise and old ones will expand, in the west and south especially. As pressures upon resources rise, we will see movement to areas where less fuel-consuming lifestyles are possible.

Table 2. Predictions of the Population of the United States 1970–2000 A.D. Using Four Assumptions (in Millions).

	Production Level (Fertility Estimates)			
	A	*B*	*C*	*D*
1970	211	209	208	206
1980	252	245	236	233
1990	301	288	271	261
2000	362	338	309	291

Source: Statistical abstract of the United States, Washington, D.C., U.S. Government Printing Office, 1965.

- New systems of transportation, communication, and infra-
  structure will be required. The problem of environmental
  pollution and the social pressures that come with crowding will
  grow.
- New businesses and industries will emerge especially in the area
  of services.
- Population growth will not occur equally among all groups,
  for the lower income groups have the highest fertility rates.
  The proportion of Hispanics and blacks in the population is
  likely to increase, with this effect slowly dampening as these
  groups are integrated into the economy and join the middle
  class. Once in the middle class, a population's birth rate tends
  to decline.

Whatever changes occur in the American population,
demographics will remain a vital factor in considerations of human
capital.

The Formal Education System and Human Capital

In 1983 a national commission studying education excellence
reported the results of a major study of public and private education
in America and concluded that we are on a course leading to
mediocrity. Its recommendations called for a return to basic subjects,
more money for teaching, longer school days, and more school days
each year. President Reagan, long an advocate of a return to older
styles of education, called for the merit rating of teachers and the
recognition of superior teachers.

For many, this approach smacked of an attempt to return
to a time when the population was smaller, more dominated by
a white majority, and more likely to reside on farms or in small
towns. For such observers, it seemed regressive and perhaps harmful
to consider that the education of the 1920s could be suitable for
the year 2000. For one thing, there will be more people in the future,
living in new locations, more highly educated, with higher
expectations of education itself. Formal education today has a wider
range and a higher possible level of academic attainment than in
the past. The idea of adult education, which has grown rapidly

in popularity during the past decade, presumes that the upper limit of education is open ended and that learning is a lifelong experience.

Formal education is the major investment in human capital made by the society in itself. It has been customary to make a fairly direct connection between a person's level and kind of education and his or her ultimate employment status. People with high school or less education are most likely to settle into semiskilled or unskilled work. Graduates of vocational community colleges seem to head mainly into technical work such as electronics, automobile service, and paraprofessional jobs, or become skilled tradespeople, such as carpenters, electricians, and machinists. The expectation of people entering professional schools, on the other hand, is that they will occupy a high standing in society both socially and economically, becoming lawyers, doctors, dentists, architects, or consulting engineers. Business and management schools have clearly defined positions in mind for their graduates, including top management for MBAs from the best schools and other managerial positions for lesser degrees or minor schools. The supply of future bankers and accountants usually comes from this source as well. The newest development in education is the rapid growth in public and private adult education, which erupted strongly during the seventies. Here the objective is to enrich the life of the population through continued education in the arts or literature or to upgrade the skills of employees and assist them in overcoming occupational obsolescence.

Connections between education and the world of employment tend to constitute a system of economic caste, class, and cultural structure that is based upon the amount and quality of investment that a society makes in its human capital and that individuals make in themselves. One of the basic tenets of this system is that the individual personally must make the decision about the level of investment that will be made in his or her own human capital. Education is not mandatory beyond age 16 at most.

Connections between education and jobs do not always hold true, however. Distortions in supply and demand occur in the flow from school to job. The *New York Times* for August 15, 1983, for example, reported a surplus of doctors in New York City and other major population centers, growing out of a heavy enrollment in medical schools during the seventies. Many specialists failed to find appointments in hospitals or were forced to move into lower paying and less challenging kinds of practice. The excessive number of lawyers being graduated has been noted as a matter of social concern as well. When enrollment in the lower grades of school fell sharply in the seventies and pay for teachers remained low, many college students abandoned education as a major in favor of business or engineering, where more and better paying jobs appeared to await them.

Payoff from Investment in Education. Theodore Schultz (1981), as an agricultural economist, based much of his human capital theory upon his work in that field. He proposed that the growth of productivity in agriculture, especially in America, was founded on a steady infusion of new capital into agricultural human resources development. In 1864 the Morrill Act provided for land grants to each of the states to be applied to giving a college education in the "agricultural and mechanic arts" to young people. These universities were known first as the land-grant colleges, later the "ag schools," and finally as the state universities. Schultz's theory demonstrated that this "investment in human capital" produced a steady increase in productivity on the American farm. While admittedly America's fertile land and ample water, political freedom, and growing technology all helped, Schultz maintained that it was the steady investment in people and their education that produced the miracle of productivity that characterizes American agriculture.

Today less than 2.5 million full-time farmers provide food, feed, fiber, and part of the fuel for over 230 million American people. They also sell their product widely abroad. Indeed, it seems that the problem of the American farm today is not low productivity but a productivity so enormous that it generates surpluses.

In recent years, when American economists and management experts looked toward Japan for the secret to that nation's industrial productivity, especially in automobiles and steel, they often fastened upon esoteric explanations for Japanese success. Lifetime employment, cohesive group behavior, and a host of other Japanese practices were proposed as the reasons why Japanese automobiles and steel did so well in the markets of the world. Yet, at the same time, American agriculture was more than seven times as productive per worker as Japanese agriculture. This caused some to wonder why American industry was so unaware of the miracle of productivity that lay in its own countryside.

Schultz (1981) did not propose that there was a simple, direct input-output relationship between investment in education and productivity of human capital. However, there is, he said, a vast potential for increased world agricultural production. Enlightened government policy is needed to aid this development. Modernization of our productive capacity must include an all-inclusive definition of capital, the absence of economic disequilibria, entrepreneurial ability, and an increase of economic knowledge. At the heart of this revolution is investment in human capital. Reconciling of social and cultural values with economic values must be done in a way that is attuned to this investment.

Driven by the excitement of a new concept that invaded traditional economic and accounting theories, numerous researchers explored various facets of Schultz's idea. Some measured the payback from investing in higher education. Others explored the economic poverty of the south from the perspective of the human capital concept. Still others dealt with the effects of human capital ideas upon the economic status of blacks and women in the work force.

During the sixties and seventies an explosion of community colleges across America led some institutional researchers to develop justifications for state and local community college expansion with specialized applications of human capital theories. Others studied statistically the personal income levels of college graduates compared with people who had not graduated from college, demonstrating that the human capital theory worked in practice.

In tangible social and individual instances, human capital pays a return which exceeds investment in other forms of capital. G. A. Moore's (1978) study showed that the State University of New York had a "redistributional" effect on lower and middle income families by providing widespread education to the young from such families. Moore's findings suggested that widespread education at the college and university levels could make de Tocqueville's image of democracy in America come true. The child of the workman, the butcher, the mechanic, the bartender or the taxi driver could become a lawyer, doctor, engineer or tycoon through the state's investment in human capital. Because investment in education is based upon performance and intelligence, it could create a meritocracy of talent rather than either egalitarianism or an elitism in which only the children of the rich or the middle class would be able to afford the education that would provide access to the richer rewards of the society. Furthermore, S. T. Mennemeyer (1978), after studying the incomes of physicians, lawyers, and dentists, concluded that the higher the level of education, the greater the return on investment. Numerous studies demonstrating the levelling effect of equal educational opportunity upon income distribution followed. Makin and Psacharopoulos (1976) concluded that not only did human capital growth have a favorable economic effect; it was also a socially profitable investment. The theory of human capital did not suggest that such investment was permanent and unmoving like a mountain. Rather, it depreciates like other capital assets. Puett and Roman (1976) suggested, in corroboration of Schultz, that educational needs, technological factors, and human resource development also have a component of obsolescence that must be taken into account for true balance sheet changes in human capital. Valuation must include some kind of actuarial assessment—a human audit—as well as a listing of the benefits of human resources development. There is also a need to include a human component in defining "wealth," suggested Richard (1975), adding that the individual must assume personal responsibility for protecting his or her own skills as personal wealth.

Not just any education, and not just any job training, will produce high return on human capital, wrote Dittman, Juris, and Revsine (1976). There are possible unrecorded human assets, they noted, due to employers manipulating technology, wages, and job mobility of employees. Thus, the firm that operates an isolated mill, pays lower than average wages, and trains people only for specific tasks related to their own technology might in fact be hiding unrecorded human assets. This tends to verify the findings of Welch (1975) that not all skills are equally valuable in making up human capital and estimating its returns. Two qualities, Dittman and coauthors noted, seem to affect the distribution of wealth and life cycle earnings; that is, earnings at various stages of one's career. Those two qualities are "durability and malleability." Permanent skills, or those that are readily adapted to new technologies, new firms, or new jobs, have the greatest capital asset value to the holder. Equal amounts of time and money might be spent by two students, one learning computer programming and the other blacksmithing. The equal investment would not produce equal value in human capital, however, because of the limited durability and limited application for blacksmithing.

The social class from which you come also has an effect upon how much value you accumulate in human capital, a report by World Bank (1977) concluded. Based on a Brazilian study, it found that upper-class youth not only had better educational opportunities but also had a higher rate of return on education than did children of lower-class groups. This was due in part to the quality of the education and was further affected by the increased opportunity for children of the upper class to obtain high-paying jobs. This means that the measurement of return to education includes a great deal more than a simple ratio of inputs into education to outputs in income; it must include social factors as well.

Schultz's original thesis was agriculture based and largely historical. A more current picture of the way investment in human capital actually works was presented by Kocher and Fleisher (1979). They described rural development in modern Tanzania, where 90 percent of the population is rural. They found that many elements in addition to education affected economic growth. These elements included social stratification, land tenure, agricultural policy and planning, the extent to which people lived in villages, health and nutrition, income distribution, labor supply, the role of women in production, mechanization and innovation, and marketing and price policies. While these elements are not all independent variables—many emerge from education and training—all have an impact upon the return to education in human capital growth.

The measurement of investment in human capital is also blurred by the extensive migration of labor from one nation to another, according to Newland (1979). Some 20 million workers now live in countries other than their homeland in order to find better job opportunities. The flow of southern Europeans to Germany since 1945, of Mexicans to the United States, of Filipinos to the Middle East, and similar migrations make it difficult to measure the true return on education and to distinguish it from the training offered new workers by foreign employers. The highly educated professional in Pakistan or India, for example, might be unable to find work at a professional level at home and might be forced to take lower-level work elsewhere. This constitutes a loss of human capital to the investing nation. Such analysis might also work between regions within a nation, for instance when physicians trained in one state move to another where greater opportunity to practice exists. This represents a transfer payment of human capital from one economy to another.

Federal spending programs in the United States during the sixties and seventies, which aimed at building human capital through health, education, and manpower development programs, seemed to have a strong urban bias, reported Deavers and Brown (1982). The changing face of rural America, including diversity and isolation, made conventional measures of human capital more difficult to apply there.

Whether in the city or the country, it takes a strong economy to exploit the full value of human capital. Thus reported the Council of Economic Advisors to the President (1980). Concerned with full use of the nation's human capital, the council noted that slower birth rates change the age of the population and might also change the use of human capital. With an older work force emerging, longer work life may depress opportunities for some highly educated young people. The council also suggested that many federal entitlement programs in human services were justified on the basis of human capital theory rather than on motives of charity or compassion.

Community Colleges as Investments in Human Capital. Economic theorists, such as the council, were quite restrained in approaching the concept of human capital, compared to educators, who were enthusiastic about it. It provided educators with a whole new set of arguments and a respectable theory to support the ever-increasing expenditures for higher education. This was particularly true for community colleges. Community colleges are two-year colleges with lower admission standards than most four-year institutions and with strongly technical and vocational curricula. By 1978, when overall expenditures for higher education were beginning to decline, public budgets for community colleges were still rising. A host of studies drew upon the idea of human capital to demonstrate statistically that investment in community colleges by state and local governments had a high yield. As one study put it, "On the average, community college students will receive almost a 27 percent return on their investment in higher education during their lifetime" (Linthicum, 1979). Other studies aimed at legislatures and voters showed specific returns to individual students for investment in community college education that were far in excess of money market returns on investment. Similar studies reported equally great returns for public expenditures on community colleges. In what was cited as an apparent direct verification of the human capital theory, Jackson (1981) reported that in Washington state, for every dollar paid by the state into the general community college expense budget, the state received back a return of $1.78 (or 178 percent) in the form of "personal disposable income." Similar results were reported in New York, Virginia, Maryland (Bowman and others, 1978), and other states and localities. Indeed, it seemed that not only was the human capital theory right, but it was possible to use it to empirically verify immediate gains.

Social Impact of Education as Investment in Human Capital. Not only was the general idea of education as investment in human capital worthwhile, but specific instances were reported in research showing how the absence of education could have deleterious effects upon the people so short-changed. Huffman (1981) reported that southern black farmers, who were denied both educational opportunity and the free advice of county agents on how to farm, were less productive than white farmers, who had access to both formal college training and extension teaching. This, he concluded, was driving blacks from farming in the south. Bellante's (1978) studies showed further outmigration of blacks northward and into cities due to lower levels of education and hence farm productivity.

Furthermore, investment in human capital was found to have an important impact on the family as an institution. Catsiapis and Robinson (1981), in their theory of the family, declared that it was investment in human capital in the child that produced inter-generational upward mobility. In other words, families who educated their children provided them with an endowment of human capital that was paid back to the next generation in the form of increased upward mobility. Nitzan and Paroush (1980) were even more sweeping in their analysis of the impact of human capital. To the extent that informed people make better decisions as citizens, they said, investment in human capital improves the quality of majority rule. Bowles and Gintis (1975) indicated somewhat less enthusiasm for human capital theory, however. Stating a Marxian viewpoint, they noted that human capital theory generally leaves out social relations and the theory of reproduction of the capitalist class structure.

Investment in human capital was seen by some as a vehicle for easing the effects of past racial discrimination. It has been pointed out that managers in general advance their careers by building up human capital and concluded that black professionals and managers in particular should concentrate on building up their stock of human capital in terms of technical mastery and managerial ability in order to advance. Colberg (1975–76) went further, explaining that both race differences and age differences in income cause subsequent envy by the lower-income groups in terms of differences in the stock of human capital each group amassed. Similar adverse effects of lower education on Chicanos and blacks were reported in a series of surveys made by Adams (1977) in Georgia, Louisiana, Texas, and Mississippi. Adams connected the absence of human capital investments with low productivity, discrimination, poor health and outmigration among minority populations. A more affirmative note on the effect of investment in human capital by racial minorities was sounded by Young (1977). He noted that Asian-Americans, who traditionally have invested more heavily in education than other minorities, have incomes that exceed not only those of other minorities but those of the white majority as well.

The idea that having lots of human capital was good, and that having less of it was bad or produced bad economic and social consequences, was further supported by studies on the economic and social status of women. Low expectation of continuous employment may influence the decision of many women to invest in practical kinds of learning experiences rather than more formal education. This, reported Sandell and Shapiro (1980), produced a kind of self-fulfilling prophecy. Based upon interviews with young women between fourteen and twenty-four years of age, the study found that the women's lower educational expectations led to their being ill equipped to share fully in the fruits of the economy and enjoy the social status that attends upon full participation. Thus, it seems, human capital theory can explain women's lower status as well. For married women, who are more apt to work part-time jobs than males, the effect was similar, as reported Jones and Long (1979). The ways women and men choose college majors can have an impact upon the human capital accumulation for each. So stated Polachek (1978), further supporting the idea that sex differences in human capital investment produce sex differences in the labor market. Women traditionally have been channelled into majors in college that in turn channelled them into traditional women's labor markets. Chiplin and Sloan (1974) had earlier made the same point more strongly: In order for sexual equality to exist in the labor market, not only must equal pay for equal work be guaranteed, but women must also invest in themselves as human capital. Rather than focusing first on income and earnings, which are effects, government policies and programs aimed at helping women and minorities improve their social status should link together occupational affiliation, human capital formation, and wage rates, wrote Oaxaca (1978).

Treating Education Budgets as Human Capital Creation. The use of human capital theory to prove that a college education is a sound public investment became commonplace during the late seventies. During that time, population figures made it clear that the boom days for education were waning. Children born during the baby boom ending in the early sixties went through the school system, leaving behind a vacuum of empty classrooms, surplus school buildings, and redundant teachers and administrators. This vacant classroom phenomenon struck first in the elementary schools in the late sixties, then progressed to the high schools and finally to the colleges and universities by the early eighties. As the visible bulge passed inexorably through the educational system like a pig eaten by a python, hard-pressed local taxpayers began to urge their elected officials to cut back on expenditures for buildings, classrooms, and teachers. The educational establishment, dismayed at the prospect of reduced budgets, responded with a barrage of studies and political actions designed to stem the decline.

Traditional lobbying and public relations efforts were mounted, with bumper stickers suggesting "If you think education is expensive, try ignorance" and similar persuasive messages. The battle was clearly against the tide, however, and school budgets dropped as the clientele dried up. It was during this period that extensive writing and research demonstrating the value of "investment in human capital" began to flow forth. For many, "human capital investment" was intended to mean "bigger budgets for education."

In an article apparently aimed at parents, Johnson (1978) found that in instances where wages and loans were not available, subsidies from "patrons" such as parents encouraged students to remain in school. The larger the allowance, the longer the student stayed in school. In a more direct linkage of time in school to return, Cooper and Bruno (1975) focused on the rising number of high-technology firms and the reasons for their success. They concluded that such firms are characterized by high survival rates that can be attributed to the relatively advanced levels of education, coupled with managerial experience, of the founders. The industrial renewal of greater Boston, for example, is explained by the spinoff of newly formed high-technology firms from research programs in universities in the region. These firms were founded by university-based scientists and engineers with advanced degrees who turned scientific concepts into going concerns.

For most researchers, human capital was considered a product of schooling, more was better, and human capital investment meant high budgets for education. If the number of students declined, no matter. Keep increasing expenditures, for an increase per student was as good an investment as an overall increase. In one remarkable case, that of New York City, the school board and the union requested a 49 percent increase in budget despite a 15 percent decline in enrollments. Expenditures at both school and college levels are important determinants of earnings, wrote Wachtel (1976), and the skills gained at all levels have a lasting effect upon productivity.

Few researchers found contrary evidence, although one of those, Freeman (1977), found that there had been a sharp drop in the economic rewards to college education, affecting mostly young males. But Witmer (1978) denied that the "Golden Age of higher

education had come to an abrupt end" and found little evidence
to support Freeman. Agnello and Hunt (1976) advanced a more
realistic solution to the problem of fewer students in their suggestion
that part-time evening business education paid off in increased
earnings, especially if taken at a young age. Such a proposal
presented continuing adult education as a fertile field for increased
investment in human capital. The use of models to show favorable
net cash flow to community college students, especially commuters,
was presented by Bowman (1978) as evidence of a fast return on
human capital invested in Maryland community colleges. Taxpayers
actually receive a return that is double the return to the individual
student, reported Kastner (1977), with the payoff to taxpayers for
investments in community colleges running over 12 percent. The
National Academy of Education (1980) has suggested that human
capital formation goes beyond calculations based on traditional
education; we should think of all forms of education as human
capital.

Despite the faith that higher budgets would pay off, not
everyone accepted this one-to-one correlation of budget to returns.
Daymont (1980) admonished educators to consider why blacks and
whites—and why men and women of equal education—received
different levels of pay in the labor market. The cost content of
education might be affected by the in-house practices of schools
and colleges in regard to teaching and administration, said McKenzie
(1979). Among the practices that could affect output were student
preferences, professor preferences, the relationship of teaching to
learning, the effects of grade inflation, faculty evaluation and pay
methods, the internal governance of universities, intercollegiate
sports, and the impact of cheating, McKenzie proposed. The return
on investment might also be affected, Fulton and others (1980)
suggested, by the quality of manpower planning being done for
college-educated people. Studies in three Eastern European nations
and three Western nations found that planning to produce
convergence of supply and demand was possible as part of
educational planning. Without such planning, surpluses or
shortages of holders of specific degrees could easily occur. People
who became alienated from their own society because of
overeducation were described by Johnson (1981), based on a study

of higher education in Jamaica. When faced with such a situation, overeducated people usually try to leave home and move to places where their education may be put to better use.

Unemployment was pointed out by King (1980) as a further limiting condition upon returns to investment in schooling. King noted that unemployment and business cycles affect human capital returns greatly. Shortages of a skill enhance the returns, while surpluses reduce it. For business school graduates there is another factor that affects starting salaries, reported Wacker and Teas (1979). Human capital theory must be matched by a "screening hypothesis" that affects decisions concerning who shall be hired and at what rates, the authors state. The authors are referring to the practice of screening out some qualified graduates on the basis of race, sex, national origin, or the prestige of the schools they attended.

The investment per student should not be considered as the same for each grade or extent of attainment, reported Ritzen and Winkler (1979). The investment is higher for graduate-level work than for undergraduate work, for example. Generally, the higher the level, the higher the educational costs. This was borne out by the findings of Mennemeyer (1978) for investment in medical education, which costs more than any other education and also pays the greatest return. This study concurred with the report by Makin and Psacharopoulos (1976), which reported a positive relationship between the rate of return and the number of years of schooling. Both the amount of education and the quality of education have a bearing upon the return as well, reported Link and Ratledge (1975), using data from young white and black males for evidence. Faced with drastic cuts by the Thatcher government in England, Jackson (1981) decried budget cuts for education by the conservative government there as being contrary to human capital theory.

An Uneasy Look at Education's Payoff. Von Recum (1981) reported from West Germany that in affluent societies the effects of investment in human capital tend to be blurred, and such investment is more like a consumer good than an investment in a fixed asset. This same division of investment into "working capital" and "fixed investment" in human capital was suggested by Odiorne (1969) for the division of expenditures made by corporations for training of managers. Some expenditures, such as product knowledge training for salespersons, should have a payback during the immediate fiscal year in which they occur. Expenditures for other kinds of training, such as the cost of sending executives to university executive development programs in the hope that some of those trained will be ready for senior executive positions a decade ahead, will not pay off for many years. The latter, with no direct or immediate return, is an investment of human capital, whereas the former resembles Von Recum's consumer good.

Despite many educators' claims, research showed that it was not schooling alone or even primarily that constituted investments in human capital. Griffin (1977) reported that a longitudinal study of young adult men begun in 1955, with a followup in 1970, indicated that life experience of people entering the labor market right out of high school contrasted with that of people who continued formal education showed a significant portion of the gain came from suitable job experience. Griffin also found that work experience acquired during formal education—"working one's way through" with part-time jobs—counts for little in human capital value. An even more skeptical report about the effects of college on earnings and return to school budgets was produced by Griliches and Freeman (1977). Working from data in a longitudinal study, produced as the so-called "Parnes Tapes," they concluded that college training may no longer be as sound an investment as it was in the past. Rather, the role of on-the-job training seems to be more significant than previously thought. They noted further than neither family background nor measured ability accounts for the major portion of the variance in economic success of individuals. The labor market itself has an impact on what majors students choose and how long people stay in school, and this relationship in turn has a bearing on how human capital accumulates from education, reported Dresch and Waldenberg (1978).

Reporting on a study of the national education system in Brazil, Bills and others (1978) found a different outcome of educational growth. Their "Elite-Mass" theory runs contrary to the industrial model, under which education increases opportunity. Bills and his coworkers found that education and regional or family backgrounds (that is, social classes) were not significantly altered by the national educational system. The national system affected the polarized social structure of elite and masses less than some human capital theorists would propose. Differences in earnings are more likely to be based on market and institutional forces than on differences in education alone. Fogel's (1979) studies revealed that managers and self-employed groups appear to have a favorable position in earnings, whereas service and female-centered occupations pay lowest, irrespective of education.

Still further splits between those who get a high return from education and those equally educated who do not were pointed out by Conroy (1980). He noted that the work of a "valiant 77 million" people supports the remaining two thirds of the population, which does not enter the work force. This conclusion opens a new dimension in the estimation of the return to education. Indeed, if the educated person never enters the work force but becomes (for example) a homemaker, the return to that person's education cannot be calculated under present methods. This leaves a significant gap in human capital theory. Greenfield (1980) found that functional competency was the most important element in labor market success for young people. In other words, people who had learned something in school were probably going to do better in the job market than people who had simply served time without adding functional skills.

As educational budgets, especially budgets for higher education, continued to face austere times, it became apparent to many that treating four or more years of college solely as an investment in human capital was too simple an approach. As elementary schools and high schools closed down for lack of clientele, for example, and pay remained low for teachers, it became apparent that four years in a teachers' college, leading to a degree in education, could hardly be considered a gold-plated investment for a young man or woman.

Engineering presents another example. Following Sputnik's launching by the Russians in 1957, a vast explosion in science and engineering education took place. New engineering schools sprung up like crocuses, and engineering enrollments bounded upward as America entered the Space Age. By 1969 human beings had reached the moon. Then, suddenly, interest in space went into a steep decline. Thousands of engineers were thrown out of work, and it became apparent to young people choosing a major that training for an engineering degree wasn't an investment that would automatically pay handsome dividends. Vacant seats in engineering schools were plentiful by 1975. By 1981, however, increasing defense expenditures and a revival of space programs under the Reagan administration generated more demand for engineers, and enrollments rose.

The need for applied research had similar effects on the supply of mathematics and science teachers in junior high and high schools, who became attracted by high salary offers from industry. By 1982 science and engineering administrators were declaring a "crisis" shortage of math and science teachers in junior high and high school. Here again, the "investment value" of a particular degree had fluctuated wildly during a single decade. The degree was essentially the same, but the labor market had changed its value.

Is the Best Education Vocational? A chronic debate in education centers on the merits of liberal arts or general education, compared with the values of vocational or professional education. During the late seventies enrollment in liberal arts colleges and universities fell, while the number of students seeking vocational learning was on the rise. Some might suggest that the more vocational the education, the more applicable to it the theory of human capital becomes. Apprenticeships for skilled occupations such as machinist, carpenter, millwright, electrician, mason, and plumber are the sort of cost-effective investments proposed by Woodward (1975) that make cost/benefit evaluation easier. (Cost/benefit analysis refers to the ratio of outputs, such as pay and benefits to the worker, to the costs of providing that education.) The financial reward of vocational education does indeed exceed that of education in liberal arts, declared Quattrociocchi (1980), while at the same time suggesting the importance of the social values of a liberal arts degree. Meyer (1980), in a book on the economics of vocational education, took a less doctrinaire view of the idea that only vocational education pays off; he noted that some forms of vocational education are more valuable than others. The student should be steered toward those areas of vocational education where the economic contribution will

be highest and the most jobs will be available, and knowledge of
economic principles should be taught along with technical topics.
Vocational training is more effective than conventional education followed by on-the-job training from the viewpoint of the
economic return on education, reported DeMoura (1979). The re-
vitalization and reindustrialization of America calls for substantial
investment in work force training, proposed Jones (1981) in
advocating the passage of some then pending vocational training
laws.

   While studies of vocational education, like those of
community college education, indicate a statistical return to such
investments that substantially exceeds that usually earned by
ordinary investments, these studies leave unstated the effect of such
education when it is carried out in connection with general education. Studies that show a return of over 25 percent on vocational
and community college education often do not include other factors
that contribute to the return on education. If, indeed the return
to community college investment is 178 percent, as Jackson claimed,
one wonders why the nation would not be made boundlessly rich
by simply covering its entire surface with community colleges rather
than building steel mills, chemical plants and the like, which show
a more modest return of 10 to 15 percent. Clearly, vocational
education, community college education, and even medical school
education pay off only when they fit into an economy and culture
that make such returns possible.

   The importance of general education, which teaches people
to read, write, and understand mathematics and science, was pointed
out in a 1982 study by the Center for Public Resources, which
reported that industry in the United States is being severely undercut
because young people entering the work force lack basic skills in
these areas of knowledge. These basic skills are unrelated to any
vocational skill such as auto mechanics or electronics, but they
underlie all vocational skills as a core competency. The center's
survey relied on responses of both employers and school systems
for its conclusions. Companies tended to report deficiencies in
basic areas, while school systems insisted that their graduates
were properly prepared to enter the work force. But bookkeepers
who can't add or do fractions and managers who can't write

grammatically correct sentences are a fact of life. Thus, the role of education in investment in human capital isn't really all that clear.

Human Capital Investment and the Quality of Life

This book focuses on the world of work and on ways human assets are treated in that context. From the individual's point of view, education can be a personal investment whose payoff and output are likely to show up in the position he or she ultimately occupies in an employing organization. For the employer, the treatment of human capital encompasses more than devising lucid and productive personnel policies and programs.

Clearly, the quality of life includes the quality of work life. The quality of work life, then, is a function of the quality of the entire society—its demographics, its migrations, the quality of family life, the population's level of education, and people's ability to renew themselves when renewal is needed. Investment in human capital in all of its stages determines our values, what we seek or are repelled by, and the ways in which we rule ourselves, relate to one another, and generally live the life we live.

2

---∽---

Analyzing
Human Resource
Investments:
How Portfolio
Analysis Works

A cynic knows the price of everything and the value
of nothing.   —*Oscar Wilde*

Analysis of an organization's human resources by regarding them
as part of a portfolio is more than simply a schematic way of
categorizing employees. It does three useful things: It assesses
employees' *value* to the investing employers, it appraises the *level
of risk* for each of the classes of different valuations, and it sets
forth some *strategies for managing* personnel according to their
valuation and risk. This approach considers people in their jobs
in the same way that investors view nonhuman assets.

Of course, regarding people as a portfolio of assets is only
an analogy. It is one that many might disagree with. However,
you need to accept this analogy for the time being and follow through
the descriptions of portfolio analysis as developed in financial or

product investments in order to see the full range of meanings involved in human capital portfolio management.

If you are to use portfolio theory to analyze your employees, you need to have some idea of the ways in which conventional investment portfolios are treated by investors and analysts. You must also explore the analogy between financial portfolios and portfolios of human resources. Limited space allows the coverage of only some fundamentals of portfolio theory in abbreviated fashion. We will describe the meaning of the major financial terms used, with a translation into the language of human resources, and then briefly discuss valuation of assets and portfolio theory as they apply to human resources and human capital.

Some Financial Terminology

The portfolio theory of human capital requires us to think in two kinds of language at once. The first is the language of finance, and the second is the human-oriented language of personnel administration, employee relations, and human resources management.

Davids (1978), in his *Dictionary of Banking and Finance*, lists nearly 5,000 specific terms. Obviously we can discuss only a few of them here. Those most relevant to this book are defined as follows.

- *Asset:* An asset is something of value represented by a credit balance. It is usually a property right, a value acquired, or an expenditure made that has created a property right. A *capital* asset is one that cannot be readily converted into cash, in contrast to a *current* asset, which can be. A *contingent* asset is one whose value depends on future events, which may or may not occur. A *dead* asset is one not productive of income under normal operations. An *intangible* asset has no physical substance; this includes such incorporeal "goods" as goodwill, patent rights, or other rights. A *nominal* asset is one that is difficult to evaluate. A *wasting* asset is one whose value is eroding, such as a mine, timberland, or an oil well. A *working* asset is one whose value is fluctuating, such as a common stock traded daily on the stock exchange.

- *Portfolio:* A portfolio is a cluster of valuable holdings belonging to an individual or an institution. Usually it contains common or preferred stocks or bonds, but it might include other assets as well. In this book we treat people as assets to be managed as a portfolio.

- *Default:* Default means failure to do that which is required by law or to perform an obligation. In the case of an employee, default means failure to perform duties as expected because of quitting the job, being fired, and so forth.

- *Discount:* This term describes the amount of money deducted from the face value of a note calculated at an agreed upon rate of interest. Thus, securities bought below par value are said to be discounted. The discount of common stock is the percentage below the par value of the stock. Discount can also mean the rate of earning or return, stated as a percent of the value of the asset. *Discounted value* means the "present value of future payments" computed on the basis of a given rate of interest. In the case of an employee, this "present value" refers to what you as an employer might earn from selling products or services produced by the employee.

- *Interest rate:* The interest rate is the percentage of a principal amount that is annually charged for its use. It is often referred to as the "rate of return," which is the yield obtainable based upon the purchase price or current market price. The yield from an employee is the employee's productivity.

- *Capital:* Usually capital means the amount subscribed and paid in by stockholders—in other words, their equity. In this book we expand the concept of capital to include humans in the employ of a firm. *Capital assets* are fixed assets. *Capital expenditures* are cash investments made in exchange for property, buildings, or other fixed assets. *Capital gain* means the increase in the value of a capital asset. *Capital investment* is the amount invested in capital. These concepts, we suggest, can also be applied to human capital.

- *Owner:* The owner is the person or organization having a vested or contingent interest in the property in question. In human capital theory, the owner is the employer.

- *Depreciation:* Depreciation is gradual conversion of fixed asset cost into expense, spread over the asset's remaining life. As employees' skills decline or become obsolete, they in effect depreciate as economic assets.

In this book we treat employees as assets that are part of an employer's portfolio. They resemble capital assets economically in that they cannot be converted into cash. They are contingent assets, since their value depends on events that may or may not occur. They are also intangible assets; they resemble goodwill and may in fact be carried on the financial report as part of goodwill. As working assets, employees may fluctuate in value. Lamentably, on occasion they may also become wasting assets. By treating a firm's human capital as a portfolio of assets to be managed, the employer tries to enhance the value of the whole portfolio and minimize the parts of the portfolio that become wasting assets.

Valuation of Human Assets

In both conventional investment theory and human capital portfolio theory, the valuation of assets is the key decision area. The two dimensions for valuation of human capital are *potential* and *performance*. These are adaptations from two basic concepts of portfolio valuation; investments are bought and sold on the basis of their expected income and their price appreciation, or growth.

Growth in portfolio valuation refers to changes in the value of assets over some future time period. In human capital theory, growth translates into the idea of potential. The young employee freshly recruited from college is ordinarily hired (services bought) because of his or her potential for future contribution to the firm. The employer expects these employees' contribution to continue over time and to grow each year.

Discounting to Take Account of Time Value. Time value refers to the future value of a present asset. How would we value an asset that will pay us $8,000 a year for forty years? Similarly, how would we value a human who might earn such a sum for us over the same period of time? The earnings from $100,000 owned today might be lower if the interest of 8 percent were for ten years than if it were for twenty or thirty years, or forever. This is called the "stream of expected income" in the future. At the time Lee Iacocca became president of Chrysler at age fifty-eight, his future contribution to that firm might in fact have been less than that of a younger employee with a similar personality, who might have forty years of potential contribution at a somewhat lower return. The hitch comes in the uncertainty of assessing an employee's potential.

Present and future dollars can be compared by discounting the sums of present value equivalents. If we assume a 6 percent discount rate, we assume that one dollar today is worth $1.06 a year from now, or $1.1236 in two years. Likewise, a promise to pay $1.00 a year from now is worth $0.944 today. An asset that promises to pay three annual payments of $100 at 6 percent is worth $267.30.

In valuation of human assets we may have to assume that the annual payments to the investor won't be equal each year. In such cases the calculations are more complex and may require a table of expected values or a programmable calculator. The basic idea, however, is that the present value of an employee is a function of the discounted value of his or her expected income stream. While this may seem impossible to calculate for, say, trainee salesman Jones, it can be estimated by studying the experiences of other salespeople who have been hired and trained by similar methods. The investment we make in training Jones should be related to the surplus Jones will produce after the initial training is complete.

The assessment of potential for a human asset must thus include the length of time over which the asset will be working and the estimated annual contribution to the organization during the years the asset is held. The method used in estimating this future contribution becomes an important ingredient in the portfolio approach to valuation of human capital.

College recruits' value may be discounted and their present value be less than their face value during their year of acquisition. Hiring a Baker fellow out of Harvard or a Leland Stanford fellow out of Stanford Business School may cost the firm $45,000 the first year, which is the student's face value, but the student's discount value is considerably less. The student's market price reflects his or her income stream over the expected holding period. The income stream and the holding period are less fixed in human capital than they are in financial investments, where laws of property and contract provide more certainty of return, but both can be estimated for the newly hired person. If an employee is likely to remain for only a short time period, that person's income stream needs to be higher in order for the employment to be profitable, and the employer might want to contract to guarantee a minimum employment period.

Discount Rate: Some Examples. For certain occupations it is possible because of employment contracts to find a fairly accurate income stream by fixing its discount rate. For many jobs in service occupations, the rule of thumb employers apply is "double the labor cost as a charge to the customer." Thus, if the customer pays $10 an hour for labor, the worker will receive $5.00 and the balance will be gross income to the employer. For higher-level jobs, such as professional services, the multiple will be more than double the labor cost; it might run to 300 percent. Thus, if an accountant is paid $500 per week in total compensation, the typical CPA firm will probably bill the client $1500 for a week's worth of labor. This leaves a gross margin of $1000 for the week to the firm. You may recall that *discount* can be defined as the "rate of return as a percent of the value of the asset." How do you estimate the capital value of this accountant? The easiest way would be to compare the return to that on alternative investments that would produce the same return.

This calls for us to figure the "expected income stream," which in the case of the accountant would be an estimated $50,000 a year gross margin, projected as far into the future as the accountant remains with the firm or the firm has the ability to keep that person fully employed. How might we estimate the capital worth of this human asset then? One way would be to consider how much we would have to invest in a *riskless investment* such as a bond or government treasury bill that would return us an equal amount. It would take a cash investment of $500,000 paying 10 percent riskless return to equal the income from employment of this accountant. It is unlikely that it takes $500,000 worth of training and recruiting costs for the CPA firm to hire one journeyman accountant; thus, the investment in human labor pays a higher return than alternative investments. This gross margin of course isn't net profit, but it is a worthwhile economic calculation for an employer to undertake.

Auto mechanics or beauticians are often paid 50 percent of the income produced from their work. If you take your car to be serviced, the mechanic gets fifty cents and the dealer fifty cents from every dollar of the labor cost of the repairs. In such arrangements the discount rate can be figured with some degree of accuracy. If a constant amount is to be paid forever, a very simple formula relates the market price to the discount rate: $PV = CR/r$, where PV equals the present value of the income stream, CR equals the amount to be received each period, and r equals the appropriate discount rate.

For most jobs, however, especially technical, managerial, and professional jobs, the discount rate can't be so neatly estimated; it may vary widely. The cost of professional engineers working on government contracts may have been incorporated into the bid, for example, so their discount rate is clearer than that of the engineer who simply works on projects chosen at the will of the chief engineer. In truth, many firms fail to estimate the returns expected from paying key people, such as engineers.

Usually, the more certainty attached to the expected income stream, the lower the discount rate, and vice versa. Low risk in the expected income stream should be valued more highly than higher risk in the expected stream. For example, the farmer's sons who expect to stay on the farm and perhaps inherit it may work for low wages or none at all, whereas the combine operator who comes and goes by the season may charge extravagant wages. The permanent employee who has many years of service usually receives lower daily rates of pay than the consultant who comes on the scene, makes quick studies and recommendations, and departs after a few days or weeks. The permanent employee, with seniority and limited ability to change jobs, has a more certain income stream than the consultant and thus has a lower discount rate.

How Risk Affects Value. Usually the riskier elements in a portfolio are priced higher than those of lower risk; that is, they have a higher discount rate. One form of risk is known as *default risk*. This refers to the possibility that the issuer's obligation will not be fulfilled. In the case of a bond or stock this could be because of bankruptcy or repudiation. In the human resources portfolio, default risk is high because of the freedom of many employees to quit on short notice. The employee serves at the pleasure of the employer and in turn remains only at his or her own pleasure. Thus, the human asset has a much higher default risk than the conventional investment unit. In some employment situations the default risk is reduced by long-term employment contracts or by limited job-switching opportunity.

A unique default risk of human assets is the mortality of humans. They can die, become ill, grow old, retire, or decline in performance interest, skills, or motivation while they are still being paid full pay.

Market risk is still another basis of risk estimation. A bond being sold on the money markets, which must compete with heavy refinancing of government debts, must pay more interest in order to sell the entire issue than one that has no such competition. Similarly, when there is a glut of workers, such as occurred with auto assembler and steel workers in 1982, their value goes down. Union contracts that year produced a rash of wage "givebacks," in which union members agreed to pay cuts in order to protect their jobs.

Similarly, hiring rates for new college graduates can vary widely among specialties. A newly graduated Ph.D. in history may welcome a job offer at $15,000 a year, while a graduate whose degree is in tax accounting may be offered $35,000 a year by the same institution. This is in part because the tax accountant is a "risky asset" for his or her employer, in the sense that the risk of that person's leaving (defaulting) is higher than that for the historian, who is likely to have few, if any, job alternatives. In portfolio terms, the value of the riskless asset (the history teacher) is the norm, and that paid above it is the risk premium. Should times change and history become popular while tax accountants are in oversupply, the positions of the two teachers might reverse.

In summary, to value a human asset, the employer must calculate the riskless rate of hiring, assess the risk of the assets (how long they will stay) and estimate the risk premium. These factors are harder to calculate for human resources than for, say, bonds, but skilled employment managers can often estimate them on the basis of past experience. This information is useful in defining policies for hiring, paying, and providing motivations for employees for whom a risk premium exists. Calculations of risk also suggest that "equal pay for equal work," using conventional job evaluation methods, is often a fiction. This is because the market scarcity of any occupation has as much effect on pay as do equality between job skills or job demands. Furthermore, if strictly applied, it could cost far more than it saves.

The Present Value Approach to Valuing Assets. Much of the previous discussion dealt with value at hiring (or acquisition) of the asset. You may also find the present value of an asset by discounting its future dividend stream and future market value; this is how stock is valued by its portfolio manager. Three elements determine the present value of the asset: expected dividends for successive future years, the appropriate discount rate, and the expected stock or asset price for some future year. In other words, you estimate the value added by the performance of the human asset and then divide that estimate by its discount rate plus its expected stock or sales price in a future year.

The new element here is the sales price of the asset in future years. A trainee in the insurance industry, for example, might begin as a novice actuary. His or her contribution during the first two or three years of employment may be negligible or even negative. Yet the trainee's present value exceeds both the dividends paid to the firm in the early employment years and the discount rate, because experienced actuaries have a high market value to the industry. That possibility adds to the trainee's present value. Estimates of present value of human assets are uncertain, but knowing the basic way that present value is estimated can bring more order and rationality to the valuation of human assets.

The Market Price of an Investment. Investment prices, or the costs of acquisition, implicitly reflect the discounted value of their expected income streams. For bonds or preferred stocks, the promised future income stream is the expected future income stream. You simply add the coupon value of the item to the interest stated and subtract the expected default loss. Common stocks, on the other hand, are affected by trading supply and demand. They have no definite promise of a future income stream, have no maturity date, and are not callable; thus, their future income stream is a lot harder to predict. Human assets are much like common stock in this respect. If you are bold and trusting, you may rely on past records and extrapolate them into the future. Actual market behavior may differ from expectations, but accuracy of forecasts of labor supply and demand is higher than that of predictions for many other factors in business. Such factors as population changes and changes in supplies of labor that emanate from schools and colleges are visible in advance of their entry into the labor market.

Implications of Market Price. Investors—or employers— acquiring an asset need to consider market price and to judge how accurate market expectations may be. For human assets, the employer can draw on expert forecasts of labor supply and demand from various sources when trying to make market predictions. The U.S. Department of Labor, for one, issues periodic "manpower forecasts" for decades ahead. For example, if computer programmers are predicted to be in short supply throughout the eighties, the employer may estimate that the price of computer programmers will rise. As with stock and bond investment, human asset investment is in part a game of attempting to understand and improve on the market's evaluation. The insurance company that hires community college graduates rather than university graduates for underwriting and claims jobs is trying to produce dividends that will be equal to or better than those of competitors who follow the opposite hiring policy. The company is thus engaging in the same kind of investment strategy as an investor in common stocks. Investors compare their valuation with the market's and try to buy undervalued securities and avoid buying overvalued ones. For the employer, this strategy means choosing the right level of qualifications when hiring. It is a common error for firms to overhire, or hire people with qualifications greater than those needed for the job. They pay a premium price for this mistake. Overhiring gets the buyer an asset whose expected income stream cannot justify the market price paid. Many writers these days view with suspicion the tendency of some large employers to hire MBAs for every management position. The employers, on the other hand, may choose to pay a premium because they estimate that the potential stream of income that the MBAs will produce over their total period of employment makes their present value sufficiently high.

Just as with the conventional investor, predictions made by the employer who invests in human capital can be in error for several reasons. Income stream forecasts can be wrong; differences between the investor's estimate and the market's evaluation may be due to errors in the discount rate; default rates may not be predictable; or the undervaluing of a security purchased by the investor may be subsequently offset by a general market decline. In 1970, for example, the investment that many aerospace firms had made in engineering talent was wiped out by the rapid decline in aerospace research; the employing firms had to discharge thousands of painstakingly recruited and trained engineers because of a lack of business.

Basing Investment Decisions on Market Forecasts. The employer of human assets, like the conventional investor, must make some kind of earnings forecast in order to make a market decision to buy or sell. Such forecasts for securities have a spotty record, to say the least. For example, in the 1970s, brokers advised acquiring Equity Funding stock, only to learn that the company had $2 billion in phony insurance in effect; the company soon collapsed. Similarly, in 1973 brokers were advising clients to buy Scientific Controls stock just one week before the company filed for bankruptcy. Future short-term growth has been found to be closely correlated with past growth, but predictions of longer-term future growth are far less accurate.

Similarly, in human asset investments, accurate long-term predictions have been hard to make. Changes in school and college courses often lag well behind changes in demand for workers in specific occupations, and employers likewise are not always skillful in predicting which assets will show rising streams of income. Labor department manpower forecasts, however, have a fairly sound record of predicting which occupations will rise and which will fall in value. This is partly because such forecasts can draw on more accurate records of births, educational majors, and other population data than most employers can, and their extrapolations reflect what employers have actually done rather than intuitive estimates. Forecasts for labor supply in specific skill areas are more accurate than forecasts for labor demand, for the most part.

There are many varieties of demand forecasting for human resources. Such forecasts are often not very accurate, for in order to estimate the demand for human assets a corporation must be able to estimate the future growth of the business. The Securities and Exchange Commission (SEC) has for many years encouraged corporations to make their internal earnings predictions public. Relatively few corporations actually make such forecasts public, and their silence on the subject produces only minor repercussions, if any. The corporation that valiantly tries to forecast earnings may please the SEC but leave itself open to criticism later if the forecasts prove wrong—and there are a number of reasons why private estimates are apt to be flawed. For one thing, forecasts of profit or growth may involve mergers and acquisitions as well as simple growth in internal business. For another, growth in corporate sales dollars doesn't always reflect a proportional growth in employment. Finally, much of the growth in employment comes from the formation of wholly new businesses (such as those involved in the recent genetic technology explosion), whose appearance cannot be predicted for the most part.

Even when more mature firms expand in sales volume the location and nature of the growth often fail to produce a proportionate growth in domestic employment opportunity. When General Motors entered a joint agreement with a Japanese firm to produce automobiles in California and auto parts in Japan and have "in bond" plants just over the border in Mexico, none of the resulting plants was very susceptible to accurate long-term estimates of expected stream of income from investment in human capital. Similarly, firms that manufacture video games or other boom-and-bust products afford little solace to the person who would try to estimate the income stream from investing in human capital. Labor market skills forecasts of demand are of often questionable accuracy, hence, individual firms' human resources planning is of scanty quantity and quality. It may reflect business forecasts that may or may not be available, and if available not worthy of serious attention. Furthermore, much of the future demand for human resources is concealed behind inaccurate estimates of future new business creation, which in turn is a product of technological forecasting, a conjectural field at best.

Must the manager, then, throw up his or her hands in dismay, rely solely on wild guesses, or simply wait quietly to find out what actually occurs? No. As with conventional portfolio management, one is better off trying to forecast with whatever information is available than not trying at all.

Some aspects of human resources supply and demand can be predicted. People don't start working until they are at least sixteen years old, so the future can be forecast accurately for the first sixteen to twenty years of life. We can predict the supply of graduates from high school, from college, and from adult education courses with considerable accuracy. We know about the likelihood of people entering the armed forces and of their being discharged. Our projections of immigration and emigration within and between specific labor markets are reasonably accurate in the ten-year range. Employers should draw on these and other kinds of available information when trying to make predictions about their human assets.

Valuing Human Assets: A Summary. In summary, here are the main things to keep in mind when trying to predict the value of human assets:

- Think deeply about income streams and discount rates for the various occupations for which you hire people, and act on your best estimates when dealing with labor markets.
- Realize that an undervalued asset is a good buy, and actively seek to outguess the market's valuation of human assets.
- It is more feasible to assess the value of an entire portfolio and its sum of expected streams of income than to assess the value of any individual worker. Thus, portfolio management of human capital has considerable value to you as an employer.

Portfolio Management of Human Resources

The most common way of describing portfolios is a variation of an old analytic tool used widely in economics and social sciences, the "two by two" matrix. To use this tool, you choose two major dimensions of a problem that can be ranked from low to high and array them on horizontal and vertical axes. Often the dimensions

Figure 2. Two by Two Matrix.

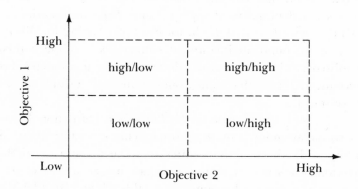

represent a combination of two equally desired objectives. The basic two by two matrix is pictured in Figure 2.

If you complete the matrix, it will give you a valuable array of information. The combination of high outcomes on both objectives (high/high) is the most desirable. A combination of low outcomes on both objectives (low/low) is the worst possible— perhaps a disastrous—mix. The other two possible outcomes are less than ideal but better than worst.

The two by two matrix has been widely used in management analysis. Blake's (1962) Grid, one famous example, relates concern for productivity to concern for people in organizational relations. Fleischman and Harris (1955) related consideration and initiating structure in a matrix or portfolio. Schoeffler (1977) used this tool widely in analyzing the profit impact of market strategies, choosing numerous variables to be correlated in the two by two format. The Boston Consulting Group uses variations of it for assessing market growth relationships. Carnazza (1978) applied performance potential axes to career succession and replacement programming.

Diversification of Portfolio to Reduce Risk. Diversifying the kinds of items in a portfolio is a common risk reduction measure taken by investors. Thus, if some industries are prospering, the wise investor builds that family of issues but does not limit the portfolio to them; holdings of other issues can offset possible losses. Similarly, a balanced human assets portfolio is best. We may balance the hiring of employees who are undervalued by the market, such as high school, state college, or community college graduates, by hiring selected numbers of top graduates from universities such as MIT, Harvard, or Cal Tech, for example. Hiring for diversity of risk is as sound an investment strategy as building a mixed portfolio of stocks and bonds or other investment instruments. Both reduce the high risks that come from holding only a single category of investments.

Assembly of Efficient Market Portfolios. The major objective of portfolio assembly is building some items, divesting others, and holding still others. This requires that the investor assemble a collection of assets that in the aggregate has an attractive set of characteristics. For stocks, bonds, mutual funds and the like, these qualities include high returns, low risk, liquidity, marketability, favorable tax status, ease of management, and similar criteria. For human assets many of the qualities are basically similar, if somewhat different in the language employed to describe them. The attractive human assets portfolio will produce a work force with high potential for contribution, versatility in skills, stability of tenure, long years of future service, and high quality of performance in relation to the goals of the firm.

Figure 3. An Efficient Market Portfolio.

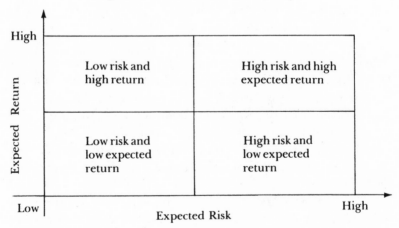

As with financial assets, human assets can be managed in portfolio form. An efficient market portfolio of human capital is divided into major classes according to risk, potential contribution over time, and actual performance aimed toward desired objectives. Risks are both market and nonmarket but in sum can be handled in aggregate variances.

An efficient market portfolio, shown on the two by two matrix described earlier, is illustrated in Figure 3. This portfolio is best for most investors because it contains no market risk. If securities have been accurately priced with respect to their expected performance, this market portfolio will be efficient in the sense that all other portfolios will offer a lower rate of expected return, a higher risk, or both. This design works as well for a human assets portfolio, in this author's opinion, as it does for portfolios of conventional investments.

In the next chapter we will explore further the ways in which portfolio theory and the development of efficient market portfolios can benefit the investor in human capital.

3

Applying
Portfolio Analysis
to Human Resource
Management

Life cannot wait until the sciences may have explained
the universe scientifically. We cannot put off living
until we are ready.   —*José Ortega y Gasset*

Human Capital Theory Enters the Corporate World

Human capital theory as it is detailed in the first two chapters
has worked its way into the world of management only recently,
and then only because of practical rather than theoretical reasons.
Even those actions that seem to reflect an application of that theory—
such as sponsoring employee education programs, long-range human resources planning, and the creation of large staffs of professional experts in human resources—have been more for business
reasons than to conform with any theory. Some of the most efficient
users of human capital theory resemble the writer who said late
in life, "I have been speaking prose all my life and only learned

48

it recently." Many large firms have applied human capital theory efficiently without realizing that they were using it—or even caring. For practical corporate executives, the system they devised has worked, and that is its major justification. As one corporate vice-president of human resources told me, "I'm happy to learn that what we invented to solve our people problems is theoretically sound. Now, perhaps, we can do it on purpose."

In reality, the theory has been most likely to be questioned by accountants, who have often resisted accepting it simply because it isn't consistent with some of the conventions prescribed by the accounting profession. It has been the managers, not the accountants, in industry and business who have used human capital theory to manage their human organization.

Corporate Training and Planning: Applications of the Theory. Leading corporations in America and Europe have long engaged in training programs for their employees at all levels. General Electric has operated a managerial training facility at Crotonville, New York, since 1951. Much earlier, General Motors had created its own college, General Motors Institute, in Flint, Michigan, with some 2,000 degree seekers enrolled by the divisions of the corporation (Sloan, 1964). In addition, General Motors Training Centers, for the training of automotive mechanics sent by General Motors dealers, were spread through major centers around the nation. This pattern was subsequently adopted by Ford, with Ford Training Centers and Ford Marketing Institute, and Chrysler, with Chrysler Institute.

From its earliest days, IBM has built much of its sales and service strength through widespread training of employees and customers. During the sixties and seventies, numerous other major corporations also erected large and well-financed education centers, staffed with professional trainers, which served customers and employees alike. Leeds and Northrup constructed such a site, for example (Eddy and Kellow, 1977). Xerox built a large facility in Leesburg, Virginia, for similar purposes. Numerous other firms had smaller schools for employees and customers, including Merck and Company, Wolverine Shoe, Dana Corporation, and McDonald's ("Hamburger U"). American Telephone and Telegraph (now American Bell) and its affiliated local telephone companies have dozens of company-owned educational facilities. The dimensions of these corporate educational efforts were usually quite large in terms of both budgets and numbers of people educated. They would seem to be excellent examples of investment in human capital, but they were almost wholly innocent of any theory of human capital, or perhaps any theory other than the ideas that revenues must exceed expense and that investment should produce a return.

Similarly, corporate human resource developers have often engaged in strategic planning for periods of up to a decade ahead. This planning was often simply a by-product of general planning for the whole business and preparation for anticipated problems (Vetter, 1968). Sometimes the plans included re-education of employees and managers as an alternative to firing them because of a business downturn. Both IBM and Potlatch Corporation, for example, required that all managers collaborate in multiyear planning for products, markets, financial requirements, and profits. They also made it a policy not to fire people when sales dropped but rather to retrain them to be ready for new business developments ("At Potlatch . . . ," 1975). *Business Week* reported that Potlatch had tripled its profits and become a leader in return-on-investment in the forest products industry by using this strategy. IBM's strategic practices have produced steady growth in sales, earnings, and market share for more than two decades.

Increased long-range strategic planning for the corporation as a whole generated more explicit human resources planning. Some proposed that human resources be treated separately and that cost-effectiveness studies of training and development programs be done. Cullin and others (1978) developed a model for determining, analyzing, and comparing training returns for both formal and informal training. Human capital theory had been developed to explain economic growth, but it was equally applicable to reduction of human losses through training of understudies and other means, suggested Neuman and Segev (1978a), who saw such measures as a part of corporate risk management. Their explanations of human resources development as a form of risk aversion was most plausible and seemed in tune with the risk-avoidance approach of many firms' strategic planning.

Again, planning and human resources development paid off. When IBM grew by more than $5 billion in sales in 1981 and by another $7 billion in 1982, its training policies provided it with sufficient people with the right skills to handle this rapid growth (IBM Annual Report, 1981). Although the sales growth did not demand a proportionate rise in the number of employees, preparation to deliver the higher level of sales and output nonetheless did place a heavy demand on the relatively small organization of 1980. Undoubtedly, the considerable expenditures that had been made on training and development reduced the risks that could have resulted from such rapid expansion.

Thus, many corporations have followed training and development practices that seem to demonstrate a belief in human capital theory. However, most did not consciously adopt the theory as a model or even seem to be aware of its existence. Certainly they showed little evidence of modifying their accounting or financial portfolio management practices to accommodate human capital theory.

Human Capital Theory and the Accounting Profession. Accounting is often said to be "the language of business." As a colleague of mine, Ronald Manino, put it, "That which counts is that which is counted." To the corporate executive, the work of the accountant is vital to measurement of both managerial and organizational success.

Certified Public Accountants are required to audit a client's books "in conformance with conventional accounting practice." What exactly constitutes conventional accounting practice is determined by a board of accountants known as the Financial Accounting Standards Board (FASB). Rulings that change the conventional methods of accounting and audit practice have considerable significance to the client corporations, for they may alter the way earnings are reported. Even a single ruling may increase or decrease the reported profits of a firm radically. As a result, changes in accounting standards are seldom greeted with enthusiasm by those being audited, for they change *reported* results for better or worse without changing the *actual* result of management. They also make comparison of figures over time difficult, since the figures may have been derived by different accounting rules.

All of this has an important bearing on human resources accounting. When theoreticians began to suggest in the 1970s that human resources should be handled through the mechanics of standard accounting practice, accountants entered into heated discussions of the theory. Some favored treating employees as assets, even though companies didn't actually own their workers. Others claimed that this innovation violated traditional accounting practices. This debate was important because it affected the ways in which client corporations might carry employees on their books.

Conventional accounting practice says that people are not assets; rather, they are to be shown on the profit and loss statement as an expense item. The proposal that they should appear on the balance sheet as assets was revolutionary—and most accountants don't enjoy revolutions. Some of the major conclusions of accounting writers and practitioners concerning this proposal are given in the following section.

Human Resources Accounting Emerges. Accounting literature from 1970 on produced some intermittent studies and some undocumented discussion of human capital theory, which was usually regarded with little enthusiasm. Morse (1975) suggested that human *asset* accounting must be separated from the human *capital* accounting and proposed a methodology for dealing with the issue, using a Markov distribution. Weiss (1975) pointed out that there are many advantages to incorporating human capital accounting into financial statements. One place in conventional accounting where such human capital might be incorporated would be in the valuation of goodwill, suggested Romano (1975). More specific suggestions were forthcoming from Trussell and Dobbins (1976), who reviewed various ways in which human resources accounting might build up (or total up) such costs using conventional accounting methods. The authors suggested historical costs, replacement costs, opportunity cost value measurement, and nonmonetary measurement as possible ways of valuing human assets, although they cautioned that none of this was an easy matter. They pointed out that there are limitations as well as benefits in all four approaches, and they indicated that extensive study was called for before human resources accounting could be incorporated into conventional accounting practices. An alternative way of handling these issues would be to value human resources in terms of cost, presumably using the four methods spelled out by Trussell and Dobbins, but, in addition, computing "economic benefit stream," according to Jaggi (1976). Jaggi's second suggestion, that the easiest way to handle valuation of human assets would be to treat them as economic calculations rather than accounting matters, would have relieved the accounting profession of the painful necessity of changing its traditional methods. At the same time, treating humans as assets would have permitted managerial decisions to be made for the benefit of the firm.

Hendricks (1976) reported that for external readers of financial statements, such as stock buyers, human resources accounting can affect investment decisions. The earnings from human capital constitute a different problem, according to Lucas (1977), who discussed valuation of those earnings according to the rate of return on human capital and suggested that such valuations could explain inequality of employees' incomes.

A review of the accounting literature from the last half of the seventies indicates that the accounting profession had little desire to change conventional accounting practices to accommodate human asset accounting. For one thing, the meticulous and sometimes tortuous method by which conventional accounting practice is changed made adoption of such changes unlikely. The FASB, which must announce all changes in what constitutes "conventional accounting practice," operated with extreme deliberation, issuing disclosure drafts for the reaction of the profession before adopting any new practice. The profession itself was under great pressure at that time from both client firms and the Securities and Exchange Commission, which threatened tighter government control of accounting practices unless self-regulation demonstrated sufficient evidence of self-control. Briloff (1972), a leading critic of his profession, summarized these problems and labeled current accounting practices as "unaccountable accounting." Small wonder that the profession failed to embrace anything novel or untried, such as accounting for human assets, during this period.

Thus, the whole cluster of ideas that sprang from Schultz's germinal concept that people were assets rather than expenses fell on hard times because the accounting profession simply wouldn't accept the notion of treating humans as assets on the balance sheet. This idea still has not been incorporated into conventional accounting practices. It has been viewed with some favor by a few corporations, but it has never gained credence in annual accounting reports.

The accounting profession generally divides its labor into two major parts: financial accounting and managerial accounting. The distinction between the two is not always clear to the layman. Financial accounting is mainly auditing clients' books; it is generally done by a Certified Public Accounting (CPA) firm. Managerial accounting is the provision to management of information that aids in making managerial decisions. This is ordinarily done by a firm's internal accounting employees, usually in a department such as cost accounting, budgeting, or cost analysis. During the seventies it seemed most sensible for human capital accounting to be handled by managerial accounting departments rather than by the beleaguered CPA firms or the FASB.

Managerial accountants, like CPAs, have their professional association, which certifies approved managerial accountants with a Certified Managerial Accountant (CMA) designation. Harris and Krogstad (1976), in an analysis of the content of the CMA examinations over the previous four years, found that exam coverage had increased in two areas, budgeting and return-on-investment (ROI) performance measurement. The two areas that had declined in coverage were cost analysis and standard cost systems. The kinds of information rising in importance to management thus seemed to be those that would assist in making strategic planning decisions, while there was less interest in current operating decisions and internal cost control.

The growth of service industries as compared with manufacturing in America also made standard cost and cost accounting areas seem less relevant. Managers in many firms needed to know where highest returns on capital were coming from and how to allocate resources to those efforts that promised the highest yield, generally measured as return on investment. Thus, profit and cost reduction were less crucial than the return on capital. This change was no mere fad. Institutional investors—holders of large pension trusts and similar vital stockholders—often bought or sold a firm's stock on the basis of such earnings ratios, and declines in earnings, even in the short run, could force stock prices to collapse painfully.

Thus, the goals of strategic planning during the seventies tended to center on returns to invested capital. Managerial accounting reflected the wishes of management in providing information needed to make decisions that would allocate resources so as to increase Return on Investment (ROI). (While ROI has been the most common measurement of profit, others were used by some firms, including return-on-equity, earnings per share, residual income, and return-on-assets.)

Because the emphasis in the seventies was upon strategic planning, this return by category of business, market, product or territory became the major focus of top management. This led directly to the treatment of each product, each market, and each business within the overall corporation as part of a *portfolio of assets* to be weighed against one another and against alternative opportunities when the allocation of resources was planned. Corporations today are slowly beginning to understand that their human capital can be treated in much the same way.

Portfolio Analysis of Human Capital

Financial portfolios are usually managed by and for investors. A mutual fund may buy stocks, bonds, or other assets and measure the return to its investors as a performance indicator of its success. The trust department of a bank, the pension fund trustee, and the investment officer of an insurance company all buy and sell stocks or other assets with the hope that the assets purchased will both grow in value and produce earnings. Unlike some individual investors who depend on earnings or dividends for their personal income, most institutional investors are relatively indifferent to the amount of growth they receive. If a security or bond pays interest or dividends and appreciates in market value at the same time, this is doubly desirable; on the other hand, the worst outcome would be that the asset not only paid no interest or dividends but also declined in market price below the purchase price.

During the seventies, there were few reported efforts to assess the impact that human capital might have on the value of investments in a stock or bond portfolio. However, Rorke (1979) studied the effect of two nonmarketable assets on the value of investment portfolios. The first nonmarketable asset consisted of government transfer payments such as Medicare, taxes, welfare, and social security payments. The second nonmarketable asset was human capital. Rorke concluded that human capital is an asset in economic terms, but it cannot be carried on the books like a truck or an office building, for its marketability and liquidation value are difficult or impossible to state. Rorke proposed that in an investor's portfolio, human capital payments are assumed to be tied to the performance of the employing firm. While this is a sensible assumption, it does little to help the employer in valuing human capital.

Defense contractors have from time to time asserted that the profit level included in billings for defense projects should include a return on human capital. In one case a large aerospace firm was charged with overbilling the government and went to court to defend its price. The higher return on assets that it had billed, the company asserted, was payment for the cost of recruiting, acquiring, training, and maintaining a unique and distinctive body of engineers whose innovative abilities constituted an asset, however nonmarketable it might have been to the firm. It asserted that the price it charged the government should include a return on those human assets. The court was partly persuaded; it allowed the firm a price higher than the government wished but less than what the firm had requested.

Other courts also have found that the treatment of human capital as an asset is less than clear. In a case involving Fairchild and Motorola, the plaintiff, Motorola, charged that Fairchild had wrongfully deprived it of human assets in hiring away a team of experts in one high-technology area. The experts left Motorola as a group and took jobs at Fairchild, where they subsequently developed a new line of business for their new employer. Despite expert testimony that human capital was indeed an asset and that in hiring away the experts, Fairchild had wronged Motorola, the judge rejected the complaint.

At least two corporations have reported on specific methods of valuation of human resources portfolios. Upjohn Company maintains a synthetic indicator of ROI for human resources that indicates their effectiveness and shows variances in costs and returns.

The indicator employed, value-added per dollar of labor cost, is the ratio of total compound value-added to total compound dollar cost of labor. Value-added is the surplus that results after all expenses have been subtracted from all income. This ratio in itself is not especially significant, but it is an excellent reflection of changes in the labor cost per dollar of value-added over time. It is also valuable in comparing the cost-effectiveness of labor in different divisions and departments or profit centers (Dahl, 1979).

Similarly, Texas Instruments uses a Personnel Effectiveness Index (PEI), which is constructed from labor costs as a ratio to return on investment. The PEI is used both to measure relative change overall for the firm from one time period to another and to compare the effectiveness of utilization of labor in different divisions, departments, and projects (profit centers). Both the Texas Instruments and the Upjohn indicators are closer to portfolio management methods than are conventional methods of measuring personnel and human resources effectiveness. Many conventional measurements are in the form of scalar lists of ideal functions that should be performed. Employees are periodically rated in terms of those functions, after which an overall rating is assigned by the auditors. In order to be a worthwhile portfolio measurement, however, cost should be related to outputs in some consistent way. Williams (1979) presented a model that evaluates education expense as an element in valuation of an investor's portfolio, but this model is not as general as either the Texas Instruments or the Upjohn model.

The kinds of ratios that characterize most labor-cost studies by managerial accountants are more germane to productivity measurement than to return on human capital. They are most apt to be in manufacturing or in specific service occupations where the output can be measured in units of some kind and the costs are clearly identifiable with the output. Sullivan (1981), in a report urging national attention to productivity, suggests that measurement of the effects of human capital investment be included in productivity measurement. Among the conditions needed to produce higher productivity, he says, are awareness of the need for productivity among workers, clear goals, effective methods for using resources, incentive systems, rewards and recognition, training, and leadership. Sullivan widens the list of conditions necessary for productivity and in so doing points out the complexity of valuation of human capital. Hiring and training of employees must be supplemented with leadership and managerial style that exploit those human assets, according to Sullivan, or the return on those assets may be lower, for reasons that vary with process rather than size or quality of inputs. Likert (1961) had made the same point earlier in stating that the process variables of leadership style can have substantial impact on the valuation of human assets.

The Life Cycle Approach. As managers of major corporations turned to strategic analyses rather than merely concentrating on operational matters of revenues and expenses, they made important changes in the ways they looked at their businesses. One of the earliest forms such analyses took was the "life cycle" approach. Empirical studies of new products and the growth of markets for them showed that similar patterns existed among many. A diagram of such a life cycle is shown in Figure 4.

As Figure 4 shows, a typical product or business life cycle consists of four phases. The *start-up phase* is the time period following entry into a market, introduction of a new product, or

Figure 4. Life Cycle of Products or Business.

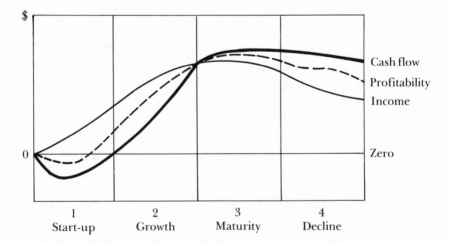

development of a new line of business. Almost uniformly, such entry produces increased sales revenues accompanied by heavy drains of cash in working capital (cash, receivables, and inventory), which grows faster than income from sales, and in fixed plant expense. Expenses for training to build up skills in the work force also drain cash. Often this cost declines with increasing experience, generally conforming to a *learning curve* in which the cost of doing things declines at a rate of 15 to 30 percent every time experience in doing the job doubles. That is, the costs of making a product during the first year can be expected to decline by 15 to 30 percent during the second year, by another 15 to 30 percent during the following two years, and so forth.

The second stage of the life cycle is the *growth phase*. During this period the beneficial effects of the learning curve can be expected to produce more sales revenues, with reduced cash drains and perhaps modest profits that grow regularly as sales and time in the business grow. Effective use of capital and people during this period can push the business above the break-even point, so that profits rather than losses appear and continue to grow.

Maturity is the third phase of the product-business life cycle. This is the time when sales reach their peak, cash expenditures as a percentage of sales level off, and cash income continues to rise. At this stage the company usually shows its best business results: earnings are high, cash demands are rising more slowly, and revenues are steady.

Decline is the fourth phase of the life cycle. Now sales revenues begin to decline as competitors enter the scene and the market becomes saturated by suppliers. As more goods enter the market and price competition trims profit margins, profits begin to wane. Often, however, cash continues to flow in at heavier-than-ever rates. Fixed plant is often fully paid off, debt may be retired, and the business contributes a hearty infusion of cash to the corporation. These results give the business an air of health, but that appearance is deceptive, for its future path will be a steady decline unless means are employed to renew the product line, improve methods of marketing, or segment the market in such a way that the firm can find a special portion (segment) of the market to exploit.

This classification of the phases of a product or business life cycle suggests specific strategies for a firm's planners to use at each stage, as follows:

Life Cycle Stage	*Indicated Strategy*
Start-up	Invest heavily in fixed plant and people and use equity or borrowed funds to seek product and market share growth and stay in front of competitors.
Growth	Pursue market share, for market share is positively related to return on investment.
Maturity	Hold market share, but don't invest heavily in fixed assets; trim back research and development and use the business as a source of cash to fund growth of future product lines. Avoid excessive expenses, control costs, and apply sound administration practices.
Decline	Be prepared to divest the business, using the proceeds to enter new growth markets and create new breadwinners for tomorrow.

Replacement Charting and the Human Resources Life Cycle. Some of America's leading firms have long engaged in a form of human resources strategic planning that employs an analytical tool called "replacement charting." Typically, this method has called for a staff department—usually management development—to prepare a special kind of organization chart that parallels the formal organization chart of the firm but is modified to reveal the possibilities of moving individuals to different and perhaps higher-level jobs. Making such a chart requires the pooled judgment of an individual's superiors concerning the individual's promotability. A decision is made as to whether the individual is immediately promotable, possibly promotable within some specified time period, or not considered promotable at this time. Decisions can be shown on the chart by means of a color-coding scheme. The backup documentation of the basis on which the decisions are made should be complete and accurate enough to be used by management development and personnel managers in initiating developmental programs, both individual and group, to accelerate the growth process. For example, it might show that few, if any, of the first-line supervisors were promotable. The organization could then initiate a program to recruit middle managers from the outside, offer added development training for foremen to enhance their promotability, or take similar actions.

Often the decision that a person was unpromotable then or ever was based on some consideration of the person's age and education and was thus a crude and somewhat rigid application of the life cycle strategic planning approach to human resources. Few firms, however, actually laid out the inventory of their manpower to fit the life cycle model of analysis. Such a display of the human resources of an organization would resemble the product life cycle model, as shown in Figure 5.

Figure 5. Human Resources Life Cycle.

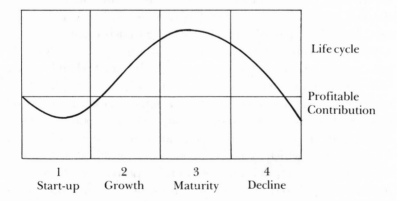

1	2	3	4
Start-up	Growth	Maturity	Decline

Start-up level employees include those who were recently hired or those who are young or inexperienced. Employees at this level are a kind of human resources investment. Vestibule training, early assignments to acquire experience, classes for supervisory or management education, and rotated job experience plans would be useful for this group.

Growth level employees are beyond their apprenticeship and are beginning to acquire higher-level skills and experience at a rapid rate. Middle managers, project managers, staff department experts, and specialist executives fit into this category. It usually includes people whose experience in years or in the firm is between five and fifteen years.

Mature level employees are usually between forty and sixty years of age and have arrived at the level of professional competence and abilities at which they are making maximum contribution to the firm. They may perhaps have reached the limits of their growth. They are not to be considered undesirable, but their potential for further growth is usually limited. This category would include most of the senior officers of the firm, as well as senior unit chiefs whose probability of further promotion is limited.

Decline level employees are those whose usefulness to the firm has begun to decline. The decline may occur because of fading health, technological obsolescence, diminished energy levels, or loss of motivation. The degree of toleration given to such employees depends on the humanistic attitude of the firm. Often they are shunted into easier jobs where they remain until they are quietly retired or "disemployed." Dynamic young leaders often attack this category of deadwood when they take over a new leadership role in an organization. The replacement charting method and the life cycle method for strategic management of human capital have definite limits, however. For one thing, replacement charting assumes that rigorous and thorough analysis of potential has been devised and is in place. It also ignores individual differences, recognition of which is necessary to make meaningful decisions affecting human capital. Furthermore, the process invites lawsuits under the Age Discrimination in Employment Act of 1979, which places people over forty years of age in a "protected" category. This law states that people cannot be fired or passed over for promotion because of age alone; they must be dealt with on the basis of performance and other job-related factors.

These methods have other drawbacks as well. Stereotyping may easily take the place of individual performance and appraisal judgments, with all people under thirty being considered as a negative investment, for example, or all people over sixty as deadwood. Also, seniority rather than job-related factors can take on a heightened significance and discourage able young people from making the effort to demonstrate ability. The Japanese management system is said to stress seniority in this way; people can never expect to gain high posts while they are under thirty unless they have some special connection, such as being related to the owners (Ouchi, 1981). Such a system presumes that age and experience have a direct correlation with ability until the point of diminishing returns is reached, at which time the old soldiers are expected to decently fade away. The portfolio approach to human capital, which is similar to the approach taken for products and markets, is far more useful than the replacement chart or life cycle methods for making key personnel decisions.

Combining Life Cycle and Portfolio Analysis. A new variation of the life cycle approach to strategic analysis was created by the Boston Consulting Group (BCG), which rearranged the same elements into a different format. This portfolio approach, which has been used with adaptations by General Electric, Shell, and others, involves constructing a two by two grid similar to the one shown in Figure 6.

Along the horizontal axis of this matrix is the objective of market growth (whether the entire market is growing slower, equal to, or faster than the economy as a whole), and along the vertical axis is the share (percentage) of the market that the company holds. This creates a four-cell matrix into which various businesses (product and market) can be classified. IBM, for example, is in a growth market, computers, and holds some 65 percent of that market, so it would be in the upper right-hand corner of the matrix.

BCG named the products in each of their matrix's four cells. *Dogs* are products that are sold in slow-growth or no-growth markets and for which the company has a low and perhaps declining share of the market. BCG proposes that when a firm discovers a "dog"

Figure 6. A Product Market Portfolio.

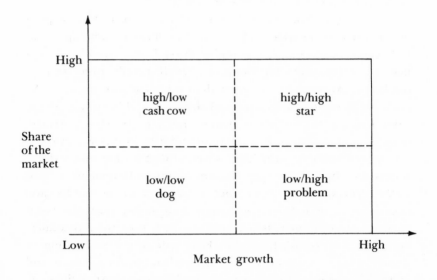

in its product line, it should divest itself of that product or market by cashing it out and transfer its resources to more fruitful applications.

Cash cows are products for which the firm has the leading share of the market, but the market is neither especially fast-growing nor especially stable. Examples are products such as Vaseline petroleum jelly (Chesebrough Ponds) or Ivory soap (Proctor and Gamble), which dominate a special market that is relatively stable. BCG suggests that firms not invest large sums in such products in an attempt to increase market share, but rather hold the share and "milk the cow" as a constant source of cash for building promising new product and market lines.

Stars are products for which markets show promise of being fast-growing and for which market development money can help to gain an increasing market share. These are the breadwinners of tomorrow and should command the best marketing development efforts of the firm.

Problem children are products for which a high potential exists because the market is growing but for which the firm has a less than average market share. BCG suggests that these products be analyzed intensively with a view to turning them into "stars" or, if there is no feasible way of doing that, turning them into "dogs" and abandoning them.

The Boston Consulting Group's system of categorization (for which the preceding is a terse and wholly unauthorized explanation) has attracted the attention of senior management and strategic planners in many major corporations. It also suggests a model for managing portfolios of other kinds, including portfolios of human resources.

Classifying Human Assets in Portfolio Form. It's apparent (at least to this author) that human capital theory has valuable contributions to make to a corporation's strategic management of its human resources. It seems equally apparent that looking to the accounting profession to produce the procedure necessary to incorporate the theory into managerial decision processes is likely to be a waste of time. Replacement charting does not seem promising, either. The application of portfolio analysis to assessment of human resources seems far more likely to produce a useful and prescriptive strategy. Although the portfolio format for rating businesses and markets is only indirectly relevant to people, it does suggest a model for analysis that can be tailored to strategic assessment of the performance and potential of people in specific jobs in specific organizations.

A model of a human resources portfolio matrix is shown in Figure 7. The matrix has the same form for human resources as for products, except that its two dimensions reflect the two major objectives of human resources management: performance and potential. *Performance* refers to the actual achievements of the individual as compared with the objectives of the job that are agreed to in advance by manager and subordinate. It is desirable that some form of management by objectives (MBO) be in place before measuring performance. MBO is the system under which job objectives are defined and then used as a basis of performance appraisal. *Potential* refers to the likelihood of the job holder making a future contribution of value to the employing organization. Evaluation of this potential may be based on the number of years over which performance may be expected or on the possibility of

Figure 7. The Human Resources Portfolio.

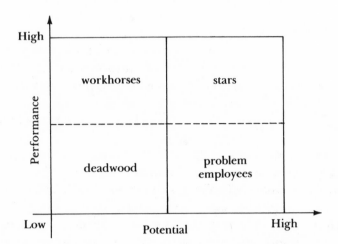

the employee making one or a few contributions that will advance
the purposes of the firm in a significant way.

Like the product portfolio, the human resources portfolio
can be divided into four cells with distinctive names. (Note that
not all the names are suitable for public labeling, however!)
Deadwood refers to people whose performance and potential are
both low. They have little potential for growth, and they do not
live up to even that level of potential in their actual performance.
Such people are unqualified or incompetent; often they are not
even trying to perform well. Only a small percentage of people
on the professional or managerial payroll is likely to be found in
this category.

Workhorses are people who have reached a high peak of
performance but have definitely limited potential. This is the largest
classification for managers; it is akin to the "cash cow" category
in financial or product portfolios. People in this classification have
probably reached their optimal level of performance, but a person
should be placed in this (or any other) category only for a given
year because of the possibility of human change. A new assessment
is made each year, and people who appear to have made a sudden

breakthrough can be moved. The best thing to do with workhorses is simply keep them abreast of the cost of living through salary increases and assure them that they are secure in their jobs (at the same level). In a study I conducted (Odiorne, 1978) of more than 1,500 managers, 79 percent were placed in this category by their assessors.

Stars are people of high potential who are performing at the highest level of that potential. Often they are young people of considerable ability who have exhibited a high level of motivation, but they may also be senior technical people or staff experts who remain creative and productive. The category might also include a general manager of great potential whose performance includes taking over troubled divisions and turning them around and whose performance is both high and growing. Fifteen percent of the managers assessed were placed in this category.

Problem employees are people who have great potential but who are working well below their capacity and with mixed results. In some instances they divert their energies to making mischief, engaging in harmful actions, or wasting their time on trivial tasks. This is the most complicated of the categories of human assets. It includes young people who have great ability but who are hazy on career potentials as well as older people who show flashes of brilliance interspersed with stretches of disappointing failures. These people should command the best attention of the management development specialist, the counselor, and perhaps even the company psychologist. Sometimes people end up in this category because of unfavorable past experiences in the organization, such as bad management by prior (or present) bosses. Recommended managerial action includes sound counseling, job reassignments, and new challenges. Problem employees are worth saving because of their high potential and occasional excellence, but individual assessment and analysis is necessary. Failure over many years should be considered a signal that perhaps the person really is lost. If problem employees don't grow into stars or settle down to become work horses, they may become deadwood.

Why Categorize? Common sense and caution are needed to prevent quick lumping together of people into categories without good reason. If an organization has no intention of taking actions to change people's behavior or move them into more suitable work, then it has no reason for assessing their performance or for categorizing them.

At the same time, it is useful to classify people in this way because each category requires different managerial action. As an officer of one firm using the portfolio approach described the system in a delightful oversimplification, "We polish the stars, fix the problems, feed the workhorses plenty of hay, and shoot the dogs."

Furthermore, many recurring tasks in human resources management can be made easier by such an annual classification. They include the following:

- selection of people for employment or for new jobs within the firm
- promotion of people to higher levels of responsibility
- rewarding of performance through merit pay, bonus, or incentive systems
- recording of performance information in the salaried personnel file to become part of a performance inventory
- identification of training and development needs of individuals and organizations
- provision of means for appraising managers and for using those appraisals in judging managerial competence and potential
- preparation of guidelines for the coaching of subordinates by supervisors
- identification of problem employees so they can be marked for special treatment.

All of these managerial decisions must be made in some way. Making them in this fashion substitutes system and rationality for sentiment, intuition, bias, and favoritism. The criteria for measuring performance proposed in this book are job objectives, discussed in detail in Chapter Fourteen.

Part Two

Managing High-Performing Employees: Workhorses and Stars

What do we mean when we say "Let the best man win"? Can an egalitarian society tolerate winners?
—*John Gardner*

4

Keeping Workhorses
Motivated and Productive

> Growth is the only evidence of life.
> —*John Henry Cardinal Newman*

The creation of formal, planned programs aimed at developing managerial talent in ordinary people is a relatively recent occurrence in business history, having begun mainly after World War II. During that emergency period, most young men were inducted or enlisted in the armed forces and thus were out of the main stream of manpower. Senior managers who would normally have retired during the war years remained on the job and then retired in exceptionally large numbers during the five years following the end of the war. The creation of managerial vacancies caused by that retirement surge, the growth of large firms through mergers, the steady decline of family capitalism and postwar growth of the national economy all generated a need for more managers.

In addition to these factors, there was a rise in the ratio of managers to workers at this time. Wholly new managerial occupations were created. Senior staff positions in such areas as personnel, labor relations, traffic management, purchasing, and research and development were added to the managerial complement in many firms. The result of all this was a severe shortage of managers. Because of the shortage, the idea of management development or management education became a formalized, standard part of the human resources functions of most large corporations.

In the wake of the postwar manager shortage, university executive development programs blossomed, tuition refund plans were installed to allow younger managers to attend evening degree-granting programs, and association programs for management development sprang up in every quarter. Many firms created their own management development centers where middle managers were sent to be trained in executive and managerial skills. General Electric's center at Crotonville, New York, created in the 1950s, was a precursor to numerous similar centers established by other firms. Today, hundreds of corporations and government agencies have management development programs. The cost of such programs run into the hundreds of millions of dollars annually, and tens of thousands of people participate in them. The American Management Association and numerous other trade associations have made management seminars and courses a staple of their member services.

Training and Development: A Growing Profession

Today, employee training, and management development—training for managers—constitute a growing professional specialty. When economic times get tough, functions perceived as nonessential are the first to be eliminated from an organization. During the depression of the midseventies, however, training was not as severely cut back as many other functions. By contrast, in earlier years (say, during the fifties) even a slight reversal in budgets, sales, or profit picture often produced disastrous cutbacks in training. Thus it appears that corporations recognize the importance of employee training and management development. Many firms now have separate corporate training departments or management development offices within their personnel administration departments.

There is persuasive evidence to show that the field of management development has attained a solid professional level. For example, membership in the American Society for Training and Development (ASTD) not only did not drop sharply in the most recent economic downturns, as it had in past ones; it actually rose! Attendance at the ASTD national convention in 1983 was one of the highest on record, despite the fact that the convention was not held in any of the major population centers where the bulk of the membership is located.

Furthermore, the number of available openings in placement columns and in the search organizations that handle training and development "head-hunting" is higher than ever. The salaries being offered are higher than ever, too. During the fifties you could have counted on one hand the number of professional training directors who made over $25,000 a year. Today high five-figure salaries are very common for experienced professionals in behavioral technology. Even allowing for the effect of inflation, this is quite a change. Corporate training is now a career—and a profitable one.

Training Programs that Work. What is behind the success of this training and development revolution? Why are today's employee training programs better than those of yesterday? What, in fact, makes a training program work? Here are ten answers.

1. *Successful programs focus on behavior rather than on personality.* Much corporate training in the fifties was aimed at changing personality. Supervisory training tried to make people trustworthy, loyal, helpful and the like, rather than making them behave in ways that were productive, creative, or skilled.

Much of the change in emphasis from personality to behavior—from the intangible to the measurable—grew out of the theories of B. F. Skinner, the language laboratory, and the programmed instruction (PI) movement. Trainers soon discovered that it was not the hardware, the PI text, or the teaching machine that was important about these techniques. Rather, programmed techniques demonstrated a new way of organizing knowledge that allowed it to be taught more effectively by any means. Skinner and his disciples also contributed a useful definition of behavior: "Behavior is activity that can be seen or measured."

2. *Successful programs are designed for results, not process.* In many training programs of the past (and some present ones), the process was the only thing of interest to the trainer. Today's trainers, however, define a result that serves organizational ends and then plan a program that will produce it.

This distinction between process and result is the major difference between the now-defunct "sensitivity training" and the new and more useful form of training called organization development (OD). Sensitivity training often centered on process, while OD focuses on result. Sales training, which often focused upon entertainment, was also process-centered training. All training uses processes, to be sure, but modern programs use processes as a means to a result, not an end in themselves.

3. *Successful programs relate training to its context.* All too often in the past, training was conducted on a "copycat" basis: When one organization reported success with a training topic or process, dozens of others immediately set up something similar. Now, however, trainers recognize that behavior change, in order to persist, must be supported by the environment in which it will be returned. Thus, it is as much a technique of sound training to study the context of the organization as it is to conduct a well-executed class or conference. The organizational culture and managerial climate to which the trainee must return should have characteristics that will support the behavior that training induces; otherwise, the training will fail.

4. *Successful programs recognize that not all management problems are behavior problems.* The ancient faith that education is a solution to all problems has often been carried over into industrial and administrative training, with some unfortunate effects. Good sense requires that the training professional ask some hard questions before setting up a program: Is there really a problem? What is it? Is it caused by lack of knowledge or skill, or is it caused by something else, such as bad organization, weak policy, or irresolute supervision? If the problem is not lack of knowledge or skills, training is not prescribed. Rather, the system that created the problem must be worked on.

One of the best things for trainers to learn is how to say NO when people rush into their offices demanding a training solution to a problem that is patently not a training problem. For example, training salespersons in "how to close an order" won't help a firm if its general marketing plan is weak, its prices are noncompetitive, or its product is inferior.

Current thinking has caused more and more training departments to see themselves as behavior change departments. If a behavior isn't amenable to being changed by training, then the professional won't use that method of changing it.

5. *Successful programs have specific objectives and criteria.* Before training begins, its objective(s) should be spelled out, approved, and presented to everyone concerned. "As a result of attending this training session . . ." should preface every announcement, invitation, or course description. This procedure gives the firm's management full knowledge of what it is buying. It lets the program's attendees know what they are in for and whether they are attending the right program. It helps teams of instructors shape their efforts toward a common purpose. It also provides the best yardstick for evaluation after completion of the training.

Objectives must be clear, and criteria for evaluating success in achieving them must be explicit; otherwise, both will be worthless in practice. Criteria might take the form of examples of the behavior that should result from successful completion of the training. They might include statistical changes in job outcomes that would be evidence of behavior change. They might be ratio changes that should be produced by training, such as a change in the ratio of complaints to compliments from customers that would be expected to follow an employee customer-relations training program.

Criteria are often presented in the form of "go—no go" statements, such as "The Palo Alto store will be turned around in sales and profit, thus avoiding its closing in 1976." The weakest criteria are those that consist of adjectives, for their meaning is often ambiguous. A good rule for formulating training criteria is, "Measure the measurable, describe the describable, and eliminate the rest."

Two further important changes have occurred in defining criteria for success in training. First, it is no longer considered sufficient to "find a training problem" and solve it. Problem solving merely restores normality. The training professional, however, should be an agent of change and betterment. Thus, important criteria for training should relate to innovation.

Second, training professionals now agree that a good training criterion must include a statement of the present condition as well as the desired condition. Without a definition of present behaviors, training may boast achievements that it should not claim, for the desired condition may have already existed before the training took place. For example, trainers could promise to make a company "safe from tigers" and then boast for years after, "Surely we must have succeeded, for no tigers have attacked the company since our course was held." To avoid this situation, criteria for training should include statements of a "from-to" character.

6. *Successful programs often use simulations.* Experience has shown that simulation is frequently the best means of changing behavior. Role playing, the management game, case studies, family group OD sessions, incident process, the flight simulator, and many other forms of simulation have proved extremely useful in training. The reason for the success lies in the closeness of the simulated behavior to the actual behavior demanded on the job. A pilot in a flight simulator enters a flying environment, emits behavior, and receives specific feedback related to flying skills.

By this same token, however, simulation will not work unless it is realistic. Asking managers to work in teams to assemble horses from magnetic pieces has merit in simulating team behavior only if such behavior is ordinary or desirable on their job—a highly unlikely state of affairs. Trainers who persist in unrealistic simulations often are merely lazy. It takes work to prepare training that simulates reality. For example, it requires that the trainer get out into the plant, field, or office where real things happen in order to find out what will make an effective simulation.

Simulation is also a good example of the advantages of action over talk. Hours of gabbing about the theories of behavioral scientists of one school or another produce nothing but trainees who can, in turn, talk about the leading father figures of training directors. The trainer might better spend time in simulating behavior expected of trainees on the job, thus applying those theories in action.

7. *Successful programs break the total training objective down into successive stages.* One of the more effective training techniques developed during the past fifty years is job instruction training (JIT), which was used in World War II to train millions of people in new work skills for wartime industry. JIT was fantastically successful, largely because it broke down each job being taught into many stages. This job breakdown was detailed enough to allow trainers to check their own progress and that of the trainees

at every step. Modern adaptations of the JIT approach, such as the Keller System or Personalized System of Instruction (PSI), apply the same logic to new training problems.

The major advantage of breaking down tasks prior to conducting training lies in the increased ability of the trainer to teach for mastery of the competencies sought. If the learner hasn't acquired the behaviors required for a particular step, he or she can be recycled through that step until mastery has been achieved.

8. *Successful programs require that the learner emit some action during training.* Passive behavior may produce some learning, but training that relies on such learning is likely to have limited effectiveness. If every person involved in the training is required to engage in some kind of action, there is plenty of opportunity for feedback to reinforce the desired behavior. Action also makes the effect of the training easier to measure.

9. *Successful programs give trainees immediate feedback for their actions.* Some trainers, especially behavior model theorists, say that the pure act of learning takes place when feedback occurs. The "hot-stove principle" of learning suggests that the cat that jumps on a hot stove will never jump on any stove again. This principle demonstrates feedback in its purest form. However, many cats will be required "on the job" to learn to jump on cold stoves, avoid hot ones, and discriminate correctly between a hot and a cold one in advance of the jump. Feedback thus needs to be specific.

Feedback is most useful if it is given in a simulated environment that is closely related to the actual environment in which the desired behavior will be performed on the job. For example, in a flight simulator, the pilot sees the plane crash if a serious error is made.

Some guides to successful feedback in training might be helpful here:

a. Fast feedback is more effective than slow feedback. The more nearly simultaneous the behavior and the feedback are, the greater the learning effect will be.

b. Relating the feedback to the behavior explicitly increases the learning effect of the feedback.

c. Favorable or pleasant feedback has a better effect than punishing or negative feedback. Pleasing feedback issued for desired behaviors not only produces the behaviors but also increases the desire to learn more. Unfavorable or punishing feedback may extinguish undesired behaviors, but it may also produce a desire to get out of the training situation immediately and remain away from it in the future. For example, forms of behavior modification that are largely based on negative feedback have attracted severe criticism even when applied to criminals.

Of course, behavior modification need not be regarded only in the narrow sense drawn from the experimental psychologists. In a broader context, all training that works is behavior modification. This includes the freshman English course that produces better writers or the team building course that produces better engineers. However, even in the case of pleasant feedback, the fact remains that effective use of feedback can change behavior. This places a great responsibility on the trainer to consider the moral and social consequences of the programs he or she designs.

10. *Successful programs measure results against goals.* Evaluation of training is a hotly debated topic today. The problem seems to be finding criteria against which to measure training effort and expense. Rating a course in terms of participant opinion, top management impressions, and similar measures misses the main point. Training should change behavior in ways that are relevant to and desirable for the job environment. The desired behaviors should be defined in advance, broken down into small steps, and simulated in the training. Criteria for evaluating these behaviors should also be spelled out before training begins. Thus, at the end of the course, evaluators can pull out the original statements of objectives and compare the new behaviors against the old behaviors and the objectives. If the objective of a course is mastery of certain skills, then the extent of mastery of these skills is the extent of course success.

Why Some Programs Don't Work. In spite of all these successes, doubts began to be raised about whether management development programs actually developed managers, especially about whether they developed star-quality managers. Robert House (1969) studied the effects of management development programs and found that they were by no means universally successful. Some, in fact, seemed to cause lower morale, increased managerial turnover, undesirable behavior on the part of participants, and conflict with superiors when the participants returned to their jobs.

In part, this was because the architects of such programs often failed to improve present job performance by training to prepare participants for higher-level responsibility in management. House defined management development as "a social influence process of change." More than just training in classes, House explained, it might include coaching, understudy assignments, job rotation, selected reading, planned experience, performance appraisal, or any combination of these. Such techniques would produce good managers, however, only if five key variables were controlled. These variables are participant characteristics, quality of development effort, leadership climate on the job, formal organizational structure and practices, and organizational culture. Since so many of these variables were either hidden from the planners or impossible to control, management development efforts often failed to produce managerial stars or even to improve participants' performance on their present jobs.

House's five variables relate to the circumstances that must be present in order for a management development program to affect the behavior of a participant in a useful way. First, the participant must be motivated to learn and have sufficient intelligence to understand the ideas presented (participant characteristics). Second, the program must have sufficiently important content to be useful (quality of development effort). Third, the work environment to which the trainee will return at the end of the course must include a superior who is willing to accept and support—or at least refrain from opposing—the trainee's new behavior (job leadership climate). Fourth, the whole organization's culture, policies, procedures, and climate must also be supportive of the new behavior taught by the program (organizational structure, practices, and culture). Otherwise the trainee's new behavior will be extinguished upon return to the job, and he or she will be frustrated and probably worse off than if training had never occurred.

Another problem is that simulation and many other modern techniques tend to work better in training people for present jobs than in training them for future jobs, the content of which may be uncertain. Simulation or management exercises, as Despres (1982), for example, describes them, draw on the principle that "What you do, you understand." Such exercises have value because present responsibilities can be defined. But to be effective in preparing people for future jobs, which is the task of management training for stars, the trainer must have some clear idea of the nature of those future responsibilities—and that is not always possible.

Different Training for Different Needs. A few years back a large firm conducted an opinion survey of its employees. Among the questions asked was a series related to employee expectations concerning opportunities for higher levels of responsibility. To the chagrin of the management development staff, over 90 percent of the managers and supervisors responding indicated that they not only desired but expected to be promoted in the near future. A cursory survey of growth prospects in the firm made it apparent that no such quantity of promotions was remotely possible. A stable and sound company in the food business, this firm could reasonably predict that higher-level jobs would be offered to about 10 to 15 percent of its management team during the next five years—but certainly there was nothing close to the level of expectation that the survey revealed. Thus a high level of disappointment was bound to occur among those whose expectations had been somehow raised.

Further study showed that the cause of this disparity between reality and expectation was a vigorously executed management development program that had stated clearly and unequivocally that the course objective was "to prepare you for higher-level responsibility in the future growth of the corporation." In other words, the course designers had promised something that the organization could not deliver. Furthermore, the course had been conducted with considerable skill and imagination and had therefore done all too effectively something it should never have attempted: It had treated every manager—whether workhorse, star, problem, or deadwood—alike, raising the hopes of all. A careful portfolio analysis of the firm's managers, made before the program was begun, might have averted this lamentable situation.

This example demonstrates an important principle for management development: Different objectives for development should be framed for different categories of people. (1) The great bulk of a firm's managers will most likely fall into the workhorse category. Their training should aim at improving job performance in their present position or one of comparable level, rather than raising hopes that cannot be fulfilled. (2) Management education for stars should be aimed at increasing and developing their potential in expectation of positions and job responsibilities that will exist in the future but may not be evident today. (3) Management development for employees classified as problems should be remedial in scope and purpose. The potential of these people is high, but their current fulfillment of that potential is low because of situational or personal factors that need fixing. (4) Time and effort spent on trying to train people definitely identified as deadwood is fruitless, wasteful, and probably productive of more harm than good.

Training and Development for Workhorses

Early management development programs presented an appealing idea. They suggested that just about any normal person could become a manager, maybe even a star. Crawford Greenwalt, president of Du Pont, expressed this theme when he stated, "We need to get ordinary people to do extraordinary things." Management development was pictured as a vehicle by which some middle-of-the-road workhorse might, after undergoing a training course, become a star. According to this theory, silk purses could be produced from even the most nonsilky materials if only the skilled management developer were given the resources and the time to do the job. It was a modern version of an old American dream: Any kid could grow up to be President. No notion seemed to exist that many people would always be workhorses and only a few would be stars; such an idea seemed to smack repugnantly of elitism. The result, unfortunately, was that management training for all—or almost all—caused many workhorses to be mistrained.

What Training Do Workhorses Need? Because of the rapid changes that can occur in even the most mundane job, persons with little likelihood of promotion to higher ranks should not be slighted when a firm plans for employee training. Nichols (1982) proposes that training be defined as a "planned effort to improve job performance." Training in this sense is needed for all employees.

Employees need to be trained to be more productive; they also need to be prepared for changes in the organization. Training, however, is different from education. Education, in Nichols's view, refers to the kinds of planned development that advance a person's career. In the portfolio approach to human resources management, "education" would be reserved for potential stars, whereas every employee would be "trained."

Who should decide whether a person should be prepared for career advancement rather than simply being trained to do a better job in his or her present position? At Lawrence Livermore National Laboratories in California, employees are offered opportunities to explore that question for themselves in career/life planning workshops (Hanson, 1982). A self-assessment inventory is one of the key instruments used in assisting employees to arrive at their own level of aspiration and career planning. This inventory uses a tool called the System for Identifying Motivated Abilities (SIMA), which measures the combination of an employee's ability and motivation. Similarly, Smith-Kline Corporation, a pharmaceutical and medical products firm, conducts career planning workshops for its employees to assist them in relating their personal goals to their career plans (Tavernier, 1980).

While the overall effects of such programs on company profits and growth have been salubrious, they also have caused some employees to decide to leave the company. Such mobility is apparently increasing. During the seventies, when jobs were relatively plentiful, many Americans quit stable jobs to seek out second careers (Sager and Kipling, 1980). Although the decline in job opportunities reduced such voluntary turnover during the recession of 1982, the trend is nonetheless still present, and it becomes higher when ordinary workhorses review their career prospects and don't like what they see in their future. However difficult starting a second career may be, it apparently is more acceptable to many people than being dead-ended in boring and unsatisfying work because of lack of education or other qualities associated with potential or simply because of company promotion practices.

For employers who have important people doing important work but who have limited potential for promotion, two alternatives seem to present themselves. The first of these is training for the people to improve their present job performance. Boylen (1980) concludes that such training has beneficial effects beyond improving productivity and facilitating response to change. Training, he states, can help to solve problems of boredom, poor attitude, and job turnover. The second employer option is offering training that is aimed at career enrichment. Such training needn't always be conducted in the classroom, proposes Kaye (1983); informal training can occur on the job through such methods as job rotation, special projects, and employee mentors. Such enrichment can remove some of the discontent that comes from feeling trapped in a dead-end job.

Training to Improve Present Job Performance. Many management development experts feel that most management development courses, seminars, and other training efforts should aim at improving the performance of participants on their present jobs rather than attempting to enhance their promotability. It is quite possible to add to people's knowledge and skills in ways that will enhance their competence, widen their knowledge of the organization and its functions, let them expand into new areas, raise their value as human assets, and provide them with more job satisfaction and success without falsely promising them managerial stardom. At the same time, well-designed courses can open doors to permit the rise of the few workhorses who have the potential for upgrading themselves into the star category.

Training for Job Change. Often we train today's workhorses for yesterday's jobs. Three concepts must characterize training for today's jobs, Livingston (1983) proposes: relevance, application to the job, and payoff in results. Beckhard (1982) focuses on perceptions of the present job as the key to improving the effectiveness of management training in a world that is changing rapidly. Studies like these suggest that applying sound learning theory even to the training of workhorses for present jobs is difficult. Jobs are fluid and dynamic, while definitions of training objectives often remain static and thus become obsolete.

Beckhard's analysis of training needs as being shaped by the viewpoints of both management and workers suggests an important conclusion about the kind of management development needed for workhorse people: Even though these workers probably won't get promoted, they must learn to live and work in a world that is changing constantly. Even the most stable jobs today have important elements of change. Rather than pounding a typewriter as in the past, for example, today's secretary is likely to type into a word processor. The new technology has brought important changes to this most traditional of workhorse jobs. The change from typing to word processing has led to increased office productivity, greater efficiency, and cost savings, according to Jones (1983), who studied the effect of word processing on the insurance industry. In order to gain these benefits, however, companies had to sponsor extensive retraining for their secretaries. Because word processing technology is constantly being upgraded, further retraining can be expected. Many similar changes are taking place in other workhorse positions.

Preparing workhorses to deal with change involves more than simply training them in new technology. Change also is the source of considerable personal stress. In the New York Telephone Company, the effects of stress at work were found to be so great that in the late seventies the firm began to offer meditation programs called "Clinically Standardized Meditation" (CSM). Coming at a time when the entire Bell Corporation was facing breakup into new units, coupled with the arrival of new technology such as word processing, fiber optics, and communications satellites, this program apparently was both necessary and beneficial, according to McGeveran (1981). Many telephone company employees who took part reported improved physical health and job performance.

Improving Workhorse Motivation

Take the case of John Smith, age thirty-five. John graduated from high school and then served in the Navy, where he learned to be an electrician. Upon discharge he went to work for a large corporation. After seven years as a journeyman electrician, he was chosen from among several candidates to be foreman of electrical maintenance for a medium-sized plant. John is married and has two young children; his wife works in a retail sales job. They own their own home. He is a member of the Elks and the Presbyterian Church, and he owns a boat and a camper. His hobbies are hunting and bowling. He is also fond of watching professional football on TV and makes an occasional trip to the city to see a live game. His family all reside in the same area. He takes part in parent-teacher meetings and has been chosen as a deacon in his church.

John is convinced that he has a pretty good life. He doesn't expect to be promoted to Chief of Maintenance, a position usually held by a graduate engineer. He attends occasional supervisory training courses offered by his company, as well as some technical training courses to keep up with new technology, but his ambitions are not burning ones. He would like to be able to buy a vacation home by the lake and perhaps add another room to his house. He'd like his kids to go to college. That's about all.

John's potential is limited, but his performance is quite satisfactory. He even has occasional moments of excellence. An objective observer would predict that John will remain in approximately the same level and role he now enjoys until he retires, which will be twenty-five to thirty years from now.

In other words, John is a typical workhorse. People much like him make up the largest portion of the work force in most companies.

Unlikely as it seems on the surface, John may have a motivation problem. While the evidence doesn't seem to indicate that he will become apathetic or alienated, his future could still be murky. Perhaps new technology will overtake his skills, making him a misfit. Maybe social changes such as affirmative action will bring his older values into conflict with new ones. Preventive action in the motivational area is surely not out of the question for Smith, although opinions vary on whether people like him really have a problem, or, if one does exist, what strategy for dealing with it is indicated.

Locke (1982) reviewed motivational methods and found that goal setting, participation in decisions, job enrichment, and increases in pay are the major methods now in use. He concluded that money and goal setting are the most successful.

Older generations of managers saw money as the major and perhaps the sole motivator for workers. The prevailing theory among behavioral scientists, however, suggests that more than money is required. People without potential for rising in an organization often feel trapped, which can lead to a sense of powerlessness, frustration, and apathy. These feelings, in turn, can impair job performance.

The form of training called Organizational Development (OD) has been applied to this problem of workhorse motivation and continues to be used widely. "Organizational development" is a broad term that covers a wide range of group development activities about which practitioners are not in agreement. Now about twenty years old, OD is an "applied theory of behavior," according to Weisbrod (1981). It works because it tends to improve work life, he concludes, and adds that it works because it is an ideology based upon science, democracy and learning, and it works in a non-literal, subjective sense. Its goals are the improvement of productivity and worker contentment. John Smith might be a highly suitable subject for OD training.

Motivating workhorses by reshaping work group membership has also been suggested. Within any organization there are certain individuals who provide a special kind of information flow. Tusheman and Scanlan (1981) call them "boundary spanners." Such people reach beyond the bounds of their own work responsibilities to give and seek out information that could have an impact on the internal workings of their group. Deliberately constructing a work group so that it contains boundary spanners can have beneficial effects on the functioning and motivation of the more narrowly oriented members of the group, the authors conclude. At present, however, the presence of boundary spanners in a group is usually accidental rather than planned, for the ways that boundary spanning and information flow work in an organization are imperfectly understood. Thus, boundary spanning cannot be relied on as a major motivational tool.

Workers paid by the hour, especially those in unskilled jobs, are commonly thought to be the most likely to suffer motivation problems. However, any person who has leveled off, even in middle and executive management ranks, may have such problems. Executives may suffer when they become shelf-sitters at a level that falls below their aspirations, reports Thackray (1981). In contrast to the "organization man" described by William H. Whyte over twenty years ago, such executives are not content to simply serve their time and become conformists to organizational policy and practice. Looking for more challenging work, bored and discontented, they would welcome more attractive features in their jobs.

For all of these groups—the unskilled worker on the assembly line, the supervisor who will go no further, and the executive who has leveled off—some action to improve motivation appears to be indicated. One of the best ways to improve these people's motivation is to make their present position, the one in which they are stuck for life, more fulfilling. This is the purpose of the technique called job enrichment.

Job Enrichment—Antidote to Workhorse Apathy? Job enrichment aims to improve the motivation of the worker or manager who is stuck for the foreseeable future in one organizational niche. The importance of motivating such people lies in their large numbers in most organizations. After all, only a few of a firm's employees can expect to rise meteorically or become fast-track careerists.

The major early theorist of job enrichment was Frederick Herzberg (1966). Drawing heavily upon studies done with nurses, purchasing agents, and others in important but often static job roles, Herzberg found that such people were motivated not only by money and benefits but by a need for achievement and recognition. The key to increasing motivation and productivity, he said, lay in developing each worker's individuality.

Herzberg (1981) claimed that job enrichment could utilize an individual's ability, motivation, and sense of responsibility to generate higher productivity and worker satisfaction. His plan for job enrichment had five major elements: doing a whole job rather than a piece of one; knowing for whom each job is being done; getting feedback on one's work; having personal contact with other people, including the boss; and having some discretion in choosing the way the work is done.

Responsibility for implementing job enrichment usually lies with the personnel department of the firm, suggest Franke, Harris, and Klein (1982). They point out that the personnel department has the power and the skill to improve working conditions for individuals through such measures as incentive awards, opening better lines of communication between workers and management, setting up programs to improve employee-supervisor relations, and reducing union influence. Certainly some specific administrative center that is responsible for job enrichment is needed, for without such a center, job enrichment is unlikely to occur, claims Hodgson (1982). "Nothing seems to have taken hold," he laments. Programs, however laudable, that are left for everyone or no one to implement usually fall by the wayside under the pressure of more important or more specific responsibilities.

Herzberg's concept of job enrichment is founded on the idea of "individual differences." Job enrichment, he says, should foster a climate in which individuals are able to utilize their abilities fully. Self-fulfillment and the need to develop competence and personal dignity are the major themes of Herzberg's approach. "Productivity begins with the individual," he concludes.

The best way of making job fulfillment work is to increase communication, feedback, and rewards for results, according to Quible (1981), although redesigning the workplace may also be useful. "Every employee can be a winner," says Kafka (1981) in apparent agreement with Herzberg; this happy state results when employees are given feelings of purpose and responsibility. Management attitudes rather than specific staff programs create this pleasant climate. Kafka espouses a "Perceptive Management System" (PMS), the target of which is improved worker perceptions of their jobs. O'Connor and Barrett (1980) propose that individual differences call for "informational cues" that come from management, peers, and the job itself; for example, systematic praise, reproof, rewards, and punishment.

While higher-level managers and professionals on the way up may live a life of anticipation, this is not advised for workhorse people whose future is to be stalemated in one job. For such people, the best strategy is one that enables them to "make the most of now," according to Beaudine (1980). Workhorses should be encouraged to think less about the future and more about immediate gratification of their needs in order to gain satisfaction and pleasure from their present jobs. Beaudine's conclusion is a cautionary one for trainers or administrators who preside over a large number of workhorses. Don't breed anxiety and frustration by holding up rosy prospects of better things to come. Rather, work harder at making these employees happy where they are.

The role of the immediate supervisor is vital in keeping this sense of "nowness" in the workhorse population. The new breed of supervisor is adept at directing "self-organized work groups," for self-organization of the work situation can use up time and energy that might otherwise be spent in speculation about lost opportunity. It is possible for individuals to realize their potential in their own jobs if they do not have their aspirations raised by false hopes.

From Job Enrichment to Job Design. Somehow, during the early eighties, the philosophy of job enrichment with its emphasis on individual differences became refocused in the direction of industrial engineering and behavioral engineering. Many managers felt that there were simply too many individuals in any large work force to permit the needs of each to be dealt with separately. As a result, there was a shift toward a more systematic, procedural, and engineered approach to job enrichment. The objectives were the same: increased productivity and quality, which would be accompanied and perhaps caused by increased worker satisfaction. The best way of achieving these goals, however, was now held to be better designing of jobs and working conditions.

Scientific management and efficiency experts had used a similar idea during the thirties, but their goal had been to eliminate waste and excess cost from the job. Methods engineering, work simplification, and time and motion study were all part of that early scientific management movement. In these early schemes, the industrial engineer or management scientist figured out the most efficient way to do a job, and the worker simply went along and benefitted incidentally by suffering less fatigue and earning more money. Job enrichment took on some, but certainly not all, of the dimensions of this earlier system.

In this new form of job enrichment, its advocates proposed, jobs would be rigorously and systematically studied and redesigned to produce better quality output, more productivity, and, at the same time, more satisfied employees. As a result of this increased satisfaction, employees would refrain from resigning to seek greener pastures elsewhere. Rather, they would stay with their blind-alley jobs and continue to happily produce more and better products.

This theory presumed that jobs could be designed, much as cars and appliances could be designed, to fit the functions required of them. One of the newly prized functions was making people feel fulfilled, satisfied, "self-actualized," and responsible. Rather than starting with individual differences and fitting jobs around them, however, the supporters of this approach proposed that standardized features of job design be applied. The result, they claimed, would benefit employees and also bring high economic payoffs to the firm.

Albers (1982) spelled out some of the worker-centered features of the new job design approach. Each job would have more variety, require a higher level of knowledge and skill, and give the employee more responsibility for planning, directing, and controlling his or her own work activities, thus providing opportunity for personal growth. These goals could be accomplished by breaking the job down into four major components: work content, methods content, personal content, and organizational content. "Enhancement" methods (or "job enlargement") would be introduced for each component. McGee (1981) described to the American Institute of Industrial Engineers (AIIE), which ninety years earlier had heard Frederick Taylor present the principles of Scientific Management, a case study in which Du Pont utilized job design as a "tool" to improve company productivity as well as employee satisfaction. The results were reported as gratifying in both areas.

McGee's description was perfectly suited to the industrial engineer. You start with a problem: needs for greater productivity and quality and for lower costs. The cause of the problem is diagnosed as "diminished enthusiasm" on the part of the people doing the work. The solution is to engineer a four-step program that fills the needs and solves the problem at the same time. This is a considerable distance from the original concepts of Herzberg, who saw work as being distorted by a management system interested only in "hygiene," or prevention of bad things on the job.

New Approaches to Job Enrichment. Attempts to refine job enrichment techniques proliferated during the eighties. If job enrichment failed to produce all that was expected of it by its proponents, the fault lay in a lack of planning and implementation skill, suggested Smith (1981). Moral commitment as well as technical competence was necessary for job enrichment, he concluded. One study of attitudes of eighty-three supervisors about staffing insufficiency showed that the degree of understaffing was related to workers' attitudes toward their jobs (Vecchio and Sussman, 1981). Employees considered their jobs more or less enriched depending on how overworked they were. In another empirical research project, conducted in a confectionery factory, Wall and Clegg (1981) devised and tested a system for building motivation, job performance, job satisfaction, mental health, and lower turnover through job redesign.

Alternative work patterns such as flextime, gliding time, job sharing, weekend work, night work, work sharing, four-day weeks, and permanent part-time arrangements were part of plans proposed by Nollen (1980) and Mundale (1981). Labor unions were suggested as necessary partners in job change plans proposed by other authors. Quality-of-work-life (QWL) programs, which were cooperative with labor unions, included not only job redesign but also plans for improved health and safety of workers and for enhanced worker participation in decisions (Bolweg, 1980). Office efficiency and the creation of systems and procedures for clerical people caught in boring jobs became a melding of rational engineering analysis and psychological job enrichment for Lee (1981). Enrichment methods suggested included team competitions, job rotation, changing of job contents from time to time, and balanced work loads.

The way to cure the boredom and apathy that come from repetitive work is to build more complexity into individual jobs, suggested Kemp, Clegg, and Wall (1980). Simplification of work, which has been the heart of industrial engineering and the division of labor in an industrial society, must be reversed, they maintained. Instead, diversity and complexity should be added in order to enrich the job. This calls for work reorganization, restructuring of tasks, and job rotation, resulting in autonomous work groups.

Before trying to redesign jobs to improve motivation, managers should consider three important motivation variables suggested by Milbourn (1981). First, he claimed, people who come from rural settings are motivated by different things than people from the city, so workers' origin is important. Second, different people place different values on work itself. People with a high overall need to work can be more easily motivated to do a given job than those whose desire to work is less strong. Third, people's psychological needs differ. Some people want money badly, others less. Some need ego satisfaction from their jobs, others find it elsewhere. Some work to meet social needs, others do not. Some people seek self-fulfillment in their jobs, while others merely want a paycheck that will buy their satisfactions in outside activities. Milbourn pointed out, however, that all people—in spite of their differences— need meaningful work, responsibility for the outcome of their work, and knowledge of results. Jobs, Milbourn said, should be redesigned to provide these three basic elements.

More openly advocating the use of industrial engineering techniques, Schacter and Walker (1980) suggested that refurbishing the physical workplace was an important part of job redesign. "Environmental graphics" means using graphics and design principles to spruce up a factory or other industrial environment. Lighting, color, and esthetics in the workplace are part of job enrichment and can provide better job satisfaction to people who face the prospect of going there every day into an indeterminate future, these authors claimed. But such job redesign actions cost money, cautioned Kelly (1980), an aspect of job enrichment that has often been overlooked. Kelly recommended cost evaluation of job redesign proposals, with productivity gains being related to job satisfaction and total gains weighed against costs.

Recognition of the problem presented by workhorses in the human resources portfolio, then, has brought many suggestions for motivational action by management. The differences in approach to the problem lie more in emphasis than in ends. The originators of job enrichment focused attention on individual differences in needs and proposed redesigning jobs to suit those differences. In more recent years, however, the emphasis has shifted to the approach of the industrial engineer, the systems and procedures expert, and the personnel researcher.

Workhorses are an important part of the workforce, and their motivation remains a difficult and important problem. The failure of some systems, such as the backfire of job enrichment at the Oklahoma assembly plant of General Motors (Roham, 1980), indicates that solutions to this problem are not simple. The prepon-

derance of evidence, however, suggests that attempts at job enrichment have had beneficial effects.

A much smaller percentage of the human resources portfolio
are those we call stars; people with high potential whose performance is also high. They need treatment very different from that
given to workhorses, as we shall see in the next chapters.

5

─────────────$\mathscr{S}$─────────────

Identifying Potential
Organization Stars

That which is in disorder has neither rule or rhyme
like the stars at Heaven's Border.   —*Francis Carlin*

A few years ago a national corporation went through a rigorous
search to identify its highest-potential younger performers. Its
managers screened, interviewed, reviewed, tested, appraised, and
assessed possible candidates exhaustively, and when the final roster
of stars was produced, they were convinced of its validity. They
presented the list to the president and chief executive officer with
considerable confidence. They were therefore dismayed when he
asked, "How about young Harry Smith?"

No Harry Smith was found on the list. Someone did recall
that such a name had appeared in an earlier version, but its owner
hadn't stood up through the tests and screens. A junior engineer
with an MBA degree, Harry was presently working as an assistant
product manager for a small product line in a minor division.

"Harry became engaged to my daughter last weekend," the
president explained happily. "I was just wondering what kind of
prospects he had for the future."

With amazing aplomb the vice-president of personnel began
recounting lists of the virtues, abilities, talents, accomplishments,
and potentials of young Harry. In fact, he explained, Harry was

so exceptional that he didn't belong on the ordinary list but rather would merit special handling. Needless to say, Harry (who was in fact a competent fellow) made fine progress on his way to the top after that.

The point here isn't that relatives or insiders are the only, or even the major, source of high-potential people in an organization. In some organizations, being a relative can even be a handicap. The story does illustrate, however, the sometimes subjective and personal standards by which potential management stars are identified.

The choice of future management stars is difficult in many ways. It is also vitally important. "Who will get ahead" is not merely a concern of the company and its stockholders any more. Many public groups feel that they also have a stake in such decisions. They insist that such choices should be made fairly, on the basis of merit and accomplishment.

Identification and treatment of stars in large organizations are also, of course, of upmost importance to the individuals themselves. People wrongly identified can be severely damaged. They may work all their lives at levels lower than their potential, or they may be thrust into responsibilities beyond their ability, suffer great stress, and end as failures.

The present top managers in most organizations have the power to decide who shall succeed them. Even when this power is limited or constrained by law or custom, the weight of decision still rests there. The decision may be made intuitively, on the basis of personal interests and biases, or it may be made systematically and rationally.

Many top managers say that they can instinctively recognize potential in people. They easily mark the brilliant young performer who "could go all the way." It may be the person's appearance, manner, education, or startling early achievements that produce such a rating.

Once identified as stars, people are not easily dropped from that category. Their progress is faster, their assignments more laden with opportunity, and their paths smoother as they waft through the organization on their way to a vice-presidency. Sometimes this is as it should be. The fact remains, however, that the identification of star-quality people is anything but an exact science.

Methods of Identifying Potential in Stars

Stars are people with high potential whose performance lives up to that potential. They have a capacity for great growth both as people and as professional managers. This is not to say that one would want an organization composed entirely of stars. To use portfolio language, that would not make an efficient portfolio. Few organizations, if any, can afford to give every employee the opportunities provided to a star. Thus the management of stars is the management of a relatively small group of people whose qualifications are especially valuable to the organizational culture in which they work.

Three methods for systematically identifying the level of potential in managers are widely used today. They are the assessment center method, the review board method, and the staff analysis method (see Figure 8). Let's examine each of these in a little more detail.

The Assessment Center Method. The assessment center method was imported from England in the 1960s (Dulewicz, 1982). It was first used in the United States to select supervisors in the Bell Telephone system and spread widely thereafter. The method consists of assembling recommended managerial candidates for the specific purpose of making assessments of their potential and arriving at subsequent decisions about their promotability within the organization. It is a kind of career examination. Groups of half a dozen to a dozen candidates meet to work on simulated management problems such as case studies, role play, and in-basket exercises (absorbing and responding to a simulated in-basket of letters, reports, and the like) under the eyes of observers who are higher-level managers in the same firm. Unlike earlier situational stress tests used by the Office of Strategic Services (OSS) in World War II, the situations presented at the assessment center are quite realistic. Candidates' behavior is watched and rated on job-related scales as they undergo the assessment exercises so that an overall rating indicating high or low potential can be made. They are evaluated on their decision-making and problem-solving skills, their social-relationship abilities, their leadership qualities, and other evidence of ability to function at a higher level. Often they are interviewed,

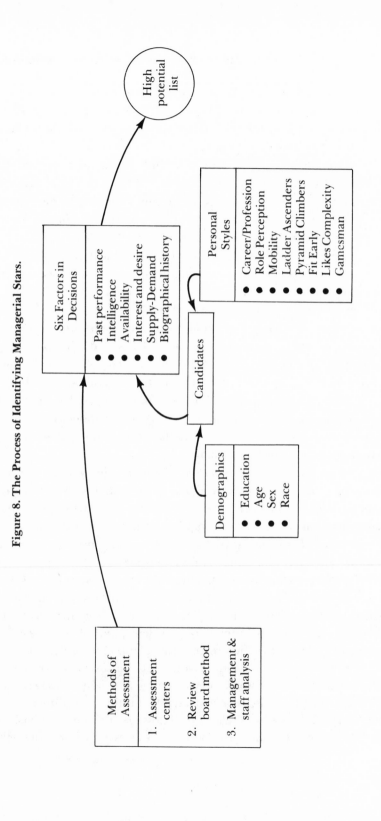

Figure 8. The Process of Identifying Managerial Stars.

Methods of Assessment

1. Assessment centers
2. Review board method
3. Management & staff analysis

Demographics
- Education
- Age
- Sex
- Race

Candidates

Six Factors in Decisions
- Past performance
- Intelligence
- Availability
- Interest and desire
- Supply-Demand
- Biographical history

Personal Styles
- Career/Profession Role Perception
- Mobility
- Ladder Ascenders
- Pyramid Climbers
- Fit Early
- Likes Complexity
- Gamesman

High potential list

and their work records are also available to the assessors. Those passing the assessment center evaluation join a pool of managerial candidates, while those who fail are returned to the lower-level positions they presently occupy.

The advantages of this method, Dulewicz states, show mainly in the assessment of long-term potential. The method can save an organization time and money by minimizing unsuitable career appointments. The cost of setting up an assessment center is high, but most consistent users report that it is worth the expense.

Because the rating scales used in assessment centers are job related, they have so far avoided charges of race or sex bias, unlike some psychological tests used for identifying potential. This may not be true in the future, however, Zemke (1980) suggests. In a world where only white males under forty are legally "unprotected," and pressures to promote more women, blacks, and other protected categories of employee are rising, any system of selection and identification of potential must be constantly revalidated in order to retain its defensibility. Although it has been held to be valid and reliable in the past, the assessment center method will require constant revision and adjustment to stay abreast of legal and social requirements for promotion standards.

The Review Board Method. Another widely used way of assessing potential, the review board method, involves the top management of a firm in making decisions about which subordinates shall move ahead more rapidly than others. The choice of assignments, development plans, and even compensation progress (rate at which pay and benefits increase) is made at special meetings of these senior officers. As practiced by Ford, Sears, and several oil companies, the review board method requires that division general managers and major department heads meet annually with the chief executive, executive vice-presidents, and often the chairperson of the board to review managerial talent. Extensive notebooks filled with information about personal qualifications, performance reviews, and work history, previously prepared by management development staff, are made available to the board members. Sometimes there are hundreds of such dossiers. Taking one division or department at a time, the officers go over the records of each

person in it, with face-to-face presentations by division and department managers to recommend future actions for the high-potential
members of their teams. As Henry Ford II is reported to have said,
"We take a week off premises with the notebooks and division
managers to be sure that they all know their people very well."
This annual grilling assures that personal attention to the performance, potential, and development of their staffs will be raised
to the highest level of priority in division managers' minds. As
an officer of one large company reported, "I think it would be
a major mistake for department heads to come before the senior
officers of this corporation and not demonstrate a rather intimate
knowledge of who their high performers were."

As a result of the review board meetings, people who are
identified as having high potential will find their careers accelerated
by the highest officers of the firm. The meetings highlight the
importance of human resources to all levels of the firm's management, for they demand a high level of study and preparation on
the part of all managers who must face the review board. The main
disadvantages of this method are the enormous amount of staff
paperwork and time of senior people it involves. It also presents
the possibility that "crown princes" may emerge simply because
they have unusually vocal or persuasive bosses, while the star
performer with a taciturn or hypercritical manager may never be
noticed. However, the cross-examination of the top managers and
the comparison of opinions held by different managers can go far
to assure a rough kind of reliability and validity for the final choices.
Because all of those being rated are managers who are being
considered for higher responsibility, there have been few, if any,
legal challenges to the process.

The Staff Analysis Method. For many firms, staff analysis
by the management development director, a staff psychologist, or
some similar professional is the main way of evaluating management
potential. Several methods or combinations of methods may be used
in the analysis. For example, a section asking each rater to describe
or rate the promotability of the individual may be incorporated
into an annual performance appraisal form. In some firms, including General Mills, a form for the "analysis of potential" is completed

separately from the performance review based upon MBO. On this form, each manager is required to rate the promotability of each subordinate and to explain and perhaps defend that rating. The ratings are then tabulated by staff, and a list of high-potential people is prepared. The system ordinarily calls for a review by one or more levels above the individual being assessed, and it is sometimes made part of the firm's review board deliberations. Caution is required to assure that the person who is rating potential is applying standards comparable with those of other managers, and staff review is needed to guarantee equity and balance between judges.

Psychological tests and interviews, conducted by a trained psychologist, may make up another element in the assessment of potential by staff analysis. Many such tests have come under fire due to accusations of "culture bias," however, and laws now require that any test administered be free of bias, conscious or otherwise, against protected groups such as women, minorities, and older workers. Revalidation of tests is a regular and costly requirement of this method.

The values of staff analysis are many. Professional staff analysts are often specifically trained in evaluation of human behavior, including psychological assessment; many are clinicians. The process is not a one-shot arrangement but a continuing professional occupation for people whose careers depend on their ability to make sound assessments. Such people develop experience and skill in making judgments and learn to be influenced more by objective data than by personal impressions. Finally, they deal with behavior on a longitudinal basis rather than relying on single or episodic examples.

The limitations of staff analysis lie mainly in the isolation of the staff analyst from the jobs of those being evaluated. It is a rare staff expert who has experience in the jobs of a firm or who gets out into the field to uncover the actual conditions of such jobs. Rather, analysts tend to work in offices and use text materials and theoretical models alone. As one dismayed manager reported to me, "Some stranger sitting in a cubicle in Chicago makes judgments about me and my future without ever having met me or visited my workplace and seen what life is like in the trenches."

Six Factors in Assessing Potential

Any forecast of the future is by definition conjectural. This is especially true for assessment of potential in the managerial star. Nonetheless, practitioners of all three methods of potential assessment tend to agree on certain points.

The first point of agreement is that potential is situational. Rather than being the sum of a fixed list of traits or qualities, potential (and therefore also its assessment) depends on the environment in which the work will be done. Since this environment changes, over time the needs of the managerial job also change, and so must estimates of potential. Such estimates are merely "snapshots" taken annually, based on the best information available at the time they are made.

Users of all three assessment methods also tend to agree on six basic factors that are important in assessment of potential. Each can be measured in one or more relatively objective ways.

Performance. Performance is the first basic factor to consider in potential assessment. People who have not performed well in the past are unlikely to perform well in the future, and current weak performance is a legitimate basis for limiting an employee's potential rating. The minimal requirement for high-potential people is that they do a good job and meet job objectives in every position they hold along the path to the top. Good performance alone does not indicate potential, however, for it may be that an employee has reached his or her maximum level. Many people succeed at lower levels, only to fail at higher levels when promoted.

To measure performance, assessors need a sound performance appraisal system, preferably one based on MBO. Such systems are discussed more fully in the chapter on performance review (Chapter Fourteen).

Intelligence and Adaptability. Studies show that optimum levels of intelligence are a characteristic of high-potential people. Optimum intelligence in this case doesn't mean genius-level brilliance. Rather, it is the kind of learning ability that makes for easy adaptation to a changing world. Adaptive behavior means learning new skills, new technologies, and grasping the essentials of a new situation.

Paper and pencil tests that attempt to measure personality traits have had a poor record in assessing potential. Where they are used, they must be administered by trained professionals and must be valid and reliable. Accusations of cultural bias leveled against such tests have further dimmed the enthusiasm of many managers for their use. Interviews are probably better, if more subjective, ways of assessing personal qualities.

Availability and Projection of Tenure. The chapter on portfolio valuation made it clear that an important element in potential evaluation is the estimation of an expected stream of income. The person who is likely to stay around and perform up to full potential for a long period of time has a higher value than one who is likely to leave the organization. Factors that may affect length of tenure and income stream include age, health, mobility, sex, and race.

Obviously, younger people have a longer expected stream of income than older people, other things being equal. While this is of little value if a young person is apt to leave the organization or shows poor performance, it is still one element in potential. Older persons must demonstrate a higher discount value in order to be considered as having high potential.

Availability and tenure are sometimes dependent on people's physical condition. A person with debilitating health problems may be a high default risk and thus have lower potential. The sixty-five-year-old with a heart pacemaker or some other serious health limitation obviously has less potential than a perfectly healthy young person.

Compulsory annual physical examinations paid for by the company are useful in both assessing and improving employees' health. Fitness programs, once a form of recreation and personal pleasure to a few employees, are now considered an important part of enhancing human potential, especially those programs that aim at improving cardiovascular fitness.

Mobility is a further factor in rating availability. The talented person who refuses to move to the home office from the plant in Keokuk places a limit on his or her potential. In the eighties, when both men and women often have careers, being part of a two-career family affects the potential rating of many high-talent people, for their willingness to move may be limited by the need to find an opportunity for a spouse as well.

Sex, race, and similar affirmative action factors will have a strong bearing on potential in the corporation of the eighties and nineties. Pressures from new laws and affirmative action programs will require that certain "protected" groups be provided new opportunities. Data about the availability of minorities and other protected groups will enter into the assessment of availability of promotable persons. The only unprotected category today is that of white males under forty. Ironically, this once-favored group may discover that its condition places a limit on its members' potential, regardless of personal qualities or organizational need.

Interests and Desires. In an organization where specialists are employed for entry-level positions and spend considerable time on their specialties, it should be no surprise that many will choose to remain with their special area of expertise, whether it be engineering, accounting, or traffic management. Such a choice is perfectly acceptable if it is consciously made, but it has the effect of limiting the potential of the individual. Candidates' feelings about specialization can be discovered through interviews.

Supply and Demand. Since the assessment of potential is a valuation of a human asset, supply and demand will always affect that assessment. If there is only one candidate for a top position, that person obviously will have the highest potential for gaining that job. If the labor market has provided a surfeit of applicants for higher-level positions, however, even people with great talent may have a relatively low value. As we enter the second half of the eighties, the dramatic drop in college graduates that will begin in 1987 will produce a shortage of college-educated people for many jobs. The worth of all graduates, especially the top ones, is likely to increase simply because of that shortage. When the baby boom that began anew in the 1980s moves onward and a rush of new applicants comes forth by the year 2000, even the best will have more competition, and the relative worth of each graduate will decline or level off.

The demand for particular skills also has a bearing on the valuation of human assets. Manpower and human resource planning for the organization of the future may call for kinds of employees different from those needed today. Predicted demand for human resources, as ascertained by organization and labor market reports, therefore has an effect on assessment of potential. If a low demand for certain types of people is predicted, those people's potential will be rated lower than it would be if demand for their skills were expected to be high.

Biographical History. Last but certainly not least, the best predictor of management potential is a full review of candidates' early behavior. The successful achiever in early life is likely to continue that pattern later on. High grades in college have value in this context, apart from their measurement of intelligence or learning ability, because they are evidence of achievement. Richard Husband (1957), studying the graduating class of 1920 from Dartmouth, found that achievement in grades, extracurricular activities, or both was highly correlated with subsequent career success. Thus, a pattern interview to bring out a detailed personal biography should be a major part of the assessment of potential.

The Changing Definition of Stardom

The definition of star quality tends to change with time. The star of today is very different from the star of the 1950s, and the star of tomorrow will be different still.

The Star of the Fifties. In the 1950s, the typical management star was a youthful graduate from a major college or university, most likely Harvard, Michigan, Yale, New York University, Stanford, MIT, or Cal Tech. Studies by Lloyd Warner revealed that the chief executives of the thousand largest corporations during those decades shared such a background. Almost all of them at that time were males. Usually they came from an upper-middle-class family headed by a professional such as a doctor or engineer. More than three quarters of them were college graduates, and of that group some 15 percent held advanced degrees such as a law degree or an MBA. Graduates in liberal arts outnumbered those in any other area by a small margin. Some 14 percent were engineers, and slightly fewer held law degrees. Majors in business and science accounted for less than 5 percent of the presidents.

Interestingly, this favored group did not necessarily distinguish itself by high levels of scholarship in college. The American

College Testing Bureau in Iowa City compiled more than a dozen studies on the effects of college grades on subsequent career success and reported no significant relationship between the two for the chiefs of that era (Warner, 1960). Rather, the typical successful-executive-to-be was much involved in college activities of either academic or extracurricular kinds. In a few large firms, notably the Bell Telephone system, grades in college were adopted as a basis for selection of managers above certain ranks, but this was more of a self-fulfilling prophecy than a scientifically determined method of choosing leaders. Having decided on and diligently maintained a policy that only those from the upper 10 percent of a graduating class would be elevated, Bell found after twenty-five years, unsurprisingly, that its top managers all shared one characteristic—high grades in college.

Choice of major and grade point average in college, then, did not appear to be significant factors in subsequent career success. Having come from the right family, however—not super-rich but middle-class—did. Likewise, no particular type of early job experience seemed to provide an advantage in the climb to the top. It was the first management role that seemed to count.

The Warner studies and similar statistical research projects in the 1960s had substantial impact on definitions of "high potential" in both business and government. College graduates were pushed ahead of people with only high school diplomas, and in some firms it became a corporate policy that only college graduates should become managers. Cultural factors dictated a preference for males and an almost complete exclusion of Jews and blacks from high positions.

Some businesses had additional requirements for success. In certain firms where chemistry was the major product line, such as Du Pont, a tendency developed toward hiring chemical engineers or chemists from the better engineering schools as potential managers. Similarly, accounting majors from leading business schools usually joined a large Certified Public Accounting firm, but a few moved laterally into large client firms as controllers, in some cases going on to the presidency of the firm (Odiorne and Haan, 1961).

Through the decade of the fifties, the importance of family connections as a basis for moving into the "high-potential" category declined with the decline of family capitalism (Warner, 1960). While many major executives of the time did have the advantage of being born into the controlling family of a firm, the growth of professionally managed firms made family ties increasingly irrelevant. Those who did rise in family-owned or controlled corporations often had to perform at competitive levels in order to move ahead against professionally trained outsiders. Young Henry Ford II automatically rose to head the firm bearing his family name, but once in charge he also demonstrated exceptional managerial skill and was noted by Fortune Magazine as a "managerial superstar" in 1970. Similarly, the Dayton Hudson Company of Minneapolis grew into a leading retail corporation while reserving its highest ranks for family members. Nearly all of those who rose to the top proved to be exceptional executives who would have done well even without the birth advantage they held. Corporation-owning families who wanted their children to inherit came to recognize the necessity of training them for leadership.

Changes Brought by the Sixties and Seventies. The tumultuous decade of the sixties brought many changes to the corporate opportunities race. Two major revolutions occurred during that decade, the revolution of the nation's minorities and the revolution of middle-class college students. Black youths turned their backs on their parents' passive acceptance of segregation. At about the same time, college campuses erupted in a convulsion of antiestablishment rioting and demonstrations. Student hostility to the war in Vietnam became generalized into hostility toward the whole corporate society. Corporate recruiters on campus were often picketed and prevented from making job offers to the young men they considered to be their firms' primary source of future leadership. This reversal of the traditional routing of the best college graduates into corporate life was especially strong among liberal arts undergraduates. It was less noticeable among business and engineering graduates, but even with them, attitudes concerning the social responsibilities of business toward the environment and toward minorities were changing.

Both revolutions soon made themselves felt in new laws against discrimination in hiring for reasons of race, sex, religion, or national origin. Aggressive implementation of affirmative action policies produced significant changes in hiring practices, pay, and promotional opportunities for members of society who had previously been left behind. Court decisions upheld the laws, and their strict enforcement impressed employers with the changing character of the employment relationship. Although the impact of the laws and court decisions failed to reach the higher level of management at first, some long-run fundamental changes were clearly in the making.

Significant increases in enrollment of blacks and women in colleges of business and engineering began to be seen in the 1970s. The number of black students enrolled in colleges of business rose from 41,000 in 1970 to 221,000 in 1978, with comparable figures for engineering and medical schools. By 1980 there were over 1 million blacks enrolled in all colleges, compared with 282,000 in 1970. The number of women entering business schools leaped from 204,000 in 1970 to 819,000 by 1978, and applications for admission to business programs rose even faster in the following years. Many leading business schools report that a majority of their applicants are now women. The total number of women enrolled in college rose from 2.8 to 4.71 million between 1970 and 1978, and by 1983 there were more women than men enrolled in college. Furthermore, deans and registrars reported that many women were making top academic accomplishments (Odiorne, 1980a).

Inevitably, corporations found that their traditional preference for the young white male of middle-class upbringing was no longer possible to implement at lower levels. Pressure from law, from court decisions, and from burgeoning new sources of supply brought new dimensions to the idea of "managerial potential," with more women and blacks coming to occupy prominent places in the line of candidates for such ranking. Many firms, especially those that had lost costly suits under equal employment laws, began to identify high-potential younger women for accelerated programs of management development. Being a woman or a black now joined youth and high grades as an earmark of the high-potential star.

These changes in law and culture have made a strong impact on lower levels of management, but effects on the highest levels of organization are still minimal. Very few top corporate officers are women, and fewer still are blacks or other minorities. This is in large part due to the length of time it takes to work up the ladder in a large organization. It is further explained by the fact that the present crop of chief officers and vice-presidents choose their own replacements. Whether the impact of changing laws and customs on manager selection will ever reach the very top level is still to be determined. It will depend partly on the choices today's top managers make, and the evidence to date is that they tend to pick people who are like themselves.

Star Qualities for the Eighties

Just as the definition of star quality changed in the past, it promises to change again in the future. By 1979 the United States Department of Labor had set forth a clear view of the changes in the shape of the labor force expected to occur during the 1980s. White-collar jobs were projected to increase by 25 percent accompanied by a corresponding decline in blue-collar occupations. The demand for unskilled labor would decline further as automation, robotics, and computer control of production processes grew. More people would work for large corporations; employment in small proprietorships and self-employment would decrease.

What is today's star like? Definitions differ, but certain characteristics seem extremely likely to be part of the winner's personality. As times change ever more rapidly, adaptability to change becomes a more and more important requirement for climbing the executive ladder. When times change and we don't, we become "misfits" and pressures which would have been normal and useful turn into stressors. People who are becoming managerial stars will need to stand the stresses of change and respond to them in positive, creative ways. While no single theory appears to encompass all star behavior, the following are some of the prevailing characteristics.

Balance Between Organizational and Personal Career Orientation. There are some people in organizations whose orientation and loyalty are given mainly to the firm in which they are employed. This seems to be a common pattern in Japan, for example. Other people are oriented toward their profession or occupation, with much less regard for where they work. Robert Merton (1957) referred to these two groups as "locals" and "cosmopolitans," with the locals being company people and the cosmopolitans being profession-centered people.

Today's star often has a strong orientation to both company and career, and he or she manages this balancing act with equanimity and skill. As an organization member, the star is fiercely attentive to the company's goals and is committed to achieving personal goals through helping to achieve company success. On the other hand, the star is likely to be willing to move boldly from one organization to another if his or her career can be thus advanced. If star-quality people are caught in a blind alley or trapped on a shelf behind an immovable boss of the same age or younger, they will foster their management careers by moving out. They do not make such moves lightly, however, for their preference tends to be to make a career by mastering the hierarchical maze in the firm where they began.

Because they have balanced localism with cosmopolitanism, stars can play the two influences against each other skillfully. By making it clear that they have attractive potential for the market at large, they increase their attractiveness to and their progress within their present firm. Stars often have the adaptability to play the game of being visible outside only to the degree required to keep their desirability level high inside. They recognize that acquiring an external reputation is a good way to ensure that their star qualities will be recognized and opportunities for advancement will be provided to them in the company where they currently work.

Ability to Manage Impressions of Self. Star quality is to a large extent an image in the eye of the beholder, and this crucial fact is well known and used to great advantage by true stars. They recognize that they are actors on a stage, and they know their role, those of the other players, and the way cues and dialogue relate to plot, stage, scene, and other features of the drama in which they play. As skilled actors, they never overplay their roles, "pose for holy pictures," upstage other actors needlessly, or play to the critics alone. They recognize that the other members of the cast are as important as the audience, and their costume, body language, and script are carefully orchestrated.

This attention to what Erving Goffman (1959) described as "the presentation of self in everyday life" is an important part of the skill of the star. David McDonald, one-time president of the United Steel Workers' Union, is reported to have attended a drama school to improve his ability to play his roles as workers' leader, organization chief, and public spokesman of his union. Many army generals are most careful of their choice of uniforms, command style, and image in the eye of the public. Corporate executives likewise control the appearance of their offices, the tone of the conferences they conduct, and other matters of personal style. Intuitively or through trial and error, they become experts in dramatic techniques and role playing. This may require the mastery of several roles, including those of subordinate (bright young man or woman), supervisor (aggressive but considerate leader), and well-liked colleague (Good Joe or Joan). Years of early practice, often beginning before their entry into the world of work, usually preceded their rise. The most dramatic illustration of this idea of star-as-performer may be the rise of actor Ronald Reagan to the Presidency of the United States. In short, stars realize the dramatic function of stardom, and they play it competently.

Mobility. At least two social scientists have observed that a quality of top management people is their upward mobility. Eugene E. Jennings in *The Mobile Manager* (1965), from his own clinical studies of top executives, reported that they relate to their organizations in a way that makes them "mobile managers." The mobile manager is one whose principle motivation appears to be success within an organization, as shown by climbing the bureaucratic hierarchy to increasingly high levels. This motivation is often such a strong influence on stars that they let little else besides those factors that can assist in their rise govern their behavior. From the start of their careers, perhaps even before they begin work, they perform well, because good performance is required for upward mobility. They often share with others the chores of lower and middle management, but in doing so, they keep an unsleeping fixation upon the next level and the level beyond that.

Robert Presthus (1962) classified managers into three groups, based on their organizational behavior. The first group is made up of those whose adaptation to the organization is "indifference."

Most organization-centered people, and indeed most employees, belong to this group. Presthus estimated that 90 percent of the employees in many organizations fit this category. Indifference is often created more by situation than by personality. Presthus felt that half the indifferents are created by bureaucratic systems that have shut them off from participation in the organization's decisions.

A second group described by Presthus is the "ambivalents." These are people whose aims vacillate between loyalty to the organization and personal and creative urges. Such people are often plagued by conflict between desires for conformity to the organization and for application of personal or professional skills. They may find relief by becoming specialists and experts or by pursuing other intellectual interests.

Most likely to be classified as a star is a member of the "upward mobiles," the third group in Presthus's scheme of things. Sensitive to the political machinations of the bureaucracy in which he or she operates, the upwardly mobile manager develops high levels of interpersonal or human relations skills in order to placate different interest groups. Upward mobiles are characterized by high morale, unfailing optimism, and strong identification with the organization—to the extent that often their jobs and firms become indistinguishable in their own minds from their own egos and personalities. They seek power, and in acquiring it they feed their egos and their desire for more success. They seldom question the organization's goals, internalizing the system and throwing themselves wholly into its achievement. No lurking thoughts of dissent impede their work. This all produces "the capacity for action despite conflicting alternatives and contradictory aims," Presthus stated. The upward mobile adopts the roles needed to succeed, manipulates the environment and the people in it, and often plays a game of human relations without really letting underlings have much participation in important decisions that affect them and their jobs.

Ability to Climb. Researchers often query present top executives about the qualities that they feel brought them to their present lofty level. While this may not be a perfectly sound method of identifying what actually got them there, for subjectivity may bias the replies, it is often informative nonetheless. One of the more cogent reasons for studying such statements is the method by which top management is usually chosen. For the most part, the people who will rise are those who are chosen by the present top managers. For that reason, a 1961 study by Roy Lewis and Rosemary Stewart (1961) is still useful in identifying today's star criteria, for the managers chosen at that time are likely to be the top managers of today. To the extent that these managers will choose their successors, their words are of value in identifying star quality.

Based on interviews with top executives in American, British, and German corporations, the study concluded that the fit between manager and organization is close. Their ethical values are congruent, their personalities seem to match. The aspiring manager usually feels that the company is doing worthwhile things with its products and services, has growth potential that affords opportunity, and has a favorable bias toward the young, for example.

In British firms, "pull" (nepotism) is more prevalent than in American firms, where "push" counts more. Conformity with the criteria of those who have already succeeded is what really pays off in both cases, however. Development of contacts, association with successful rather than unsuccessful people, and keen attention to status symbols such as desks, office size, and the like are similarly important. So is being associated with new ideas, whether they are one's own or not. Obvious toadying is banned for the star, but artful use of flattery and adeptness in sincere praise of higher-ups are important skills. "Have weight, caricature what you are supposed to be, and never let your brains show," advised the authors.

Knowing how to reckon the odds is another quality that Lewis and Stewart reported as essential to the climber of managerial ladders. The first hazard is the choice of an immediate boss. Find an able person who will serve as mentor and foster your career and help that person look good, the authors said. Finding the proper route by entering the right departments is likewise important. In Proctor and Gamble, for example, all top management came up through marketing, whereas in high-tech businesses the route to the top is most likely to be through engineering or science. A willingness to take inevitable risks is essential, but by choosing the route where the odds are highest, one's potential is raised.

One important risk is that of changing one's organization. The young manager who aspires to top management must avoid getting stuck too long in one job. Three to five years is the longest one can afford getting stuck in a single position, the authors felt. Moving must be approached carefully, however. Loyalty in subordinates is highly prized by top managers, and the move must be made to look like something that couldn't be refused. To move under what appears to be one's own volition may seem disloyal, but accepting offers thrust upon one and agreed to only after reluctant deliberation will appear sensible and sound.

Stars often have a better ability to relate to their organization than do others who are not stars. The shape of most organizations resembles a pyramid, according to Vance Packard's *The Pyramid Climbers* (1962), which was popular during the sixties when today's top managers were rising. *The Pyramid Climbers* told how young people, mainly men, rose in organizations in that era. Certain groups, Packard noted, were simply beyond the pale. They included those without college degrees and those of the wrong sex, national origin, or religion. The prevailing criteria have been expanded to include more women, blacks, and Jews since Packard's book was written, but the statistical evidence against such aspirants is still strong, since they must be screened by the male, white, Protestant college graduates who occupy the vast majority of top management positions in American industry today.

Being identified as a high-potential manager by one of the leading search ("head hunter") consulting firms is an important step forward, Packard said. Having several such firms on your trail seeking to hire you for one of their clients is a giant boost for your career.

Showing the right behavior in interviews is also essential. Packard cited psychologist Johnson O'Connor's three important characteristics for potential executives: "Being slow of speech, impressive in appearance, and completely lacking in a sense of humor." Being well packaged is a related quality. Eccentricities of dress, varying from the dress code of the present top management, are apt to result in one's being pushed quietly aside.

Packard suggested four rules for pyramid climbing: (1) *Be dedicated,* which means shutting out almost everything except the business. (2) *Be loyal.* This is especially important in explaining the company to subordinates. Treat the company as your own mother and father. (3) *Be adaptive.* Subordinate your personal likes and dislikes for those of the organization. (4) *Be quietly deferential.* Recognize that rank has its privileges, give the top people their due, and avoid disagreements with superiors.

Early Achievements. The way management stars relate to their organization and its challenges was studied over a period of many years at the Standard Oil Company of New Jersey. Beginning in the fifties and continuing through the sixties, selected managerial personnel were tested, interviewed, and assessed in other ways, and their subsequent progress was checked longitudinally. Assessments used included a Miller Analogies test, a Guilford-Zimmerman temperament survey, and an autobiographical statement. The purpose of the study was to find out whether any of the tests used could identify traits or behavior patterns that marked high-potential people when those people's careers were just beginning. The term Early Identification of Management Potential (EIMP) identifies the study and names its focus. The candidates and their bosses were not informed of the test scores in order to avoid the "self-fulfilling prophecy" error.

The results showed that 33 percent of people who scored in the top 20 percent on the tests ended up in top management positions. People who scored in the top 20 percent were nineteen times more likely to gain top jobs than people who scored in the lowest 20 percent. The most powerful predictor of success, however, was the individual's autobiographical statement, which included verifiable facts about his or her previous life and accomplishments. It was found that those who had accomplished many things early in their lives were more apt to rise after maturity than those who had accomplished little. People whose youthful behavior showed incidents and achievements that marked them as mature and emotionally independent usually continued to succeed throughout their adult lives. As psychologist Saul Gellerman described the same phenomenon in a different study, "They were . . . no strangers to success; and for the most part they achieved success by pursuing it, having made such a pursuit a habit for most of their lives" (1968, p. 110).

Mental ability was the second most accurate predictor in the EIMP process of testing and evaluating. The project directors equated intelligence with learning ability, which in turn was important because executives at higher levels constantly need to learn new things. In sum, the study concluded that the qualities that enable a person to handle an executive job effectively can be measured while the person is still young by using a combination of biographical, situational, and mental ability tests.

Ability to Work in a Web of Tensions. While such firms as Jersey Standard and IBM were focusing on the qualities of future executives, others were pointing out the complexity of identifying stars. Harlan Cleveland (1972), whose management experience was principally in the public sector, wrote of the star's need to relate to complex and evolving situations. The world of the executive, he proposed, was becoming a "web of tensions" created by conflicting pressures that tried to push the organization in mutually exclusive directions. "Complexity has a bright future," Cleveland stated. He pointed out that organizations are evolving from bureaucratic hierarchies to globules of interests and pressures that need to be attended to from the top. Detailed planning is no longer important, he claimed, for in this web of tensions the need is for people at the top who can respond to changing pressures by improvising.

Cleveland didn't hesitate to suggest the qualities of individuals who would rise into the ranks of top management, especially in public service. The future executives, he proposed, will be those who have first climbed the ladder of success as specialists and experts and then have demonstrated generalist ability on top of those expert talents. They will be people who have mastered a "low-key" style of giving orders or stating directions rather than those who feel impelled to shout their commands. Consensus rather than directives or votes will prevail, he said, so future leaders will become consensus makers. The future executive's task, proposed Cleveland, will be to "establish, maintain, advertise, and continually amend a sense of direction."

Gamesmanship. One of the more interesting recent descriptions of executive star qualities is that of Michael Maccoby (1976), who based his findings on psychiatric interviews with 250 managers (all men) from twelve major U.S. corporations. Managers, he concluded, can be divided into four major classifications: Craftsmen, Jungle Fighters, Company Men, and Gamesmen.

The *Craftsman* holds traditional values in high regard, especially hard work, respect for other people, and concern for quality and thrift. These people enjoy the process of making or building things. They hold few of the values which Cleveland suggests will be present in the future executive, for they make little effort to build teams of followers or collaborators. They prefer the pleasure of doing work well where they sit.

Jungle Fighters view the corporation the way the late Jimmy Hoffa viewed it—as a hostile jungle, crawling with enemies. In the Jungle Fighter's perception of corporations, the rule is to eat or be eaten, and the goal is power. Peers are either accomplices or enemies, and helpers are objects to be used, maintained as long as they are useful, and then discarded. When Jungle Fighters are successful, they build empires; when they fail, they may die.

The *Company Man* is the modern form of the Organization Man described by William White some twenty years before Maccoby. This person's role is centered in working for a powerful and protective company. The most successful Company Men create an air of congenialism and collaboration and resemble Cleveland's Future Executive. The weaker ones in this category find a comfortable shelf and survive by their dedication, integrity, and loyalty to company purposes.

The *Gamesman* is the "new" person whose major interest is in challenges, competition, and winning. Attracted to risk, these people are impatient with lesser persons, although they find pleasure in motivating others. They communicate enthusiasm, are attracted to new and fresh ideas, and are spontaneous in their work. At the same time, they are organization people—team players whose lives center around the corporation and who will often subordinate their egos to the goals of the firm. Maccoby concludes that while corporations need Craftsmen and Company Men (they could get along without Jungle Fighters), their future depends most of all upon the mature development of their Gamesmen.

Flexibility and Ability to Generalize. Although much of the material on identification of managerial potential was written during the sixties and seventies, the search for high potential in management continues, and new findings are being produced. On the whole, the search's methods and results seem to be similar to those of the past. James Hayes, longtime president of the American Management Association, writing in *The Director* magazine (1983), advised its board member readers that there are "eighteen competencies in management," clustered into four major groups: goal and action management, directing of subordinates, human resources development, and leadership. More than knowledge is needed in these areas, Hayes added, for the success of the manager lies as much in what he or she does as in what he or she knows. That these skills can be learned, however, is testified to by D. L. Niehouse (1983). Niehouse proposed that close observation of role models, coupled with a personal assessment of one's strengths and weaknesses, is a practical means by which the aspiring star can rise through a kind of self-nurturing process. Treese (1982) suggested that the aspiring manager who wants to rise in the organization should turn his or her interests outward and attend to the organization itself. The lower-level manager can master the details of a single department to the extent that few if any problems will arise that he or she cannot solve, but this knowledge may not be useful in other departments. Treese's prescription is to acquire a mastery of the total operation of the business that could be invaluable when crises occur and the organization needs someone to step forward with possible solutions. "Broadening your perspective" with respect to the whole organization can pay off in promotions, Treese concludes. When the higher-level managers who make the decisions on promotions note that one person stands out as well informed and well prepared to deal with organization-wide issues, such a person will be favorably rated.

Niehouse, in another article, advises aspiring stars that breaking the promotion barrier will come easiest to those who maintain a "flexible style of leadership" (1982). This flexibility means mastering different styles of leadership, such as varying the amount of direction given to subordinates. Being flexible, maintaining a strong goal orientation, and developing promotable people among those under one's charge can all enhance one's chances of breaking through into higher levels of management, Niehouse suggests.

The Star of the Future

How will tomorrow's star manager differ from today's? What changes will he or she have to face?

One area of change will be in office equipment and communications, suggests J. J. Connell (1982). The manager of the future will live in a technologically sophisticated office, surrounded and aided by complex electronic equipment and communication devices. Such "Star Wars" offices will have a far greater impact than simply that of the hardware and its attendant speed and complexity. They will require new roles for managers, calling for people who are comfortable with high-level decision making and problem analysis and who do not need to be occupied in routines and paper-bound activities. Less time will be required for travel as communications improve, and the span of control will probably widen. The star manager of the future will be one who can flourish in such an environment, Connell proposes.

The notion of a changing work ethic, often discussed by popular sociologists, gained some support from a study done inside American Telephone and Telegraph, reported by Howard and Wilson (1982). The Bell system repeated a similar study that had been done in the fifties. The group studied in the fifties scored significantly higher in the motivational part of the survey than the eighties group. The fifties group had higher expectations for the future and were willing to put more of themselves into their work than today's work force. The explanation of this change, according to the researchers, lay in the early childhood experience of the workers coming to adulthood during the seventies. After a childhood and adolescence characterized by considerable instant gratification, they had replaced the pursuit of achievement with the pursuit of pleasure. If this proves to be a continuing trend, a major change in the supervisory behavior of leaders will be required. So far, companies have responded to this change by altering the ways they organize, including arrangement for more diffused responsibility and more participation of workers in decisions that affect them. This new attitude toward work, found in a major American corporation with over a million employees, suggests that a more participatory style of leadership will be needed in such arrangements. The star of the fifties was a task leader, while the leader of the eighties and beyond will need to be more of a collaborative group leader.

Still further changes in the demands on top management are proposed by Stone (1981). Based on research by the National Academy of Public Administration, Stone's article points out the importance of finding and recruiting more innovative top management people for the future. Stone adds that top-quality managers attract other top-quality individuals to the organization, a verification of sorts on the thesis that top management is responsible for choosing its own replacements. Government especially needs to select innovative top management that can reverse its poor reputation as an employer, Stone says.

The need for better information about the requirements for the manager of the future is evidenced by plans for a four-part study to be conducted over a four-year period by the Administrative Management Society, delving into the workplace of the future and the requirements for managers in that workplace. Long (1982) defines the four areas of the study as involving "human resources, environmental factors, technological opportunities, and management strategy."

Widespread interest in the changing managerial job picture is demonstrated further by the fact that Peters and Waterman's book, *In Search of Excellence* (1982), reached the top of the national best seller list for *all* books—not simply management books. Based on three years of interviews with managers in a selected group of corporations judged to have excellent management, the book defines seven areas in which excellence is needed. It also provides a host of case studies describing how the best-run firms manage themselves. There are few surprises in the authors' findings; the unusual feature of their work is that it struck a responsive chord in a widespread public that is deeply concerned with the question of what is needed to restore American economic health. It has become commonplace now to recognize that the quality of top management makes a great difference to a corporation. Even though there is far from complete agreement about the qualities needed in today's or tomorrow's star manager or the best way of identifying such a person, at least the right questions are being asked.

6

Education, Training, and Mentoring for Stars

So faithful in love, so dauntless in war. There never was knight like young Lochinvar. —*Sir Walter Scott*

As evidence presented in Chapter Five indicates, education and early achievement are important in determining how far a star can go. There are a number of paths to the top for star-quality people. All, however, tend to have in common the requirement that the rising executive be both a learner and a teacher.

As learners, executives are collections of possibilities rather than simply of attributes that are present today. They have already passed through formal schooling for the most part, but their education is only beginning when they join a firm. The great bulk of their learning will occur through role modeling, aided by supportive leadership from present high-level executives and systematic planning for human resources supply and demand. The best executives will in turn become teachers, providing the support needed to make their subordinates' high performance a developmental experience rather than merely the result of compliance founded on fear or greed.

Seven Routes to the Top

In one sense there are as many routes to managerial stardom as there are rising stars to map them. In the vast majority of cases, however, rising executive stars use one of these seven springboards to the top: (1) graduating from a leading MBA program, (2) graduating from a lesser MBA program, (3) becoming a technological entrepreneur, (4) studying engineering or other technical curricula, (5) applying a liberal arts education, (6) possessing special education or experience, or (7) learning in the "school of hard knocks." Let's examine each of these paths to stardom in more detail.

Graduating from a Leading MBA Program. For better or worse, the MBA degree has taken on a certain fraternal cachet when it comes to advancement into upper management. MBAs usually turn to younger MBAs when they choose their successors. There's good reason for this seeming snobbishness. Simply, the degree works. It focuses on specific things that top managers do in their daily work, including strategic planning and the blending and coordination of functions such as finance, marketing, manufacturing, personnel management, and dealing with the outside world. No other degree program, no matter how academically taxing, so directly teaches the specific tasks of the executive as the MBA. More rigorous than ever before, strongly based upon quantitative skills and analytic ability, MBA degree programs from the top schools also give their holders practice in the work habits necessary for executive jobs.

Even the programs of Harvard and the other "best and brightest" schools have their critics, however. Some have claimed that the programs' rigor is often overdone, producing a course of study as stressful as some military courses for rangers, paratroopers, and other elite groups of volunteers. In 1983 the Harvard faculty acknowledged these criticisms by cutting back on the work load required of business school graduates. It has also been suggested, at least for Harvard, that its business school's methods and content are presented as "gospel" with a fervor that produces something akin to brainwashing in those who complete its courses.

Some recent graduates of Harvard have also expressed unease about the quality of the education they received there. Steven J. Buckley (1983) states flatly that even the best business schools are not equipping their graduates with two skills that are essential in the modern business world: how to react to international competitors and foreign governments and how to identify and create new business opportunities. Rather, he suggests, they are training managers to manage in a time of low government involvement and ample growth opportunities, an era that is over. The centering of traditional MBA programs on fundamentals of finance, accounting, marketing, production, and human resources is sound, he says, but it doesn't go far enough. By providing little training in governmental relations or in creativity, such programs fail to teach students how to identify and cope with new trends. Creativity, not caretaking, is the essence of management today, Buckley suggests.

Still, if there is any course of formal education that can claim to produce stars, an MBA degree program from one of the leading business schools is surely the one. For the young person seeking early identification as a star, gaining an MBA degree from a top-drawer business school is almost bound to be a giant step in the right direction.

Once MBAs have been hired, Donnelly (1982) suggests that the best way to develop their managerial potential fully is to utilize the skills they have already acquired rather than honing them further in management courses. Such utilization should include presentation of challenging jobs and developmental opportunities in order to stimulate interest and motivation to achieve high levels of performance. Donnelly suggests that goal setting that produces clear and tough objectives, coupled with a rigorous and well-developed performance appraisal system, is most likely to exploit an MBA's strategic management potential.

Graduating from a Lesser MBA Program. Whereas only 6,000 persons received an MBA degree in 1951, over 50,000 received that same degree in 1982, and enrollment in MBA programs is still rising. Faced with a declining demand for their services in the labor market, liberal arts degree holders have flowed increasingly into graduate business programs, both because of the increased job opportunities available to the graduates of such programs and because the MBA has acquired a kind of "in" quality even among those who previously would have scorned business education.

The pressures of increased demand for the MBA degree have caused hundreds of colleges without prior business education experience to begin offering the degree. Small liberal arts colleges faced with declining enrollments and rising costs started evening business classes as a means of keeping themselves afloat. Former teacher training colleges, many with low standards for admission, turned themselves into MBA-granting institutions, using part-time faculty or faculty hastily recruited from psychology, economics, statistics, law, or other behavioral and social sciences. The effect was the production of numerous graduates, all holding the MBA, whose schooling had varied considerably in kind and quality.

To begin with, the amount of schooling differed. For a few schools, the MBA was a mandatory two-year program regardless of the students' prior level of education. For many MBA programs that were held in the evenings, on weekends, or on other nontraditional schedules, one year of academic work was sufficient to earn the degree. Furthermore, in major urban centers, "executive MBA" programs offered the degree to experienced managers at premium prices, with little regard for prior educational achievement. Some allowed experienced executives to enroll without holding an undergraduate degree, thus making it possible for someone to go directly from a high school diploma to an MBA. Others allowed substantial credit for work experience through credit-for-work programs.

Beyond this, each school offering an MBA program seemed to have a special emphasis that stressed its strengths and the ease and speed with which the degree could be attained. Some, such as Carnegie-Mellon, stressed quantitative analysis. Others stressed behavioral science. For still others, a financial or marketing emphasis prevailed in the curriculum. Some colleges' MBA was a generalist's degree. Varying levels of computer competency separated the schools, as did variations in the use of lectures as opposed to case study analysis or other ways of producing general management skills.

This wide variation placed a great burden on employers, management directors, and human resource planners when they had to hire people or evaluate their potential. On paper, the Harvard graduate's MBA degree was just the same as the MBA of the graduate from Podunk—but not in practice. The Association of Collegiate Schools of Business through its standards committee, struggled to alleviate the problem by defining and maintaining standards for all MBA programs. However, these standards tended to emphasize inputs into the programs (books in the library, number of Ph.D.s on the faculty) rather than the quality of outputs—the programs' graduates. Common bodies of knowledge were defined but not always achieved. Thus, corporations' concern about the quality of the MBA degree persisted and grew. Whereas all MBA degrees used to be almost certainly equated with high potential for its holder, during the eighties a more critical examination of MBAs has emerged, although demand for such graduates continues to be high.

Along with their qualitative questions about individual MBA programs, employers began to ask how the growing infusions of women and minority groups into MBA programs affected the value of the degree as a mark of a high-potential manager. In particular, they questioned the motivation of these new MBAs. Bartol, Anderson, and Schneier (1981) compared the managerial motivation of males and females, blacks and whites at two different universities, using a Miner sentence completion scale. They found lower motivation for female business students than for males and a tendency to less preparation among blacks than among whites.

Women who are highly motivated to succeed in managerial work and who have sufficient academic credentials to be admitted to good MBA programs will certainly find their paths for advancement more open under current laws and social pressures, and no doubt they will be as good at their jobs as their male counterparts. The question still remains whether high grades and an MBA degree can be equated with the talent and motivation necessary for a high promotability potential as surely as they used to be.

The MBA degree holder is an important source of high-talent managerial help. Still, not every top executive will have an MBA, and stars may develop their careers through the effective use of other educational programs or even approaches not involving formal education.

Becoming a Technological Entrepreneur. From 1960 onward it became apparent that many of the highest-performing executives were not those who had obtained an MBA and climbed through the ranks of a large corporation. Rather, they were scientists or engineers who combined the ability to invent and develop new products with the entrepreneurial savvy needed to establish and head a successful business. Such people became a whole new class of managerial stars.

Kenneth Olsen, for example, left the engineering department of Harvard and started Digital Equipment Corporation with a modest loan in order to exploit the potential of the minicomputer. Similarly, Dr. An Wang developed a billion-dollar word processing firm from his own technical knowledge and managerial competence. In a rash of spinoffs from leading university science and engineering departments around Cambridge and Palo Alto, a number of high-technology firms were established according to this pattern. Few, if any, of these entrepreneurs held the MBA degree, although they often became major employers of business school graduates as their companies grew into corporate giants. Their abilities united to produce a new kind of hyphenated star—one who had both technical and managerial competence at a high level.

Studying Engineering or Other Technical Curricula. For many large corporations deeply committed to technical innovation coupled with managerial excellence, the major source of star-quality management has become engineering and science graduates. For example, Du Pont has long hired graduates of chemistry or chemical engineering schools for its managerial ranks; only once in recent years has a chief executive of that company been a nonscientist. For other firms, hiring engineers who will eventually be turned into managers and from whose ranks the stars will be chosen has become the *modus operandi.* Typical of such firms is Texaco, which recruits heavily among technically trained college graduates. After demonstrating high performance at a lower level, selected employees from this group are exposed to a more general overview of management functions and policies in a ten-day seminar held yearly in Florida.

For employees with technical backgrounds who have demonstrated performance at star levels, university executive development programs that convey the major content of a traditional MBA course have proven useful in training for a new managerial orientation. One of the oldest of such programs is the Sloan executive program at MIT. It admits mainly engineers and other technically educated managers between the ages of thirty and thirty-five who have been nominated by their employers. These people attend a nine-month special course that adds managerial skills to their technical training. A review by this author of major six-week management education programs at Cornell, Stanford, and Northwestern revealed that a substantial number of participants in such programs were in this category: technically proficient people whose careers were aimed toward higher-level management jobs. Clearly many corporations have concluded that brief but intensive education in finance, marketing, personnel, labor, and similar specialist areas, topped off by a middle-management or top-management executive development program, provides the best way to round out the technically trained manager.

Applying a Liberal Arts Education. Liberal arts graduates are fighting a rearguard action in the human resources marketplace, or so it would seem. The number of job openings for such graduates shrinks perceptibly each year, and their starting salaries are appreciably lower than those of business, engineering, or other professional school graduates. Partly as a result of this, enrollments in liberal arts courses have declined steadily during the seventies and early eighties, to the point where many small liberal arts colleges appear to be on the edge of extinction. Some have already gone out of business, and many others have survived only by taking on majors in management or other applied professional topics and engaging in fierce competition for enrollments. Yet Mark Twain's remark, that "reports of my demise are greatly exaggerated" may also prove true for the liberal arts college.

For one thing, economic returns to education cannot be judged only at the point of entry but must be further evaluated decades after graduation. In the long run the salaries of liberally educated students compare quite favorably with those of business graduates or engineers. This is true in part because many liberal arts majors, especially those with the highest grades, tend to go to professional schools after gaining their bachelor's degree, thus joining the MBA and technical degree holders in management. Increasingly, top business schools have abandoned undergraduate business courses on the assumption that a well-founded education before starting professional training will produce a person with higher potential than that of someone who has specialized from the beginning. This allows the liberal arts college the option of

offering its traditional broad curriculum along with some prepro-
fessional courses in such topics as economics and applied behavioral
sciences.

Many corporations have come to recognize that a liberal
education can be an admirable preparation for leadership responsibility in many areas of life—business included. When well done,
liberal education teaches people the accumulated knowledge of our
civilization, which is exactly what the executive of the future will
need. Knowledge of the arts, science, literature, history, and the
social sciences is not at all irrelevant to the executive who is making
strategic decisions that will shape the future of an organization.
The skills of rational thought, decision making, problem solving,
and ethical evaluation are no less vital to future corporate officers.
Today it is widely recognized by business and government employers
that the ability to write, speak, listen, and read with insight and
understanding is of the highest value for the executive of the future.
Indeed, survey after survey by colleges of business and engineering
indicates that the leading complaint about their graduates concerns
their woeful inability to communicate at even the most basic levels.
Remedial communication skills courses make up a substantial
portion of the training and retraining that employers feel impelled
to offer their stars.

Much of the criticism of liberal arts education as a path to
managerial success is founded on the lack of motivation that many
liberal arts graduates have for a career in business. In the sixties,
liberal arts colleges and liberal arts departments of major universities
were the center of revolt against the establishment, and this residue
remains strong. Few firms are noble enough to deliberately seek
out and cultivate people who are hostile to their values. Faced with
declining job opportunities and the changing culture of the midseventies, however, the liberal arts graduates of today are much
more friendly toward business than their older brothers or sisters
were. They want jobs. They study harder. The grade inflation of
the sixties has been halted and, in many institutions, turned about
sharply. The college recruiter is now a welcome figure, in contrast
with the sixties when many were barred from campus. Even many
sixties "flower children" now seem to have opted for an MBA or
other advanced degree and to have settled into careers in business,

government, or the professions. They may still have life-styles different from those of earlier times—husbands and wives may have equally strong commitments to their careers and yet have less regard for work for its own sake than, say, their parents did; and their standards in general are less dominated by puritanical ideas—but their rebellious views have been tempered by time and responsibility.

From an economic point of view there is a considerable case to be made for employing liberal arts graduates today. For one thing, they are currently a major source of undervalued human assets with high potential. Their motivation to work toward business objectives is often high. With clear goals and systematic performance review, they can be expected to produce more than their share of high-potential top managers exactly because of their education, which promotes ability to reason and communicate, broad capacity for learning, and flexibility in the face of change. The liberal arts education is unique in focusing upon change over time, the nature and quality of change, value shifts, and the way the process of adaptation works. Entering a world of business where history and political science are very practical bodies of knowledge, the liberal arts graduate offers much that the expert in the functional areas of business may lack.

Learning about the nature and function of government is not something to be done after the manager has arrived at the top, nor can creativity and the ability to respond to change be instilled in a quick course for middle and upper managers. Even more difficult is the attempt to patch mature, versatile communication skills onto training that stressed accounting or finance; rather, the power to communicate must come first. Because of these factors, it is likely that the star of the future will have an undergraduate degree in the liberal arts, topped off by an MBA or other professional degree. Attendance at seminars can keep such people abreast of new information important to their professional development.

Possessing Special Education or Experience. A small but significant number of stars will follow none of the usual paths to the top. They will find direct routes into top management positions without ever slogging it out at lower ranks in marketing, manufacturing, finance, or engineering.

Lawyers make up one such group. A post in the corporate legal department or perhaps a partnership in a large law firm on retainer to the corporation has proven to be a step to chief executive rank for many top managers. Three reasons might explain this shortcut route for lawyers. First, attorneys are often involved in actions important to the survival of a corporation, such as antitrust suits, patent claims, labor disputes, and the like, and they are likely to have close personal contact with top management while these matters are being dealt with. Since present top managers choose their successors, this exposure to top decision makers affords an important opportunity to demonstrate a grasp of key issues in the business. Antitrust matters, for example, often require detailed and sophisticated knowledge of organizational practices. Patent claims, product liability suits, and class action suits also afford the lawyer both duty and opportunity to dig deeply into the details of a business. When an individual is afforded this kind of access and opportunity, personal qualities of intelligence and ambition coupled with sage political skills and sufficient mentoring can often permit a rise to the top that bypasses ordinary career paths.

Accountants are another special category of managerial talent. Armed with an in-depth education in accounting, the highest academic achievers in this field are likely to enter business through a Certified Public Accounting firm. If this CPA firm is one of the "Big Eight" that provides auditing and management services for a corporate giant, it is not uncommon for one of its managing partners to move laterally into a senior executive position in the client firm. Slightly over 10 percent of the chief executives of major corporations report an accounting education in their background. Often their move into corporate life was at a high-ranking position such as financial vice-president or even president of the client firm.

Like lawyers, accountants deal with information that permeates every facet of a business. They have a unique monopoly on control of information inside the firm—collecting it, analyzing it, and disseminating it. Often data processing and other computer-related departments are part of a company's financial arm, which gives the chief of financial information even more powerful tools of information management. Information thus can become a means of accumulating power and controlling visibility and influence inside the organization, especially with top management. Add to this access and opportunity a certain amount of intelligence, personality traits that are pleasing to the present top management, a supportive executive mentor, and some political skills, and the ambitious accountant may outflank those who count on solid performance to be rewarded with higher rank.

Family members of corporation owners, top managers, and major stockholders have a unique opportunity thrust upon them. A few years back, the president of a large retail company, seeking his replacement, hired a search firm to recruit an experienced executive from a competing chain. As part of the courtship of this leading candidate, the president invited him to dinner at his home, where they were joined by the executive's family, consisting of five bright young sons. The dinner conversation turned to the retailing business, and the sons (ranging from twelve to twenty years of age) all chimed in with informed and intelligent questions and observations about retailing, the firm, and management tasks.

At the end of the dinner, the candidate left without taking the job. He said simply, "Mr. X, I think you have a team of highly talented future executives around your dining room table. If I take the position you've offered me, I can see some special problems for me over the next ten years that I am not ready to take on. Thank you for the opportunity to visit with you."

Following this turn-down, the father told his sons, "Boys, I think we are going to have to count on you for the future of the business. Therefore, you should all start planning with me right now for your careers in the firm." Subsequently the company did find important places for all of the sons, and it went on to become a multibillion dollar retail firm.

Although family capitalism has declined steadily in the past fifty years, a number of today's executives found their way to the top because their names were already on the outside of the building when they started working inside. For example, Henry Ford II, longtime chairman of Ford Motor Company, came to his post by inheritance, though later he was rated by most as a superior executive. On the death of his grandfather, the original Henry Ford, he found great responsibility thrust upon him. At the suggestion of his grandmother, Clara Ford, the company hired Ernest Breech, a vice-president of General Motors, to come into the company and "teach Mr. Henry what he needed to know to run Ford." Mentoring of this sort by experienced executives is often made available to younger family members of corporate leaders in order to teach them the business and inculcate in them the proper skills and attitudes for top management positions.

Even good mentoring cannot bring success, however, if motivation or ability is lacking. Children of entrepreneurs and chief executives have a unique opportunity, but not all of them will relish it or be able to turn it to advantage. Some may wish to follow other lines of work; others may not want to work at all. Those who do enter business will unquestionably have a head start because of their family connections, but if they do not also have the talent and the drive to succeed, others will ultimately surpass them.

Other problems may face family scions as well. Often they must work harder than people in comparable positions who are not related to the boss, for the father at the top may bend over backwards to prove that he is not being affected by nepotism. On the other hand, business-oriented children of entrepreneurs may suffer from excessive expectations. As it has been said by a long-time professional manager, "You cannot groom a man for a job without creating an expectation in him that he will receive it." The family member can more certainly expect that his or her successful grooming will be rewarded with promotion than an outsider could, but there is no automatic guarantee in most family firms that every interested member of the family will hold high rank. For one thing, the family itself would rebel at incompetence being rewarded, for their personal wealth is dependent upon skilled management of their business. For another, if the firm begins to be taken over by people whose skill and motivation to manage are too low to bring success to the company, stockholders who are not family members will protest such placement decisions. Promotion of incompetent family members can also have a devastating effect on the morale and motivation of professional members of management who are not part of the family. In family firms, a corps of developmental mentors who will tutor, guide and teach the rising family members is as important as the abilities and motivations of the family stars. The depth of motivation of the children of the rich is still another question. Will the heir dig in and work hard enough to do a good job in management?

It is in the tough business situations that the ultimate test of selection systems work. Psychologist Robert McMurry, long a consultant on executive selection, admonished that the best executives are those who are "hungry," by which we might infer they have the motivational quality of perseverance when confronted with continual stress. The likelihood of this quality being tacked on to executive habits later in life is less likely than that it will persist when it is identified early.

Learning in the "School of Hard Knocks." Last but certainly not least are those people who, lacking formal education, start at the bottom of a business and rise to the very top. In an earlier time this pattern was made famous by Horatio Alger in a series of books about bootblacks who rose to head giant corporations through admirable qualities of "pluck and grit," coupled with high intelligence and an eagerness to succeed. With more than 70 percent of today's top executives holding a master's degree and many with Ph.D.'s, the number of people who reach top management by this route seems to be diminishing. Yet many major corporations are headed by people who started their careers as machinists, truck drivers, or salesmen. Several recent presidents of General Motors never attended college, except to receive honorary degrees after their rise to fame.

Usually the successful "bootstrappers" distinguished themselves from their fellow workers in four ways: (1) They outworked everyone around them, showing fanatical levels of commitment and devotion to the duties of each job. (2) They were endlessly curious about all aspects of the business in which they were employed, learning other people's jobs as well as their own. (3) They were usually taken under the wing of some senior executive or higher-level manager who sponsored their rise in the organization and fed them instruction and opportunity. (4) They often met Robert McMurry's requirement of being "hungry"—of having high aspirations for wealth and the other benefits that come with rank and power.

The key to succeeding by this bottom-to-top route is the presence of high goals in both the individual and the firm that sponsors him or her. This must be matched by a systematic plan for performance review that recognizes genuine accomplishment.

Sponsoring mentors, supplemented by generous doses of company courses and outside seminars, can implant the skills acquired by others in college.

Sadly, many large firms now have policies that bar such unorthodox paths to the top. One large food company, for example, has a flat policy that no one who lacks a college degree will be appointed to any management position. Other firms, while keeping the door open for people rising from the ranks, show a strong penchant for hiring and promoting college graduates. In instances where the technology used by a firm is changing rapidly, technical knowledge available only in college is a legitimate requirement for appointment to top posts. In such firms, nongraduates can expect to be limited to middle and lower management ranks. Furthermore, even those older executives who rose through the ranks tend to seek their replacements among persons better educated than themselves. Mastering the intricacies of finance, manufacturing, marketing, strategic planning, and human resources management—skills required of today's top executive—is difficult without a college degree. As industry becomes more involved with government, international business, and technical innovation, the liberal arts background or the technical knowledge obtained in youth by degree holders gives them an ever-increasing advantage.

Furthermore, all too often the rate of advancement of the self-educated person can exceed the level of learning attained, and the result can be disaster for both the individual and the firm. Well prepared for every job below them, such people may ultimately go beyond their capacities to learn and adapt "to their level of incompetence," as Peter (Peter and Hull, 1969) described it. The result may be the sort of failure exemplified by John De Lorean or Robert Vesco, who eventually faced criminal charges, or James Ling, who built a $4 billion business and then faltered and failed.

Mentoring: The Best Teaching for Stars

Each route to stardom in management calls for different assessment and development procedures. However, most of them have in common the requirements for superior performance on each job held on the way to the top, setting of challenging goals, careful appraisal of performance, and personal coaching. Levinson (1968) asserted strongly that business must be an educational institution, "an institution for problem solving and learning," if it is to survive. In the case of stars, the best learning is likely to be that which takes place under the tutelage of an experienced mentor rather than in formal courses.

Can Star Qualities Be Taught? It is reasonably apparent that training can change behavior related to someone's present job, provided that the desired behavior is clearly defined, the person has the motivation and the intelligence to acquire the new behavior, and the new behavior will be supported by the environment of the job. If that were all there was to management development, it would be a simple process to develop managers by the score. One could provide training to a wide range of candidates and then adorn the best learner with the highest rank. As Gill (1982) has reported, however, this concept of training as just a way of changing behavior has serious limitations when it comes to developing management potential. Gill felt that only two managerial skills, decision making and setting priorities, can really be taught.

Even those skills that can be taught are often not tested. A distinctive feature of many management development programs is the absence of testing of the amount of learning that has occurred— or not occurred. At the end of one course on banking, given by the Stonier Graduate School at Rutgers and sponsored by the American Banker's Association, the participants do take an objective test on the content of lectures. In addition, between the course's first and second years they must write a thesis on a topic related to banking and bank management that will be reviewed by a panel of experienced bankers. Those who do not complete these testing requirements successfully are not awarded a certificate of completion for the course. Such a situation is most unusual for university trade-association-based management development courses and seminars, however, and even in this case the directorate of the school admits that the major purpose of the testing is to stimulate attendance at the lectures.

Participants in most management development courses are reassured on the first day that the practices of testing and grading experienced in conventional college courses will be avoided. The final judgment of the effectiveness of such a course is left to the participants themselves rather than to faculty and staff. In fact, participants are usually asked to rate the course—its lectures, faculty, contents, administration, physical surroundings, and so on—in anonymous questionnaires at the course's end. In effect, the participants in these courses are treated more like customers than like students. The high fees charged for the courses, the need to produce a steady stream of future enrollments, and expected resistance of the participants to any other approach can easily explain this deferential attitude, but that doesn't make the measurement of executive learning any easier.

Mentoring in American Business History. Good performance, with or without additional development courses, isn't enough for development of the managerial star's full potential. At every level, senior people must take a personal interest in the development of younger or lower-ranking employees who are trying to climb up the management ladder.

Many top executives have not only an impressive record of personal achievement but also a great number of brilliant subordinates who rose out of their tutelage. For example, Ernest Breech learned his craft as a chief executive from Alfred Sloan at General Motors, as did dozens of others. Breech went from General Motors to the chief executive post at Ford. There he developed such talented executives as Henry Ford II, Robert McNamara, and Tex Thornton. Thornton moved to Litton Industries, built it into a major corporation, and in turn trained Roy Ash of Dictaphone, Harry Gray of United Technologies, Fred Sullivan of Walter Kidde, George Scharfenburger of City Investing, and many others. This pattern is common enough in twentieth-century business history to give rise to a generalization: The best route to the top is to perform extremely well and find a competent, nurturing boss. The existence and importance of mentoring can also be inferred from the fact that certain large corporations such as Sears, General Motors, Du Pont, and Standard Oil seem to produce more than their share of people who go on to become senior or even chief executives in other firms. A report, called "the IBM Alumni Association," unauthorized by the company and privately circulated by some former IBM executives, states that no less than 350 company presidents started their careers with IBM. If this figure is correct (and it may well be), it suggests that something in the IBM management system produces not only enough executives for its own ample needs but an excess that can flow forth to other firms. Similarly, Harold Geneen, longtime chief executive officer at International Telephone and Telegraph, trained numerous people who became chief executives for other firms. Proctor and Gamble is still another corporation whose alumni hold chief executive positions in other companies today, including Monsanto, Dr. Pepper, H. P. Hood, and dozens of others.

This pattern has been present since the beginning of American business history. Business historian Robert Sobel (1974, p. xiii) noted many connections among the country's leading business founders: "There are interesting interconnections between the men discussed in this work, some of which are direct and some of which are not. Francis Cabot Lowell was of the Boston aristocracy, as were his associates. Their grandchildren financed railroads which competed with Hill's Great Northern, and their children were among the initial backers of Bell Telephone. A direct descendant of Lowell's became interested in the commercial aspects of flight and offered to support the work of the Wright brothers, while others were involved in the workings of Textron, Royal Little's conglomerate. Textron absorbed Bell Aircraft and aviation firms started by Lawrence Bell, who had been one of Donald Douglas's associates at Glenn Martin Company. . . . Buck Duke, the tobacco tycoon, spent the last years of his life erecting Duke Power and Light, made possible by Edison's work in electricity." It was J. Edgar Thompson, one of the founding managers of the Pennsylvania Railroad, who taught his subordinate Andrew Carnegie how to manage. John Paterson, president of National Cash Register, personally coached Thomas Watson, his national sales manager, until Watson left to take over a struggling little firm called CTR, Inc., which he renamed IBM. Similar highly personal connections between older and younger executives are common in business history.

In the early days of American business, the connections were often family ones: Fathers taught their sons. As family capitalism declined and professional managers took over, the mentoring process changed. Older managers taught younger ones of diverse backgrounds. Managerial mentoring today has become less based upon class, caste, and family connections than it was in former times.

Mentoring, past and present, is a distinctive American innovation. These days it's a habit of many consultants, writers, and academics to attribute all kinds of magical qualities to foreign management systems. Where people spoke of the "German miracle" twenty years ago and the "Swedish system" ten years ago, they now glorify the Japanese management system. I would like to suggest that if we are looking for models of managerial excellence, there are numerous features of American management strategies that are distinctively ours and are highly worthy of praise. This is the message of the current best-seller *In Search of Excellence*. Focus on such methods could lead to an American business renewal.

Certainly one of the more distinctively American management practices is the way our senior managers coach their subordinates. American coaching or mentoring practices differ from those of most of Europe and certainly from those of Japan. In more tradition-bound cultures, only a few elite young people—almost always upper-class males—have the benefit of being personally coached and trained by senior people in power. In the United States and Canada today, however, talented young people from all levels of society attempting to move into corporate management may enjoy the mentoring of the present top people. The son or daughter of the assembly line worker, the taxi driver, or the clerk can find the way to executive row with the assistance of a senior authority figure.

Who Is a Good Mentor? Most managers can easily name the person who was most responsible for helping them make their first move up the ladder. For some it was a parent or older brother. For others it was a school teacher, an uncle, a coach, or even a neighbor. The most important mentor for most successful managers, however, was usually an early boss. Perhaps that boss stirred up an ambition to rise in the organization or assured the young subordinate that he or she had a lot more talent than was being used. Perhaps the boss gave the subordinate a special opportunity or assignment that opened the door to possibilities not previously imagined. All of these are examples of ways in which a mentor, at the right time, can make a vital difference in a young manager's career.

Not all bosses make good mentors. Some bosses are people builders, while others are people shrinkers. Some bosses habitually work at putting down the ambitions and aspirations of their subordinates, advising them that they are foolish and presumptuous to consider being anything more than they are right now. Others cheer their subordinates on and encourage their growth by word and action. Only the latter, of course, should be mentors.

The most natural mentor for a rising managerial star is the star's own boss. Sometimes, however, that boss is uninterested in helping subordinates, hesitant to show special attention to one employee, or blind to the star's potential. In such cases, another manager or highly placed person with whom the star's contacts are relatively casual, but who has been favorably impressed with the younger person's work and potential, may become the star's mentor. The mentor talks to the star only occasionally, usually about business, but extends the discussion to giving advice beyond the immediate concern. The exact job relationship between the mentor and subordinate is not important, but the mentor should have a higher post than his or her protege. The mentor should also be a successful person, a role model whom the subordinate will look up to and aspire to imitate.

Business history shows that the best bosses—and the best mentors, or trainers of bosses—were people with a strong goal orientation. Success, after all, comes from unremitting attention to purposes and drive to achieve goals. This goal-centered managerial style may or may not be part of a formal MBO program. It may show itself by example, by rewarding and punishing, by setting standards, or simply by showing enough confidence in subordinates to leave them alone while they are working. The learning of a star who works for a good mentor will center around goals, expectations, standards, and the pressure to do all he or she is capable of doing. It should come as no surprise that most firms where there are good managers produce other good managers almost as a byproduct of operating a profitable and growing enterprise.

The best mentors are characterized by these qualities: (1) They are superior performers in their jobs. No one wants to imitate a loser. (2) They realize that they are examples, and they behave in ways that are worth imitating. They avoid behaviors that, if imitated, would have a bad effect on the careers of their emulators. (3) They are supportive and helpful to subordinates, but they avoid usurping the subordinates' jobs or insisting on things being done exactly their way. (4) They are good delegators. They let subordinates know what results they expect, give them help and support, and then leave them alone to work toward those goals. (5) They provide feedback so that their people will know how well they are doing in their jobs while they are doing them. Such feedback turns people into self-rewarders—or self-punishers. It teaches people to work at their tasks under their own control rather than that of their boss. This is a superior preparation for more responsible positions.

Good mentors have positive attitudes toward their subordinates and toward other people generally. They feel that many people have within them more capacity than is presently being used, and they work hard at bringing out whatever latent talent is there. This attitude need not be wholly selfless. The manager who works at bringing out the best in subordinates will benefit from better performance, greater productivity, and a more profitable business.

Unfortunately, there are still many people in top positions who see people merely as a resource to be exploited. Some see subordinates as competitors who must be batted down when they rise too fast, while others have a detached view that demands a fair day's work for a fair day's pay and nothing more. None of these bosses will gain the benefits of good mentoring for either themselves or their subordinates.

A mentor can't be exacting, hostile, overjudgmental, or punitive in dealing with subordinates if he or she hopes to elicit their best abilities. The attitude of a boss who sees people as objects to be used like Kleenex and disposed of when no longer useful will be quickly sensed by the people under him or her.

Because mentoring of talented junior executives is so important to a company's growth, performance appraisals of managers and objectives for senior executives should include items relating to the number of people who have been promoted out of those executives' units and sent to do bigger jobs. Managers who never produce high-quality people for the rest of the organization are doing only a fraction of their jobs. Thus, every performance review should include the question, "What are you doing to grow people under your charge?'' America's corporate leaders usually have such policies, as we have seen. IBM, Du Pont, General Electric, and similar firms are money tree companies in profits and growth, and at the same time they are people growers. Nobody has built a permanently strong, growing organization without becoming a people grower.

Mentoring of Women and Minorities. The mentoring process becomes considerably more complicated when one of the parties involved is a woman or a minority group member. In particular, many men find it less than comfortable to become mentors for younger women. For example, travel together can be a source of questions or gossip in a tradition-centered environment. This is less of a problem for younger men and women today, but for many senior officers the problem is major.

The notoriety of the Bendix case, involving president William Agee and his protegee, Mary Cunningham, has done much to dampen the prospects of a male senior executive taking on a woman protegee to mentor, however talented she might be. "I can handle being a sponsor for a talented young black man far more easily than I could handle being a sponsor or mentor for a young woman," reported one middle-aged company president. "I don't like one damn bit the prospect of facing a lot of cheap leers and sly remarks, even if they're made in a jovial way," reported another. As a result, many high-potential young women find that today's generation of senior people will take on a mentor role for them only under strictly limited circumstances. If all contacts take place in a controlled environment such as the home office, during working hours, a mentoring relationship may be possible. However, if mentor and protegee will be working together out of the controlled office environment, away from other people, the older man will most likely duck the whole situation.

While the problem of external opinion isn't nearly as great as it is for a mentoring relationship between a man and a woman, taking on a protege who is a minority group member also causes difficulties for many senior managers. Many older white managers are awkward with people of a different race. Young black executives have usually found that they do better in getting support from present senior members of the establishment if they are seen as "being really quite like us." This usually means that their dress, manner, and style must be middle class.

Obviously, the personal values of potential mentors will have an important bearing on their willingness to become sponsors or tutors of younger blacks or women. Some have very conservative social views and simply can't see themselves doing anything special for a minority person. Others have a strong bias in favor of people of their own religious, ethnic, or cultural background. In one large firm, for example, it was a common article of faith among younger managers that "you gotta be Italian to get ahead upstairs in this company." Some senior officers won't mentor anyone who did not go to a certain college, receive a certain degree, or originate in a certain section of the country. These kinds of barriers are fortunately declining as more liberal human relations values emerge, but they do still exist.

Instead of seeking individual mentors, many ambitious young people who happen to be women or minorities are now making an end run around traditional prejudices by using support groups, networking, and caucuses as vehicles for mentoring. These groups have several advantages over solo mentors. For one thing, they provide psychological support as well as practical help in learning the ropes of an organization. Usually these groups are informal, formed voluntarily by people who have similar career aspirations and want to get ahead but realize that they face extra obstacles. More than grievance or gripe sessions, their meetings focus on the social and business barriers that group members must overcome if they are to get ahead.

In one regional telephone company, for example, a women's support group took on a barrier that was preventing women from being considered for repair and construction jobs. Management claimed that repair and construction workers needed to be able to carry seventy-eight-pound wooden ladders. The support group looked into alternatives and found that the company could purchase fiberglass ladders that weighed only thirty-eight pounds, light enough for any woman to handle. Not only did the management agree, but the men who had been hefting the heavier ladders for years were delighted at the improvement in their own working conditions.

More typically, support groups provide feedback and counseling to one another on personal behavior, dress, and dealing with discrimination or system policies that keep members from getting where they want to go. These groups also often invite senior executives to visit with them and hold off-the-record discussions, during which the group gains the benefits of mentoring from the senior officers in a developmental and nonthreatening environment.

The Ethics of Mentoring. Mentoring has no set of formal rules or ethics, but sensible mentors follow certain basic guidelines. Here are a few.

- Don't show favoritism and call it mentoring. There are people we like and people we don't like, but in choosing people to get ahead in the business the wise and ethical executive does not use rank to reward friends and punish enemies.
- Don't let a group of permanent "crown princes" emerge. Make the mentoring relationship a temporary one, annually reviewed and based on continued excellence of performance. If a protege lets high visibility get in the way of doing the job supremely well, dump that person from his or her elite position.
- Don't extract gratitude, repayment, or services from a protege. This includes personal services, especially sex favors. A recent article in *Harper's* reported that a majority of women with older male mentors had engaged in sexual relations with them. Such situations can be devastating to the morale and confidence of other employees. Gratitude on the part of a protege should be expressed by helping somebody else later on, not by repaying the benefactor of the moment.
- Be sure that a protege is worthy of the special advice, assistance, and career boost you are giving. You can't afford to push ahead people who are unworthy or who won't work like the devil to prove that your confidence is justified. Base your choice of proteges on facts, not intuition.
- Having two or three proteges is better than having only one. This avoids the charge of favoritism. If the group is recognized as being made up of superior performers, your choices will be accepted. Their performance appraisals should reflect your high opinion of them. Your job as mentor is to provide opportunity and incentive; your "stars" must do the rest themselves.

7

Moving Stars Up
in the Organization:
The Management
of Managers

I had ambition not only to go farther than any man
had ever gone before, but as far as it was possible
for a man to go.   —*Captain James Cook*

The ultimate star in an organization's human resources portfolio
is the chief executive or top manager. This post is the goal of all
corporate pyramid climbers, and their urge to reach it impels people
to do things that go beyond even their own estimates of their ability.
The small number of people who have the talent and drive to achieve
this goal are different in some important ways from other employees
and even from other managers. In order to help rising stars who
have the power to "go all the way," older managers must learn
to recognize these fundamental differences.

The Drive for Success

Above all, Eugene Jennings (1965) suggests, the *success ethic*
controls the motivation of executives and those with the potential

to become executives. It takes the place of many of the motives that drive more ordinary mortals. The aspirations of success-driven people rise as their rank becomes more lofty. This doesn't mean, of course, that executives don't possess the same basic drives as everybody else. We can, however, distinguish special ways in which certain motives appear and impel such people. Above all, the success of the executive is centered in the job, for the failure of the organization is the executive's failure.

Components of the Success Ethic. The success ethic of the executive is likely to be compounded of eight historical and cultural values. Each component makes an important contribution to the executive's motivation (see Figure 9).

- *The Protestant ethic.* Many executives, regardless of their actual religion, are likely to be influenced by what Max Weber (1958) called the Protestant ethic. Weber attributed the rise of capitalism in part to this ethic. He claimed that the Protestant Reformation gave new emphasis to the values of self-reliance, working harder and longer, and saving money, not for the things wealth would buy, but for the emotional and spiritual satisfaction of having done a job well.

- *Benjamin Franklin's homilies.* Franklin was a model of Yankee practicality and ingenuity—hustling, working hard, engaging in little leisure, finding pleasure mostly in working and achieving. In his autobiography he expressed much of the ethic that goes into shaping many executives' motivational patterns. Franklin homilies about business include "A penny saved is a penny earned," "Time is valuable and should not be wasted," "Honesty pays off," and "Credit and character are vital to living the happy life."

- *Horatio Alger's heroes.* Americans still have a deep admiration for people who start at the bottom and work their way to the top. The theme of over a hundred books written by Horatio Alger in the last part of the nineteenth century, which sold a total of over 55 million copies, was that the son of the bootblack or farmer, through luck and grit, may become a tycoon or chief executive. Opportunities abound, and material success is a direct product of hard work and honesty, Alger taught Americans.

Figure 9. Components of the Success Ethic.

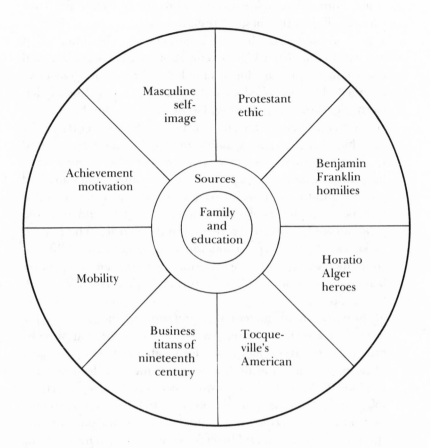

Alger's heroes remain part of the executive's culture and motivational wellspring. Each year a leading executive is awarded
the "Horatio Alger Award" for having arrived at the peak of
corporate success from humble beginnings.

• *Tocqueville's America*. In 1831 Alexis de Tocqueville, a French
  writer, toured this country and wrote of his experiences in a
  book called *Democracy in America*. He observed that immigrants
  from foreign countries hardly landed on our shores before they
  began dreaming great dreams and scheming schemes that they

never would have dared to imagine in their native lands. This frontier spirit has imbued those who rose to riches and fame through the creation of great organizations.

- *The titans.* In the freewheeling, rough-and-tumble economy that existed after the Civil War, a generation of great organizers and corporate empire builders labelled "titans" or "tycoons" emerged. They included such powerful figures as Rockefeller, Carnegie, Harriman, Stanford, Gould, and Morgan. Later many of their exploitative and often ruthless ways were curtailed by law, but their audacious ambition struck a responsive chord in others. When these men were young, they were frugal, hardworking, and wholly committed to business. They amassed great wealth through aggressiveness, vigor, and vision, coupled with personal powers of domination and mastery, and produced grudging admiration and awe even in their critics. Their lavish lifestyles, their sweep of imagination, and their ability to combine resources into organizations of a size and power never before seen became part of the culture and value system of would-be executives.

- *Mobility.* A more modern interpretation of the success ethic is that of Eugene Jennings, who has proposed that success-oriented executives seldom care deeply about the long drudgery of doing a single job or following a single profession for a lifetime. Rather they rise upward by being mobile, moving from job to job. Jennings pointed out that today's success-centered executives usually come from middle-class homes and carry the success ethic that a middle-class education engenders in its pupils.

- *Achievement motivation.* Psychologists David McClelland and David Winter (1971) researched the differences between American executives and leaders in underdeveloped societies. They found that successful leaders were driven by "achievement motivation." The need for achievement promotes entrepreneurship, which in turn is the key to economic growth.

- *"Masculine" qualities.* Much of the value system of executives—even female executives—is masculine in orientation, almost *machismo.* Michael Maccoby (1977) reports of his visit to the Bohemian Grove, a summer retreat attended only by top male executives of leading corporations and a few leading statesmen. He was deeply impressed by the extreme masculinity of the group in its conversations and behavior. Other research by Butterfield and Powell (1979) showed that the qualities that business students associated with leadership were mainly those traditionally held to be masculine in nature: such traits as physical dominance, combativeness, and willingness to confront were rated higher than sensitivity, considerateness, and compliance, and were attributed more to men than to women. This association of business leadership with masculinity was evident even among women students. Much of the success ethic of top executives originates in values of boyhood that are carried into adult life.

Inculcation of the Success Ethic. Nobody would suggest, of course, that these sources of the success ethic are presented to youngsters directly. More usually these values are induced by examples, lessons, and behavior of older family members or teachers. For example, the lad of seven who tries pounding nails in a board to make a tree hut may be stopped by his father, who tells him soberly, "Son, if you are going to do something at all, do it right! Now, let's tear down what you have done and do it over correctly." Benjamin Franklin and Max Weber are never mentioned, but the point is made.

Similarly, certain school systems teach their students that they are members of an elite group destined for higher things than the general population. The schools do not give lectures to this effect but rather convey their message through social memberships offered to students, associations with people in the upper crust, and coaching and participation in the hobbies and habits of the well-to-do or upper middle class. Children from ghettos are less likely to play tennis, golf, or polo or sail a sloop than the children of professionals. By engaging in the ordinary life of the middle class, the child acquires modes of communication, values, and beliefs that incorporate components of the success ethic.

During the sixties it was discovered that the children of liberals were most likely to be stalwarts of the campus radical student movement, although a certain number of radicals were rebellious children of the middle class who consciously rejected social pressure to become like their parents. By contrast, lower-class working parents, who themselves stood little chance of climbing to managerial levels, usually succeeded in imbuing their offspring with the success ethic.

The eight components of the success ethic make up a driving motive with considerable power for causing people to choose certain career paths, sustain a persistent course, adapt to new obstacles, and renew their efforts after serious reversals and setbacks. Many people who are driven by the success ethic are not fully conscious of their motives, for the ethic's component values were imprinted early in their lives by family, school, and personal associates. Indeed, the earlier in life and the more completely the success ethic is implanted, the more likely it is to survive bureaucratic apprenticeship experiences that will be contrary to its teachings.

Some Limits on the Success Ethic. Clearly the success ethic alone cannot explain why some people become executives and others do not. Not everyone who believes in the success ethic will be a superior performer. For example, people whose early training and backgrounds have convinced them that they are automatically entitled to high ranks may find that such a viewpoint leads to disappointment if they allow their job performance to falter.

Furthermore, not everyone who has absorbed the values of the success ethic will choose business and organizational management as the vehicle for expressing that success drive. The law, politics, medicine, teaching, or the arts may be a more compatible choice. Vance Packard points out that pyramid climbers exist in many lines of endeavor. Many of the qualities and behavior patterns that drive corporate presidents to their pinnacles are also found in concert pianists, Nobel Prize-winning scientists, or leaders in government and labor. C. Wright Mills in *The Power Elite* (1956) even suggests that people at the top of one pyramid often transfer to the top of another, as when an army general becomes a corporate chairman or a corporate executive becomes head of a major cabinet department in government.

Any peak of human achievement calls for special dedication and commitment to a goal. In sports, the arts, the theater, and government, there are always people who have a unique and uncompromising commitment to reach the top. A generalized kind of success drive, then, is necessary but not sufficient for wading through the lower levels of a business and rising to the top. Achievement of a top management position also calls for a strong desire for executive responsibility, status, power, and perquisites.

Managing the Underground Executive

Whatever else an organization produces in the way of goods and services, it must also produce a stream of talented top leaders in steady succession. Without such a succession, no amount of capital, no market advantage, no technical leadership, no monopoly can keep it from failing. Successional planning begins with a concern for the quality of the recruits that the firm brings in at the bottom. Campus recruiting results are noted anxiously by senior management. Unfortunately, far less attention is usually paid to these new employees after their arrival. As a result, there is often a high rate of turnover among college recruits in the first two or three years after employment (Odiorne and Haan, 1961). In this way not only many good workhorses but some potential stars are lost.

Because of the need for a reliable succession of top executives, the management of managerial stars is a matter of organization-wide importance. The organization must provide for its own survival through the creation of capable leaders who can rise to the top. It is in such positions that stars must ultimately come to the fore. But how is this creation to be brought about? In other words, how should an organization manage its managers?

The Importance of Early Work Environment. In 1983 about 150,000 young men and women graduated from college with bachelor's degrees in business. Another 60,000 were awarded the MBA degree. This suggests that many people are oriented toward business as a career and probably will seek management- or professional-level work. Most such people have been inculcated with middle-class values, including the success ethic. Yet only a few of these business graduates will arrive at the top levels of the organizations they join. This is partly because of differences in performance, but it is also partly due to differences in the environment in which they operate after their recruitment by a firm.

Many of these business graduates can be quite legitimately routed into middle- and lower-level staff and line positions, where they will become the organization's white-collar and managerial workhorses. Yet there are many with sufficient abilities who ardently hope to move up rapidly but fail to do so. During their first fifteen years of work experience these people are most likely to serve tours of duty as salespeople, accountants, or similar occupations. At the end of that period they have arrived at the age where they might expect to be considered for promotion into higher levels. But after fifteen years in an environment that forces them to be head-nodding, agreeable, compliant subordinates—characteristics all too frequently required for survival in lesser ranks—they have lost the ability for daring and skilled leadership that is needed at entrepreneurial levels.

The person who emerges intact from the forest of supervisors and managers who have shaped his or her responses to direction is usually what Molz (1984) has labelled "an underground executive." This remarkable specimen, throughout apprenticeship in the trenches of the firm, keeps alight the flame of the success ethic without offending others to a degree that threatens career advancement. Such people figure out the ropes of the system by themselves and use their knowledge to advantage. They are often rebels against their surroundings, able to swim upstream against the daily influences that could kill off their success ethic. Robert House (1969) suggests that such nonconformity to one's immediate environment calls for exceptional ego strength, highly saleable skills, or a wealthy spouse. It may also represent an unusually deep or early inculcation of the success ethic.

Tips for Helping the Star Survive. Successful management of managers calls for chief officers to construct a *controlling environment* within which those stars who have been imbued with the success ethic are encouraged to apply their skills to reaching their own and the company's goals. Several measures or conditions can materially assist in bringing the underground executive safely through the suppressive early employment years.

- *Early identification* of stars through portfolio analysis can be of considerable assistance in creating the proper climate for orderly and rapid growth of the highest-talent people. "Crown prince lists" have their perils, but identification of star quality early permits talented people to be placed in accelerated development programs. During the eighties the Bell System, following some adverse court decisions concerning its treatment of women, created a special fast-track program for some of its high-talent and high-potential younger women. Other firms have also created star groups through early identification. Once stars are identified, their progress is less likely to be stifled.

- *Clear goals* of a challenging nature can provide opportunity for underground executives to display their desirable qualities. This calls for keeping the best employees out of the clutches of the people shrinkers and under the supervision of people developers in lower management levels. Most people work below their potential, and jobs are often designed for the lowest level of ability in job holders. Years of underachieving because no challenges or requirements to stretch have been presented can doom the underground executive to remain in the dank regions of lower management for life.

- *Top management attention* can do much to overcome the stifling of entrepreneurial qualities. Serving as assistants or aides to senior officers can be invaluable for people with high potential, especially if those officers are people developers rather than people shrinkers.

- *Special assignments* have an unusually important role in keeping the underground executive from stagnating and dying on the shaded vines of the lower levels of an organization. Ivan Willis, longtime personnel executive at International Harvester, once reported on a study of the top managers in that giant firm. He asked these people what events in their early careers had, in their opinion, produced the greatest impact on their subsequent successful development. The most prevalent reply was a description of some special assignment, project, or task force with which they had been involved in addition to their more mundane duties. Often this special assignment had placed them in contact with higher-level executives, which greatly increased their chances of rising from the slough. They gained an opportunity to observe the higher-level people in daily work, and at the same time they became visible to them. As a result, they were often placed under the sponsorship of a mentor who assumed personal interest in and responsibility for their career progress.

- *Words of encouragement* should come often to those who will ultimately rise through the ranks of their peers. The mentor who helps a younger person keep his or her sights set high may do so directly or, more likely, by example and a sense of commonality. A statement like "When I was selling groceries like you, twenty years ago, I used to run into the same kind of obstinate customers" is a way of telling the future executive, now a grocery peddler in his or her apprenticeship, that the path to higher things is open to be traversed, thus keeping the flame of hope and ambition alive.

- Informal contact between stars and higher-level groups may be specifically arranged. Asking young, high-potential people to do detail work at executive conferences (fill water pitchers and the like) or to do administrative chores at company executive development seminars gives the young stars a chance to observe and imitate the models presented by the presently successful executives. In one large grocery firm, younger managers identified as having high potential were formed into "communication groups," each made up of ten such peers, which met off-premises once a month to discuss company business. The groups were often visited by top managers, who discussed specific functions and problems of the organization at the corporate level. The group meetings thus provided opportunities for teaching by role modelling and personal contact.

- *A junior board of directors,* parallelling the senior board, was a longtime feature of the McCormick Company of Baltimore. The junior board rotated in membership and dealt with the same issues as the senior board. This training in thinking and feeling like a senior executive is reported to have produced important opportunities for growth for underground executives in the company who might otherwise have bloomed unseen in the desert air of lower bureaucratic levels.

The Four Roles of the Executive

In the process of rising through a firm's lower and middle levels, the managerial star has probably gone through many successive screens of experience, trials, errors, and contacts with strong and able mentors. Some changes in his or her values and expectations are likely to have occurred during this time, for the work, goals, and problems of higher-level managers—especially of executives and chief executives—are different from those of managers at lower levels. For example, the higher-level manager's concept of success is likely to become centered around the goals of the organization, sometimes to the degree that the person may not be able to distinguish his or her own personal success from that of the organization.

The high-level manager or executive also becomes more actively concerned with profit. Presidents of large firms are often criticized these days for not taking a long-run view toward profit, which accounts, the critics suggest, for Japanese successes in world markets and export competition. Yet the American company president operates under a charter of goals in which profitability and the interests of the stockholders are foremost. The need for a steady stream of immediate earnings this year and next is inescapable, for if earnings fall, the value of the company's stock falls. Security analysts can make the hapless company president breathless by the speed with which they dump the stock of any firm that forecasts lower earnings for the next quarter or the next year.

It is not surprising, then, that a survey by Odiorne, Michael, and Carlisle (1983) of the presidents of the Fortune 500 largest corporations found that the top priority of company presidents is financial results. "Split a company president's head open and dollars will fall out," as one financial analyst put it to this writer. All other concerns, including management development, public responsibility, employee relations, innovation, markets, and customers are lesser priorities and, as such, are the responsibility of lower managerial ranks.

Success is by no means automatically assured for the star who reaches executive territory. Far from being a sinecure, the job of an executive requires continued high performance and, additionally, the learning of four roles for which the star's previous experience has probably provided little preparation: those of a member of a ruling class, a professional, a trustee for various interests, and a spokesperson and flak catcher. Let's look at each of these executive roles more carefully.

The Executive as Member of a Ruling Class. Only in this century has nonowner professional management assumed a dominant role in corporate affairs. At the beginning of this century, the American system still contained significant elements of financial and family capitalism. The owners, their sons and grandsons, or bankers held the reins of many major businesses. But, having been assembled in order to make money for financiers, the corporations grew to the point where full-time professionals were required to operate them efficiently. By 1918, representatives of financial houses or entrepreneurial families "almost never took part in middle management decisions on prices, outputs, deliveries, wages, and employment" unless they were trained as professional managers, reports Alfred Chandler (1977).

Railroads, mines, and utilities required huge infusions of financial capital, and the providers and assemblers of the capital retained a significant share of the decision making in most such firms through the end of World War II. The involvement of family owners in most large businesses became limited to reaping shares of dividends in proportion to their holdings of stock. Mason (1960) revealed that of the 200 largest nonfinancial American companies, none was privately owned, and in only five was more than 50 percent of the stock controlled by one family or group. Strong minority holdings, in excess of 10 percent but less than 50 percent, occurred in 26 cases of the 200. Over 85 percent of the firms were widely owned and run by professional managers. Even in the five firms where family members were ensconced at the top, all of those leaders were also trained managers.

The concentration of assets in a few large firms continued throughout the twentieth century with only minor interference from antitrust laws and prohibitions of monopoly. Today approximately 0.1 percent of American corporations own over 80 percent of the assets of all of them. The small group of people at the top of these concentrations of economic power and influence have become of considerable interest to the public. Stories about their persons, their lives, their habits, their likes and dislikes, their decisions, their rise and fall are widely circulated in the media. Their merit and competence—or lack of these qualities—become matters of popular debate.

For the small number of managerial stars who rise into lofty executive levels, the new role of members of a ruling class is both heady and nervewracking. Having been buried in the ranks of lower management for many years, they now find that they are the object of keen public attention. Their characters are scrutinized, and their behavior is judged sternly. When William Agee of Bendix, fresh from a press barrage that had pilloried him after the revelation of his personal alliance with vice-president Mary Cunningham, attempted to acquire RCA, the president of RCA was reported to have said, "We hardly think Mr. Agee is qualified to manage RCA if he can't manage his personal affairs." This was an unprecedented kind of judgment for one corporate head to make publicly of another, but it reflected what the press, government regulators, and the public appeared to think of the behavior of this chief of a multibillion-dollar enterprise.

Most top corporate executives are uneasy in the presence of the press. They are governed by a "passion for anonymity" and prefer to leave matters of public relations to staff professionals. Only a small number develop the panache of Lee Iacocca, who dramatically saved a failing Chrysler Corporation in part by appearing on the media to sell cars, and incidentally the corporation, to an admiring public.

Rather than seeing their role as baronial, typical chief executives see themselves as servants of the corporation—"just a fellow trying to do his job." For example, the chairman of General Motors, Richard Gerstenberg, when called to testify before a Congressional committee about certain engineering and design problems in the company's automobiles, brushed aside his mantle of greatness with the aw-shucks statement, "I'm just old Gerstenberg the bookkeeper." But however vigorously a chief corporate executive may claim to be just another worker with a different (albeit better-paid) job, he or she is seldom viewed as such by the public, the company's customers, its employees, the unions, the government, or the press.

Chief executives do not in fact rule alone. The corporate president shares power with other top officers, including the chairman of the board, chief executive officers, vice-chairmen of the board, and key officers who report to the president. Such people as executive vice-presidents and key staff executives in charge of finance, engineering, personnel, and manufacturing must also be included in any reasonable definition of "top management." Even the office of chief executive itself is sometimes shared among three or four people. But, justifiably or not, it is the man or woman at the very top on whom the glare of publicity will be focused.

Reasons for regarding executives as members of a ruling class are not entirely financial. True, most are well paid, and some become rich by the standards of the average person; a small group becomes very, very rich. Many are motivated by the desire and opportunity to become independently wealthy. Still, none can match the powers of acquisition of the early "titan" entrepreneurs who started small firms and made them into giant pools of wealth, such as Andrew Carnegie, who finally sold his steel company to U.S. Steel for over $600 million in 1901—with no income tax to reduce his fabulous store. Few professional managers could hope to emulate Carnegie's hobby of buying castles and importing them from Scotland or to duplicate the multimillion dollar houses built by the titans on Long Island or in Newport.

The perquisites that go with rank are seen almost as necessities by many professional corporate executives. They fly in the company Lear jet because it saves them time that would be lost in waiting for commercial flights, standing in line and perhaps having unplanned and inconvenient encounters with the public. The average work week of top managers is reported as sixty hours. Time is a precious commodity to them, and corporate funds that are spent to conserve that time are considered—or at least reported— as sound investments for the firm.

Some top managers live simple and unostentatious lives, relying on this self-effacing behavior to protect them from the pressures that afflict other public figures. For most, however, the high salary and benefits that go with their rank are a form of status symbol. Even David Rockefeller, president of the Chase Bank and heir to multiple millions in personal wealth, never spurned his high salary, though he reported that it all went to philanthropy.

Living in this world of high income, considerable power, and public attention is hardly something one is trained for by working one's way up through long years as a sales manager, plant manager, or chief accountant. It is something that the chief executive must learn how to handle by on-the-job training. The best schools for such learning are the small groups and associations that top managers enroll in after their ascent is complete. The president's course of the American Management Association stresses peer influence and "education of management by management." The Young Presidents' Organization is open only to people who became chief executive officers of firms with over $20 million in yearly sales prior to reaching age thirty-nine. At age forty-nine they must leave the organization. During their membership period they attend chapter meetings of YPO in their own states and also go to a prestigious "University for Presidents," convened annually in such posh resorts as Acapulco or Hawaii. There they engage in discussions and listen to speakers talking about them and their jobs. The instructional programs at this "university" are secondary to the social purpose of seeing others and being seen by them. Numerous other "presidents' roundtables" in banking, insurance, and industrial trade associations also help the new chief executive adapt to being a member of the managerial ruling class.

One of the main things these groups teach, directly or indirectly, is the rules of executive behavior. Many executives show concern for the reputation of management as a class when one of the fraternity falls from grace. When General Electric found itself on the front page in the early sixties because some of its senior executives were jailed for conspiring to violate antitrust laws, Henry Ford II castigated GE's chief executives for allowing violations that permitted the company's sins to be exposed to a critical press. In 1982 numerous executives were openly critical of the public battle that resulted when Bendix tried to acquire Martin Marietta and was subsequently taken over by Allied Corporation. The great merger and acquisition binge of the early eighties produced sharp comments from some corporate executives, who scolded their peers for making asset plays of a purely financial nature rather than investing in capital expansion that could have created new jobs at a time when 10 percent of the work force was unemployed. David

Finn (1969, p. 136) summed up what he saw as the official executives' creed like this: "Here then are the official rules which supposedly guide the corporate oligarch in the formation of his policies: He is profit oriented. He is growth minded. He is devoted to the welfare of the corporation and feels that by helping to fulfill the common needs of society he is serving the cause of progress."

Of course, these "official rules" do not necessarily represent all executives' real attitudes. Power, for example, may be a greater motivator than profit for some. In fact, Peter Drucker wrote in 1954 that profits were tangential to the real goals of a corporation. He claimed that profit, far from being the major purpose of business, is really a limiting factor upon it. The real purpose of business, he suggested, was to "create a customer."

Relatedly, in 1966, Senator J. William Fulbright suggested that the chief motivational force in the private sector is acquisition, while the major motivator in government is the pursuit of power. This belief is widespread among top executives, who stoutly proclaim that acquisition is the major motive that drives them. Yet they hold, accumulate, guard, and use the power of the corporations under their domain. Many see the search for power as legitimate if it is "power to produce" that is sought rather than power to control things extraneous to the main purposes of the firm.

Studies have shown that conglomerates are not the most profitable of corporations, yet mergers and acquisitions continue to rise. Growth for its own sake may well be a concealed form of power seeking, and the difference between the stated or chartered objective of the firm, to increase the wealth of the shareholders, and the hidden objective of seeking power often becomes blurred in the minds of acquisition-minded executive groups. Such delicate value discriminations exemplify the kinds of decisions that the rising young manager must deal with once he or she has become established in the territory of the top managerial stars.

The Executive as a Professional or Craftsman. As managers rise through the ranks from their first positions, the content of their jobs changes in steady increments. As shown in Figure 10, the technical content and functional objectives of typical jobs decline with each step upward, while the managerial content of the work rises.

Figure 10. The Changing Content of Managerial Jobs by Level.

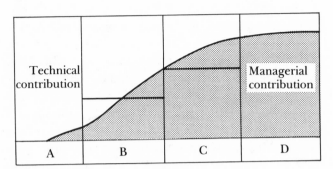

Starting as a technician (A), the employee is paid to apply the principles of a body of technical knowledge to the solution of company and customer problems such as making and selling products, producing income, cutting expense, introducing new products, or controlling product quality.

The first line supervisor's job (B) is divided into two segments. Most of the work remains technical, but certain new duties arise that call for judgment of the work of others, coordination of their efforts, organization of work, planning for the future, and coaching and counselling professionals.

At a key point in the rising star's career (C) a "vital shift" occurs, after which the managerial content of his or her work comes to outweigh its technical demands and the professional manager-of-managers emerges. The rising star may ultimately achieve a general management position (D), in which the great bulk of the work expected is managerial. It is here that the major test of managerial craftsmanship emerges. In all likelihood, success or failure at this division general manager level will be decisive in determining whether or not the rising star will move on into corporate-level ranks, becoming a senior vice-president, group vice-president, or even president of the corporation.

What are the responsibilities of the manager at these loftier levels? In 1950 Peter Drucker wrote that this level of management called for three major responsibilities: (1) The survival of the enterprise in the economy, its profitability, its market, and its products; (2) organization of the human resources of the firm and their efficient use; and (3) orderly and adequate succession to top management itself.

Top managers make decisions, but they do not execute them, Drucker explained. "Getting things done" rather than doing things is their responsibility. Their decisions may work their way into reality as much as five or ten years hence. The job of the manager, Drucker noted, "is largely a job of projecting the future onto the present." This entails both policy making and planning.

In a later work (1973) Drucker expanded upon his definition of a top manager's job. He stated that there are five basic operations in the work of the manager: setting objectives, organizing activities and choosing people to execute them, motivation and communication, measurement of results, and, finally, the development of people—including the manager's own development. Drucker also said that there are six common mistakes that impede managerial effectiveness: designing jobs so small that people doing them cannot grow, assigning people to nonjobs such as "assistant-to," designing jobs in which the worker doesn't have enough to do, designing jobs in which people must spend an inordinate amount of time in travel, using titles as rewards, and creating "widow-maker" jobs that kill.

Many writers besides Drucker have attempted to explain the complex craft or profession of the executive. Often their explanations have been mutually exclusive, rooted in the biases and expertise of the explainers rather than in hard evidence about what top executives really do. Harold Koontz of UCLA has referred to these conflicting theories of management as a "theory jungle." Here are some of the more important "trees" in that jungle.

Functional theories of management. Early writers about the rise of managerial capitalism set out to define the functions of the corporate executive. Henry Fayol (1930), a French industrialist, looked back on his own success and declared that the functions of a manager were organizing, planning, coordinating, and controlling. Between 1930 and 1950 a school of similar theorists emerged. They saw the corporation as a kind of ponderous machine, with fixed rules and principles that must be applied properly to achieve efficiency. Ideas about management functions were the basis of "management" as a separate topic, one that ultimately flowered into an academic department in many business schools. R. C. Davis (1951) combined these theories into an integrated whole, naming organizing, planning, and controlling as the three most vital managerial functions. He stated that these functions could be melded into a leadership pattern through application of such concepts as authority, responsibility, and accountability.

Behavioral theories of management. The initial intrusion of the social and behavioral sciences into management theory was brought about largely through some experiments conducted in the Hawthorne works of the Western Electric company in 1927 (Roethlisberger and Dickson, 1939). Harvard social scientists were invited there to conduct experiments to explain the causes of the productivity of workers. They found that social and psychological factors in the workplace were of utmost importance. This was a denial of certain long-held assumptions about the causes of productivity and motives of workers, which in the past had been presumed to be based upon a single-minded search for money and financial rewards.

The Hawthorne study led to numerous other behavioral studies, not only of the motivation of workers but also of the nature and behavior of groups, cliques, cabals, and organizations in business. This research as it emerged focused on three aspects of behavior: that of individuals, that of groups, and that of complex organizations. For the behavioral sciences, this new field of research was a bonanza. Having discovered the last obscure tribe, and tiring of experimenting with rabbits, rats, primates, and pigeons, the behavioral scientists discovered executives with a zeal matched only by the enthusiasm of the executives themselves for being studied. The behavioral school sees management's job as choosing arrangements that evoke a system of cooperative relationships among people who are trying to accomplish the goals of the organization. This suggests that the manager must become a talented amateur in applied psychology, sociology, and even anthropology (Gordon, 1963).

Operations research. During World War II researchers from the physical and mathematical sciences proposed that mathematical analysis, model building, and sophisticated operations research were the keys to effective management (Ackoff and Rivett, 1963). The operations research movement recommended that managers use a systems approach to running their organizations. The mathematical model—the heart of this approach—has been greatly aided by computers, which can simulate decisions in advance, allowing the quality of the decisions to be improved and failure to be avoided. Several societies and journals for professionals in operations research, management science, and management systems have appeared since 1950.

Scientific management. Even earlier, some American engineers had turned their attention to the tasks of management and had produced a body of knowledge known as "scientific management." Widely popular during the early part of the century, it was centered around the work of Frederick Taylor, an engineer, who proposed four keys to scientific management (1911): (1) developing the best way of doing each job; (2) selection and development of workers; (3) matching workers with jobs; and (4) obtaining close cooperation between managers and workers. This approach ultimately led to a more scientific and rigorous analysis of the tasks of workers and was also partly responsible for the creation of industrial engineering as a profession. Still widely used in mass production industries, it has been supplanted or modified in other industries by more modern approaches.

It would be no surprise if all these conflicting theories produce some confusion in the mind of the emergent star as to what successful executives actually do. In effect, the theory jungle suggests, the executive must be a combination of scientist, systems expert, psychologist, engineer, sociologist, and administrator.

But even if a chief executive were a complete master of all these areas of expertise and could know when to apply each one, he or she might still be more qualified to teach management courses in a college than to run a large organization. Most top managers are guided by practicality, not by theory. Descriptions of executive skills continue to proliferate, but some writers suggest that most of them are irrelevant. Henry Mintzberg of McGill University, for example, has expressed serious doubts that managers actually engage in the kinds of behaviors attributed to them. Likewise, Edward Wrapp asserts that managers are more "likely to wheel and deal" than to follow a systematic pattern of learned behavior.

The theory of *situational management* attempts to reconcile these conflicting descriptions by stating that managerial behavior is solidly rooted in the precept "It all depends." The best way of managing in a given situation depends on the company, its people, its environment, its rate of growth or decline, the age and stability of the industry, the amount of government regulation it confronts, the amount and quality of its competition, and a thousand other variables. Such ambiguity leaves only two simple rules for the manager to adhere to: define goals clearly and be adaptive in reacting to whatever comes.

The Executive as Trustee. The third major role of the senior executive is that of a trustee who fulfills the responsibility of the corporation to its four most important constituencies: stockholders, employees and their unions, customers, and the general public.

Stockholders of today are not simply small shareholders, "widows or orphans." They are more likely to be pension fund trustees, bank trust officers, managers of mutual funds, investment officers of insurance companies, or similar large portfolio managers. Such people are sophisticated investors, keenly interested in the details of any business in which they hold stocks. They are acutely aware of influences inside the firm, the industry, or the economy that could affect the value of their portfolios. As explained in Chapter Two, portfolio managers are quick to relegate a company's stock to the "dog" category if its earnings have fallen or threaten to fall. As guardians of the investments of their clients, they have both a legal obligation and a professional pride in holding assets that will grow and produce earnings (stars or winners). This simple fact of life dominates the world of the chief executive and the officers immediately under him or her. No single crisis or problem can outweigh this endless need for results that increase the wealth of the company's stockholders. The duties of this stewardship become even more complex when the pension fund of a company's own employees owns controlling amounts of stock in the corporation or when, as has happened in meat packing, steel, and textiles in recent years, the employees buy out the company and own the majority of its stock.

Employees of a firm have certain rights and interests that must be protected. The right of steady employment at fair wages and the right to organize into labor unions for purposes of collective bargaining over wages, hours, and working conditions are protected under the Wagner Act of 1935 and the Labor Management Relations Act of 1947 (the Taft-Hartley Act). Under these laws, employing firms are required to bargain in good faith with properly chosen agents of their workers, to make agreements in the form of written contracts, and to abide by the terms of the contracts arrived at.

Numerous other laws also govern the labor-management relationship. For example, firms cannot engage in illegal union-busting or discriminate against minorities in hiring, pay, promotions, or supervision. They must pay minimum wages, provide safe working conditions, and provide for unemployment insurance in the event of necessary discharge of workers. Protecting the rights of the company's employees and dealing with employee representatives are important parts of a chief executive's job as trustee of the organization.

Customers are protected against defective or ineffective products and have a right to expect that a company's claims for its products be reliable and believable (Cron, 1974). Products in certain crucial categories, such as drugs, must pass registration and approval procedures of government regulatory agencies. If they are found defective, they may be recalled at the expense of the manufacturing corporation.

The public is likewise protected from wrongful and harmful behavior on the part of corporations, and protecting the public interest is part of the trustee role of the executive. Under environmental protection laws, for example, a firm may not pollute air or water in the course of making its products, and if it does, it must remedy those evils. In the eighties it has become necessary for the corporate executive to adopt in effect the rule that governs the medical profession: "Do thou no harm." If harm does occur, the executive must expect to repair the damage.

Protection of the public extends to corporate acts that are careless, inept, and stupid as well as those that are deliberately venal and greedy. A corporation must divulge business information to any government agencies that legally request it. In addition, it must obey all criminal laws. If it does not, it may be indicted and punished like any individual.

As the ladder-climbing organization star undergoes his or her early training, the pressures of job objectives and demands for specific performance often make these trustee responsibilities seem academic and remote. The manager of the copper refinery or the coal mine may find that the pressure for tonnage is in conflict with environmental laws, for example, and under such pressure he or she is likely to treat trustee functions as an inconvenience, if not a downright nuisance. Once at the top, however, the executive finds that a need to achieve both production and protection is part of the job. Because early experience is often poor preparation for this part of the executive's responsibility, it is not surprising that many top managers attempt to either ignore or circumvent the trustee's role.

Life in the pressure cooker of a company's lower ranks, with its emphasis on immediate goals, doesn't prepare one very well for a world in which long-range, externally originated matters are of great concern. Thus it is not surprising that stars who rise to the top find the climate there very different from what they are used to and, perhaps, from what they expected.

Of course, there are numerous advantages in being at the top. Most people would agree that it is better to be rich and powerful than poor and weak. At the same time, there are also special kinds of pressures in executive territory. The rewards and stresses that make up the fourth executive role—that of spokesperson and flak catcher—are the subject of the following chapter.

8

———————— *∫* ————————

Stresses and Rewards
of Stardom

Success is counted sweetest by those who ne'er
succeed . . .   —*Emily Dickinson*

Managerial stardom usually comes to those who advance through
an organization by a long series of successes. Driven by the success
ethic, they tend to work harder and longer, study more deeply what
they need to know to get the job done, and prepare better for whatever
problems and setbacks they may confront. They learn the art of
mastery early and polish that art through regular practice, which
helps them achieve one spectacular win after another.

Take the case of Robert X, who started as a junior manager
in an automobile company. Because he had a sound grasp of
accounting, Robert was able to find cost savings that others had
overlooked. After several remarkable accomplishments he rose to
the level of department head, where he applied his cost-cutting
and profit improvement abilities to an entire department. He was
then assigned to a small and struggling division that had never
been very profitable. Through man-killing hours, some bright
innovations, and an inspiring leadership style he turned it into
one of the firm's most profitable divisions, with heartening prospects
for the future. It was agreed by all that Bob was a "real comer."

The story of Bob is typical of many managerial stars. They
succeed because they are driven, and their success breeds new skills

of succeeding that carry upward to new levels of performance. People begin to recognize the stars' special drives and abilities, and the stars in turn learn to associate with other people who have similar habits and get similar results. Their best friends are often their closest competitors for higher rank, and this competitive element adds fuel to the fires of their success ethic. They enlarge and embellish the applications of this ethic in practice, watching others for cues. As they continue to succeed, they attract the attention of senior people who have already arrived at the top. This favorable visibility opens new doors of example and opportunity for them to widen their repertory of success-producing behaviors.

In many ways these stars resemble Abraham Maslow's (1954) description of the "self-actualizing person." This person is a healthy person who makes "full use and exploitation of talents, capacities, potentialities, etc. Such people seem to be fulfilling themselves and to be doing the best that they are capable of doing." They have a clear view of reality and are comfortable with it, have high acceptance of themselves and others, are spontaneous and natural, are problem-centered, and have detachment and a need for privacy. In addition to this, Maslow stated, they have a high sense of autonomy and seem independent of the environment, yet they are active agents within that environment. They have deep interpersonal relationships and a democratic character structure, and they can identify strongly with other people. Further, they have a philosophical rather than a cruel sense of humor and are universally creative. In relating to their culture they may tend to resist enculturation in favor of an inner detachment while showing easy conformity to conventional customs of dress and manners.

All these qualities will stand young executives in good stead and prepare them for the next stage in their rise through the organization. They produce the successes that are the tangible expressions of the success ethic. Even more importantly, these qualities are also the source of the greatest satisfactions in stardom. The self-esteem that flows from each success reinforces the self-esteem needed to tackle the next challenge successfully. Harry Levinson (1968) suggests that the executive achieves a sense of mastery when "ambitious striving emanates from the sense of competence, supported and encouraged by authority figures."

For many who achieve and reinforce their stardom, contin-
uation of success may be expected as long as opportunities come
their way. The firms that manage their human portfolios best are
those that identify their stars early and continually feed them
opportunities for greater success. Upon entry into executive territory
the opportunities increase radically, even astronomically, for the
entire world of the corporation, society, and the economy lies before
the top management.

The Stresses of Stardom

More ominous opportunities also lie at the top—opportunities to fail, to suffer defeat in a big way. These opportunities are
greater than the possibilities of failure that came before, for they
often involve the unpredictable world outside the firm. Not only
does the law impinge, it changes. Critics may attack a particular
corporation or the institution of the corporation itself. In this land
of organization-wide opportunity the star may come face-to-face
for the first time with the chance of a failure great enough to threaten
the loss of everything he or she has gained.

The Executive as Spokesperson and Flak Catcher. For the
would-be executive who rises through the selection process to
stardom and ultimately into top management, there lies ahead the
possibility of crisis experiences for which lower-level learning has
provided no preparation. These are crises that afflict the entire
corporation. Often they are initiated outside the firm and cannot
be resolved by ordinary administrative practices or managerial job
skills. When a corporation's actions produce protests, lawsuits, or
adverse publicity, the press, the public, and the government expect
that the corporation's top person will respond to the criticism. The
public or government regulator, like the field anthropologist in-
vestigating a strange and remote tribe, almost inevitably heads for
the chief's hut and won't be shunted aside or mollified by lesser
ranks.

In the sixties, when a dozen electrical companies were
convicted of illegal conspiracy to fix prices for electrical equipment,
it was the presidents and chief executives of these firms who were

hailed before Congress and the press to explain. When General Motors was found to have initiated a hostile personal investigation of Ralph Nader after his disclosure of defects in Chevrolets, it was not the investigators from the firm who were marched to Washington to face the bright glare of national opprobrium but rather Frederick Donner, the chairman of the board and chief executive officer. Understandably, this role of spokesman and flak catcher, which is unique to the very highest level of the firm, is a major source of executive stress.

During the turbulent sixties, a whole new set of stresses emerged. More recently scandals have also shaken the boardroom, causing a decline in public regard for business and a lowering of organizational morale. There is open dissatisfaction with managerial decisions and continuing concern about policies regarding the environment and occupational safety, the peaceful uses of the atom, the reliability of CPA reports, and a host of other continuing problems.

As laws and standards of conduct for corporations change, so do the standards of performance for those at or near the top. Many levels of an organization share the stresses of corporate life, but the engineer, line manager, and machine operator are not likely to be hauled before a legislative committee or slapped with charges of bribing a foreign official. They are not apt to be kidnapped or picketed outside their homes or shouted at by stockholders angered by corporate losses. These debatable honors are reserved for those stars who have worked their way to the top.

The Buck Stops Here: Causes of Executive Stress. Anxiety and stress are apparently chronic conditions of modern society. Studies of patients in mental health clinics show that a near majority of them suffer from stress-related symptoms. Hollingshead and Redlich (1958) found that neuroses, which are usually stress related, are especially common in the middle class. Nonspecific pressures produce a generalized state of unease that can lead to health problems such as cardiovascular disease and hypertension. Freud (1936) defined anxiety as "something unpleasant felt by the individual." The pressures of conflicting groups, leading to the conclusion that you can't win and you can't quit, produce great amounts of stress and anxiety at the top.

For some executives the stress may grow out of a longstanding anxiety about authority figures. Having arrived at the very top rank, the chief might expect that authority over him or her will no longer exist. Yet a Congressional committee, a judge, or an IRS agent may renew deep-seated past fears. The press, seen as representing "them"—a great population of unseen and uninformed readers— may appear as another form of hostile authority figure. Facing such figures is often a most unpleasant sensation for the person whose power inside a firm is well established. Changes due to competition, new technology, or failure of employees to perform are considered to be manageable problems, well within the skills of the executive to handle. Confrontations with outside power figures are less predictable and less manageable and thus cause much greater stress.

The fear of failure underlies much of this stress. After years of unremitting success at lower levels, the star rises into the "heaven" of the executive territory, only to learn to his or her dismay that great threats to self-esteem and suppressed feelings of inferiority await. Often they come from sources wholly new to the young executive's experience.

The same success ethic that drove the executive to the top now becomes the basis for a heightened fear of failure. A business recession that dries up the market for several years and savages the company's financial statement, the OPEC oil crisis, double-digit inflation, and failure or malfeasance of subordinates that leads to public ridicule for the firm can all produce setbacks that attack the basic success ethic.

This does not suggest that anxiety, stress, and neuroses are not found in middle management, of course. But the stresses of upper management have a special quality because these people are so success oriented. Their success ethic works quite well in dealing with things under their control, less well for things that are not. Being "lean and mean" (a favorite phrase in executive suites during the recession of 1982) is a suitable response to a firm's internal problems, but it is likely to prove very unsuitable as a response to a Congressional committee, for example.

Ephraim Rosen (1959) concluded that "fear of failure" is at the root of most executive anxiety. Many neuroses, such as fear of the possibility of separating from executive territory and the executive social class, are founded on the act of separation, as Otto Rank (1945) found. Firings of chief executives, reported daily in the business press, represent an ever-present possibility of separation for the star who has made the long climb to the top. Some of the stress response of executives in crises also grows from threats to their identity, which is closely bound up with their success ethic. The loss of the sense of mastery built up in the successful climb to the top is more severely stressful than failure would have been if it had come earlier.

Executives Under Siege: Three Response Strategies. Little work has been done to find out how executives handle the special traumas of life at the top. In an effort to gain some insight into this side of managerial activity, this author interviewed sixty-one executives whose lives and jobs had been directly affected by traumatic events. They were asked what strategies they took or would recommend taking to avoid aggravating a bad situation. Once their confidentiality was assured, they were remarkably willing to discuss their crisis experiences and philosophies.

The strategies revealed in the interviews fall into three rather predictable categories.

- *Fight the adversary.* In at least two cases I was treated to an approximate recitation of Hamlet's question about "whether 'tis nobler in the mind to suffer the slings and arrows of outrageous fortune or to take up arms." In these cases and others, the besieged executives obviously relished a fight. This was particularly true when the chief executive founded the firm and perhaps saw it as his fiefdom: An attack on the company was an attack on the founder and vice versa. Furthermore, an attack on either was often seen as an attack on America, free enterprise, and so on.

- *Run away.* Those who had little advance warning of crises often reacted to them with dismay, shock, chagrin, and consternation. Taken by surprise, these executives—who usually had had records of unremitting success—frequently had heart attacks or turned to alcohol. Many avoided their employees and entered and left their offices at times when they were likely to be seen by the fewest people. Others refused to return calls or answer letters, surrounded themselves with guards, or got unlisted home phone numbers.

- *Respond professionally.* Executives in this category would step back from the predicament, analyze it, and then devise tough and adroit responses. Such professionals often anticipated the crises. Even so, one noted, "Having a personal stake in the outcome can cloud your judgment. That's the best argument for using experts to review the situation. The old saying that "the person who is his own lawyer has a fool for a client" applies to more than court cases.

   "Executives must make decisions that have an even greater impact on the lives of others than on their own. In such cases, getting all the facts and clearly examining the situation is how a rational person would proceed. But that's not always what happens. It's easy to be objective, even Olympian, about other people's problems. We all learn to suffer others' aches with considerable equanimity."

   This executive emphasized that, when an executive is directly affected by a crisis, outside advice becomes particularly important. "Oddly enough, that's the very circumstance where your vaunted objectivity is apt to desert you quickest," he said. "Getting the best possible advice from those who won't lose their objectivity is a pretty sound idea."

   Another executive told how a friend had been chased around the boardroom by a small group of hostile board members. "He was tempted to give the whole board an ultimatum and nearly forced a showdown. But he decided instead to discuss what to do with trusted and objective advisors, and they suggested options. Finally, he simply smiled his way through and let the opposition blow its game by going to excess. His first impulse would have led him astray."

   Where a decision has high personal impact, the instinct is to make an emotional response. That can be just what the people on the other side are hoping for. Tensions can build to the point where it seems necessary to take action—any action—without gathering enough data for an objective decision. The wise executive, however, avoids this temptation.

Fourteen Crisis Tactics. The three general strategies just described can be subdivided into a number of specific tactics. The following responses were all drawn from our interviews.

1. *Freeze!* Only shortly before the media reported it, the head of a medium-sized firm learned that his sales department and his controller had bribed a foreign agent to get business. Immediately howls went up for explanations and for costly remedies, not to mention the chief's scalp.

    "I didn't know what to do, so I did nothing," the chief executive said. "I froze like a pheasant in danger. I didn't do it rationally; I just froze and couldn't move." This reaction apparently worked well in his case; he avoided aggravating his critics and was able to respond quietly later.

2. *Become an ostrich.* One executive allowed us to interview his officers but not him. They reported that he stuck his head into the sand when he learned about his company's practice of dumping toxins into a river. Publicly and privately, he would not hear of the problem. When his aides went to hearings and negotiated a costly settlement, he neither asked about it nor commented on the cost. He acted as if nothing had happened.

3. *Lash back fast.* One corporate office took on the air of a war room when the SEC and a prosecuting attorney charged the company's officers with wrongful insider trading in the company's stock. News releases and press conferences were assembled with fantastic speed. The charges of wrong-doing were hotly denied, the motives of the agency chief were impugned, the capabilities of the agency's staff were scorned, the quality of its data was downgraded, and grand generalizations attacking the motives of the agency and the administration of which it was a part were issued. Sometimes this strategy works, but frequently it does not.

4. *Raise the issue to a more general plane.* This response is highly risky. It can steel the offense and perhaps expand what could have been just a lost skirmish into a major battle. For example, an executive precipitated a suit that went all the way to the Supreme Court over the right of OSHA inspectors to enter his plant without a search warrant. The cost of the suit far exceeded

the possible losses from any safety actions and fines that might have resulted from the inspection. Such actions usually are motivated by deep-seated ideologies, principles, or values that overshadow the specific situation. The long-running court fight of Vivian Kellems, the Connecticut manufacturer who for years refused to pay income taxes, didn't save her any money. The IRS simply impounded her bank account and took what it claimed, plus interest. But her fight centered on what she saw as the issue of the proper relationship between business and government; the question of actual tax payments was secondary.

Business leaders who have strong ideological casts of mind are apt to favor this response. One executive, a member of the John Birch Society, responded to threats and crises this way, and some subordinates suggested that he cultivated crises that placed him in the center of controversy.

5. *Let your lawyer handle it.* This is a common solution to ordinary crises. For example, when one company and some of its officers were charged with failure to pay income taxes properly, there was no visible effect on the daily routine of the company or its leaders.

The company lawyer was instructed to "fix up this damn mess you made," and he was empowered to commandeer any help needed. All hands received stern lectures. The implication was that "if the damn lawyers and tax people had done their jobs right, this never would have occurred." In at least one instance, even after the corporate counsel had done Herculean work at near-genius level, the entire legal department was quietly eliminated and a private law firm was retained.

On the basis of evidence collected in these interviews, it is easy to conclude that it would not be sound career policy for a lawyer or tax accountant to crow "I told you so" when crises occur. The messenger who brings bad news should keep one foot in the stirrup; prior warnings are often forgotten when the crunch comes.

6. *Tough it out.* In situations where the originators of the crisis were a counterculture group or some ethnic or racial minority, the favored response seemed to be to wait for the problem to go away or to assign a low-level staffer to meet the unhappy

group's representative. There was a consensus that if a problem would solve itself without further action, it was pointless to spend money or time on fixing it.

7. *Round up your gang.* Although crises often centered on the chief executive, one response favored by skilled professional managers was to call in key executives and announce that "we" have a problem. "This means that if I fall, somebody else is apt to fall with me, if not ahead of me," said one chief executive coolly. "I guess there are probably a couple of these guys who wouldn't mind seeing me slipped quietly over the side, because one of them might move up. I want to cool that idea very quickly. I make it clear that, as with all problems, we are going to work on this one together. I organize my defense so that they become spokesmen, advocates, and defenders along with me. I bind us together at the ankles, which helps in the battle."

One large food company was hit by charges from a Congressional committee's surprise witness, who presented on TV what he said was damning evidence about one of the company's products that is sold to children. The accuser asserted that the president of the firm knew and condoned the product's poor quality ("Profits ahead of kids") and recommended that the company officer be hauled in to explain his malfeasance to the committee.

The company president immediately rallied his team, making it clear that the head nutritionist and director of research would be the first to go to Washington and that, if he himself were called, he would immediately volunteer all of his team to attend and sit behind him in symbolic evidence of unity.

In another case, a committee for defending the company was appointed in response to a crisis, and a well-known critic of the president was made chairman. The responsibility for clearing up the mess was placed squarely in his lap, and he worked hard and successfully to refute the charges against the president and the company.

8. *Make like a duck.* The late Bill Powers of the American Banker's Association had a tactic for crisis situations—"Make like a duck: Be calm and serene on the surface but paddle like crazy underneath." When confronted with a devastating report from

an examiner or other important critic, he would calmly agree to read and study the report and would seek a delay. Then he would work like mad to limit the report's exposure, talk to key directors so there would be no surprises, and whale backs to get everything corrected as quickly as possible. This would often permit him to tell the critic, "We thank you for your report, and we can now report that everything you found has been corrected."

9. *Contain the damage.* A chief executive who advocated this strategy was a former high-ranking naval officer who said he had learned in combat that when you are hit, there is no use panicking or jumping overboard. "It's better to assess the damage, close off the most damaged compartments, and save the rest of the ship by sound emergency procedures," he said. "The objective is to save the entire vessel. It may even be necessary for the captain to accept some casualties in the containment of damage in order to save the rest of the crew. I guess the key to my strategy is to contain the damage." In short, this means sizing up the damage, writing off what may have to be sacrificed, setting up a line of final resistance, and making a strong stand there.

10. *Act like Mayor Daley.* One executive of a large Chicago firm suffered through a traumatic experience inflicted by a hostile newspaper's investigative reporting. "I learned from our late mayor how to respond to personal attacks, especially when they seemed to have really caught us short," he said. "Mayor Daley, when confronted with a smoking-gun case of malfeasance in his administration, would express shock and then fire a depart- ment head in a somewhat conspicuous way. The expendable subordinate usually understood the mayor's motives and nor- mally accepted the firing as necessary to keep the party organ- ization afloat. This managerial logic is very tough but clear: a manager must accept responsibility for his department and, if something goes wrong, he should be ready to depart."

This kind of response usually involves a private consul- tation between the boss and departing manager, in which it is explained that there is nothing personal in the firing but that the action is necessary for the good of the organization.

A generous termination settlement and strong assistance in outplacement usually are provided to help ease the transition.

11. *Attack the other's motives.* Usually more instinctive than logical, the defense of charging the attacker with the wrong motives must be used very well in order to work. "This is politically motivated" is seldom an effective response to a substantial charge; hard evidence is needed to impugn the attacker. Defamation laws must also be considered, since a charge like "He is seeking revenge for being fired for incompetence" must be defensible in court.

12. *Countersue.* While using the courts to fight personal battles is illegal, a countersuit is a defense against a noisy and troublesome suit. "I resigned from a board because I suspected the president of cutting corners in stock selling, and I joined the board of another firm that indirectly competed with the first," said one executive. "The president of the first firm filed a noisy suit charging me with conflict of interest. After some thinking and consultation with a tough lawyer, I countersued for ten times his suit, describing his malfeasance. I sent the facts to the Justice Department, the attorney general, and several other regulatory agencies. The president withdrew his suit in a hurry."

Such counterattacks should be waged only by those with clean hands. For example, after charges by Ralph Nader, General Motors had Nader's morals and character investigated. This counterinvestigation outweighed the alleged wrongs in the public's eye and put Nader on the road to acclaim and power.

13. *Pick your best option.* Anger, panic, and stupor prevent most people from listing available options, defining objectives, and weighing each option for contribution and cost. Even if you use rational analysis in your normal dealings, when your adrenalin is flowing and the media are showing caricatures of you to millions of people, you probably will have trouble being calm and logical. This may be the time to call for some detached advice.

14. *Win on a higher level.* Dissidents charged in public and in the boardroom that one company founder was not competent to be CEO and chairman because of ill health (he had had

one heart attack). The old man appeared to be defeated but made a last-gasp request that his removal be deferred for six months for personal reasons. The request was granted.

With the pressure off, the CEO put himself under the care of a leading heart specialist. He lost weight, exercised, got a tan, and surfaced three months later with his doctor. "I'm back in the saddle," he announced to his board and the press. The physician chimed in that "In my opinion, the best therapy for him would be to return to work at once." The rebels hastily retreated, leaving the CEO in charge for ten more years.

Preparation for Crisis. Our interviews suggested that an ounce of prevention can prevent a pound of panic. The ideal pattern of preparation for crisis appears to shape up like this:

1. *Manage by anticipation.* The best strategy is to be prepared— to consider in advance all plausible crises and have response tactics prepared for each. For example, lawyers usually will be of more value in response than in prevention.

   A solidly grounded public relations director will think more strategically than operationally, so an executive can expect some crises if the firm's PR chief is more of a fire fighter than a preventer. For example, the president of one large corporation donated funds to his alma mater for a building and, with a go-ahead from his PR director, agreed to speak at its dedication. The situation soured when a crowd of hostile students appeared at the ceremony, jeering and shouting insults about his company. The shocked executive did not handle the confrontation very well.

   The PR man should not have allowed his president to be caught unprepared in such a situation. The president should have been warned of the possibility of a demonstration and given suggestions for ways to handle it and even turn it to his advantage.

2. *Make good use of environmental audits.* Companies that operate in high-risk environments should be committed to surveying those risks regularly and assessing the possibilities of exposure. This requires constant staff attention to threats and consideration of ways of turning them into opportunities. The most profes-

sional executives reported that they really welcomed some of
the challenges and crises. They saw opportunities where others
might have seen only dangers or, at best, nuisances.

3. *Keep fit.* Maintenance of a steady state of physical health, positive
   mental outlook, and equanimity seemed to be a major part of
   crisis preparation for professional managers. "I find that if I
   am overtired, overworked, and overtaxed, I am apt to blow my
   cool at something rather small," one executive said. "I found
   that rage is something I fall back on when I haven't had enough
   rest—working too many hours, traveling too much, and not
   taking a vacation. I now plan a winter vacation in the sun for
   a couple of weeks every year, and I don't let anything stop it.
   I look forward to a fully occupied period with my grandchildren,
   some reading, and some long spells alone or with my wife."

4. *Develop personal skills.* Executives who faced crises that required
   talking with reporters, personal appearances before investigative
   bodies, or sessions in court reported that they fully appreciated
   any previous training in public speaking, communication skills,
   or working in front of a TV camera. Past experience as an officer
   in a trade association, conducting seminars for professional
   groups, or speaking to educational groups proved to be excellent
   preparation for these kinds of stressful public appearances.

   "I found that my evening teaching in a college many years
   before was probably the best preparation for dealing with the
   press and media," said one president. "It taught me to deal with
   tough questions from relatively uninformed people who
   wouldn't mind catching me in an error."

5. *Plan to do things right all the time.* One president of a large
   insurance company quoted La Rochefoucauld: "Perfect virtue
   is to do without witnesses everything that one is capable of doing
   in public view." Another read a quote from Eldridge Cleaver:
   "Doing right is a hustle, too."

Most stars' roads to the top of the organization afford little
on-the-job training for the kinds of crises that executives must deal
with. The most similar experience is likely to be that of isolated
command, such as being plant manager of a factory or mill some
distance away from the home office and in poor communication

with it. With modern communications technology, however, even the most distant plant or office is apt to be in almost constant touch with the home office. While this has advantages for information flow, it also reduces the opportunities for managers to acquire experience in lone, free-standing decision making.

"The best job I ever had was being a plant manager in a small plant, one of dozens, in a very large company," reported one company president. "My boss had these sixty or more plants to run and couldn't visit them all very often or even reach them by phone because they were spread over four different time zones of the country from Maine to Hawaii. As a result, we had to stand on our own feet, solve our own community problems, deal with our own unions, and show results without using the home office staff as a crutch. In fact the home office was very thin on people; we couldn't weep on their shoulders because they were too busy. I think this separate command idea is the best preparation you could get for the presidency."

The Rewards of Stardom

What awards await the star at the top, and how important is each kind of reward as a motivator? John K. Galbraith declared that money ranks first as a motivating force and "beats whatever comes second by a considerable margin." On the other hand, Henry Ford is reported to have said that "money is simply what the businessman uses to keep tally of his accomplishments," implying that it is the accomplishments themselves that count. Surveys of top management by the Roper organization found that executives listed achievement and position as the top motivators; money wasn't even mentioned.

Herzberg's (1966) studies on motivation similarly found that the true motivators for most employees were the work itself, recognition, achievement, and responsibility. There were also certain "dissatisfiers" that watered down positive motivational effects. These drains on motivation included excessively low salaries, company policies that were not clear and fair, and poor working conditions. Herzberg defined two classes of "energizers" as "motivation factors and hygiene"—hygiene being the absence of dissatisfiers.

Herzberg's research was done on lower-level workers and on professionals such as nurses, manufacturing supervisors, and scientists, but there is considerable plausibility in applying his principles to the executive. Clearly the star has hygiene needs. Indeed, because of the success ethic and the usual history of a star's career, he or she may have acquired more hygiene needs than the hospital orderly or machinist. When the president of a billion-dollar firm learns that he is making less than a basketball star, a running back, or an outfielder, he might shrug that off. But if he is making only a fraction of what another executive in a like-sized or smaller firm makes, he might focus upon his salary as a dissatisfier and become impelled to earn more.

Financial Rewards. If you really want to be rich, emulate Charles Revson, the founder of the Revlon cosmetics empire. When Revson died, he left a personal estate valued at $100 million. It would have been considerably greater if he hadn't had a penchant for spending money at a rate equal to that of people with ten times his wealth. Raised in a cold-water flat in Manchester, New Hampshire, Revson built a $4,000 a year fingernail polish business begun in a garage in the Bronx into a $400 million corporate giant that provided him with the life of an emir. He enjoyed "New York on $5000 a day," reports his biographer, Andrew Tobias (1976). His triplex penthouse was matched by his 257-foot yacht, the *Ultima*, which slept fifteen and had a full-time crew of thirty-one. For short forays it carried a launch and a speedboat, plus a little motorboat on deck. Filling its gas tank cost $20,000. The ship cost Revson $3000 a day to own, even though nobody used it for four days out of five. At his death, Revson left behind him (along with his wealth, his immediate family, and three former spouses) an industrial empire operated by "hundreds of shell-shocked, verbally assaulted, overworked, overpaid, and in some cases wire-tapped executives." He also left behind numerous admirers who marveled at the steepness of his ascent, his drive, and his imagination.

When Revson died, Revlon directors acted for the first time to make an important decision—something "Charlie" had never permitted them to do. They chose as Revson's successor Michael

Bergerac, the kind of person one might expect to be hired to head a major multinational corporation. Bergerac had the right college degrees and had climbed to a vice-presidency in the $11 billion I.T.T. corporation. His salary and bonuses as the new president of Revlon, while most ample from the ordinary person's viewpoint, would not in ten years have added up to enough to let him buy an apartment like Charlie's or relax on a yacht like the *Ultima*.

Unquestionably, the financial prize is worth the game for most ambitious young stars who climb the corporate ladder. The star who rises to the top ranks will almost surely become a millionaire. The executive at the top of an organization must receive a considerably greater salary than the people immediately below him or her. Studies by the American Management Association show that the salaries of all managers have a rather fixed ratio to those of the people below them, which turns the second- and third-level executives into ardent supporters of high salaries for the executive at the peak.

Bonus plans also have a direct bearing on the annual income of many corporate executives, and these are directly tied to overall corporate performance. While the sales executive may be rewarded for sales alone, it is the overall success of the firm in such measures as return on investment, earnings per share, and return on stockholders' equity that determines the top-level executive's bonus. The Conference Board reports that most bonus plans have several distinctive features: They are related to the attainment of individual objectives, they are based on overall corporate results, and they represent a percentage of earnings beyond a profit that allows for dividends to shareholders.

The level of compensation that executives can gain through bonus plans is not unlimited, however. The IRS scrutinizes corporate compensation plans carefully to look for salaries that exceed the norm or that may jeopardize stockholder interests. Stockholder suits, disaffection among lower-level management, and adverse publicity can all result from a poorly constructed or poorly administered executive bonus plan. Each year in Detroit, for example, union newspapers publish the amount of the bonus paid to each auto company executive, using figures that must be filed annually by all corporations with the Securities and Exchange Commission and the IRS and which are open to the public. Often these figures directly affect union wage demands.

In spite of these limitations, it is undeniable that anybody who earns from $500,000 to over $1 million a year in salary is highly paid. Add to that stock options, bonuses for performance, and numerous "perks" such as lodges, a company plane, a private dining room, and generous expense accounts, and you are not talking about an anchorite who adheres to the vow of poverty. Yet IRS figures show that among those people whose income is over $1 million a year, only a tiny fraction of that income comes from salaries. The salaried corporate executive is actually among the poorest of the rich.

Many highly paid executives have indeed built up substantial estates, in the range of $50 to $100 million, but they did this not merely through their salaries but also through shrewd management of assets. For example, John Lee Pratt, long-time treasurer of General Motors, left an estate of $90 million, but the greatest share of that estate was accumulated after his retirement through investments.

For most executives reaching a level just below the presidency, opportunities for accumulating fabulous wealth are limited. The executive's demanding schedule, running an average of sixty work hours a week, simply doesn't allow for the time or energy to pursue much side dealing. Then, too, the average age at which stars reach the top ranks is such that they don't draw extremely high salaries long enough for fabulous estate building.

Starting your own firm can produce more generous rewards if you succeed at it. High-technology firms started by dropouts from IBM, Western Electric, or other corporate giants sometimes create new products that find a niche in the market too tiny to be worthy of large corporate dealing. The founder of such a firm can build it up to a size and market position that make it attractive to a merger-hungry bigger fish and then walk away ("cash out") with several million dollars for only a few years of backbreaking and risky efforts.

Alternatively, there are firms like Teledyne, Litton Industries, Hewlett-Packard, Wang, and Digital Equipment Corporation. Their founders didn't sell out; rather, they remain firmly in charge and each has been rewarded with wealth averaging over $100 million.

While few of these entrepreneurs have followed the lifestyle of
Charlie Revson, they could more nearly afford to do so than most
salaried professional managers.

Tax considerations play an inordinately large role in determining the reward level of salaries for executives. By the time the
IRS, with state and city income taxes thrown in, has taken its bite—
in the 60 percent range—a $200,000-a-year executive's earthly store
hardly increases by leaps and bounds. The costs of tuition at the
best colleges for his or her children, a top-of-the-line car or two,
a home in an executive neighborhood, and perhaps extra payments
for child support or alimony don't leave much surplus for great
savings and estate building. The latter comes more often in the
form of deferred compensation and stock options, which don't
embellish the executive's immediate living standard greatly.

Nonfinancial Rewards. Many major rewards for high-
ranking executives are nonfinancial. In addition to benefits, which
are tax-free additions to income, deferred income, and the like, the
executive's job should provide a fair mix of the following:

Recognition. The executive has a strong need to be credited
for his or her accomplishments. This recognition is most important
when it comes from other members of the executive community.
It may include membership on other companies' boards of directors,
membership in prestigious groups such as the Business Round
Table, chairmanships or directorships of civic organizations, honorary degrees from major colleges, and invitations to address
important organizations. There is a limit to this kind of recognition,
however, for such things must have the air of being thrust upon
the person; "showboating" is frowned upon. During the early
eighties, when some company presidents appeared on national
television in commercials for their products, low-key muttering from
other executives about "overdoing" was heard.

It can also be a detriment for the rising star to receive excessive
press attention. In one large electronics firm, three senior vice-
presidents were vying for the top spot. One was covered lavishly
in a weekly business magazine, which caused him to remark: "That
might just have cost me the presidency. I had to assure everyone
that I didn't seek out this burst of fame, that it was solely the
magazine's idea. I'm not sure they are convinced." Executives at

the top know the mechanism of the public relations "buildup," and if one member of an executive-level team receives recognition that the others feel is hyped, they may quickly administer internal sanctions to the offender.

Belonging. One of the genuine rewards of success for the star is the right to join the select group at the top. This does not mean merely the notorious "key to the executive washroom" and private dining room. It means the company, approval, and acceptance of this important group of high climbers and successful people and it is an important reward. It is not given lightly. A major consideration in choosing a member of a top management team is whether the candidate will "fit in." If he or she is perceived as a "grenade thrower" or other nonteam player, that person simply won't be invited to join the club.

Status and power. There is great ego satisfaction in making things happen. The moving of people, plants, money, and programs produces a feeling of high achievement, and the ego satisfaction that comes from doing things that lesser people can't do is an important reward for the top executive group. The size and power of the corporation itself, through the process of identification, provides rewards to the executive near the top. This is reinforced by the status symbols that are usually all around the executive. The tasteful and elegant office suite, the stylish professional secretary, the quiet bustle of opulent surroundings reinforce the satisfaction the executive feels. To be sure, in their extreme form such things, which can be purchased with money, can beguile the executive, much like the buildup of public relations hype. As one retiring executive described his early experience in joining the top management: "When I first moved to the tenth floor where the executive offices are located, I was really impressed at how nice they were. Then after a while I began to feel that I deserved such fine fittings. Next I began to tell myself that after all, such amenities were no more than suited to a big shot like me." The possession of such expensive accoutrements as thick carpeting, huge desks, credenzas, paintings, and Danish furniture all reinforce the feeling that one must be adequate to deserve such status symbols.

Sense of mission. The feeling of power that comes from being an executive near the top of a large corporation with hundreds of plants and tens of thousands of employees is often accompanied by a heady sense of great mission. Doing strategic planning to perpetuate the corporation, "an immortal but fictitious person," has a strong emotional impact on the executive. It may imbue the top people with a respect and loyalty that make building a great organization and serving it well one of the best sources of executive reward.

Couple this with generous monetary rewards, and the stresses and crises that occasionally erupt in executive life will seem bearable, and the job will be worthwhile for the successful star. As one union leader remarked after a visit to the inner sanctum of a corporate officer's suite: "There ain't nobody hurting too much up there."

Part Three

Managing
Poor Performers:
Problem Employees
and Deadwood

Misfits are mismatched. One group's misfit may be
another group's star performer.   —*Philip Marvin*

9

Identifying
and Removing
Causes
of Poor Performance

> It is better to fail in exquisite things than to succeed
> in the contemptible.   —*Arthur Machen*

No matter how much we might wish the contrary, not all employees are stars or even workhorses. The less satisfactory elements in the human resources portfolio—problem employees and deadwood—also exist in every company. Handling these people requires different management skills than does bringing out the best in employees who are already doing well.

Deadwood and problem employees differ in their potential, but they have an important characteristic in common: poor job performance. Poor performance, of course, can mean different things to different managers. However, certain behaviors appear likely to get an employee into trouble in almost any company.

What are those behaviors? In other words, how does today's business community define poor performance?

Why People Get Fired: The Anatomy of Poor Performance

There have been numerous books and articles on the anatomy of poor performance and the reasons for it. Some have centered on the personal qualities of the individual employee, while others focused on the policies of management. A few years ago I undertook a more empirical approach by surveying personnel managers of about a hundred firms of various sizes. Instead of requesting general opinions, I asked for facts: "What were your exact reasons for separating each person in a managerial or supervisory position who was fired by your firm in the past three years?"

Their responses were most enlightening. I summarized them in an article called "How to Avoid Being Fired" (Odiorne, 1980a). Even when the behaviors described did not result in firing, they were likely to result in demotion, layoffs, or other disciplinary action.

An important general principle emerged from this study: Personal behavior, habits, skills, and motivation were at least as important as actual poor job performance in determining who would be fired. This was especially true of managers in the workhorse, problem employee, and deadwood categories. Stars were most often fired because they didn't achieve sufficient output or results. The others were more apt to be fired because they didn't *behave* in an appropriate fashion. Sometimes this misbehavior was related to improper emotions or attitudes. Sometimes it involved breaking safety or other rules or not following proper procedures so that spoiled work resulted.

Fourteen Reasons Why People Were Fired. When the personnel managers went over their records, they came up with the following list of the most common reasons why people were separated. Those separated ranked from foreman or supervisor through vice-president. The reasons for firing didn't seem to vary much according to rank; a vice-president was apt to get sacked for much the same reasons as a foreman.

• *Couldn't control emotions.* People who blew their tops, pouted, or became despondent at the wrong time were among the leading candidates for separation. They raged, insulted, sulked, or had one tantrum too many on the job, and their outbursts cost the company time or money. Getting emotions under control on the job and being cool under duress seem to be wise ideas.

- *Behaved immaturely.* Some people acted like kids. They were destructive of other people's interests or property or were excessively pleasure-minded, and their job performance was affected by their behavior. Immature people didn't try to see the consequences of their actions, were overly dependent on others, failed to keep promises, and were selfish. Some abused alcohol or other substances.

- *Lacked a sense of urgency.* A third category of loser was the person who simply didn't treat important things as if they were worth doing. Such people promised to get a job done but then forgot it, ignored it, or were extremely late. They let important problems go on and on, while they treated small problems or trivial items as if they were important. These people couldn't keep their priorities sorted out.

- *Was stopped by trivial obstacles.* "The accounting department never sent me the forms that week," or some similar alibi was often given by people who failed. They became experts at finding reasons why a job couldn't get done on time and within budget. If they were in sales, for example, they might say, "The product is inferior" or "the presentation you gave us doesn't work" to explain why people weren't buying.

- *Couldn't respond to change quickly enough.* People in this category didn't catch on to the fact that times had changed. They resisted company requests to attend to new rules related to affirmative action, EEO, OSHA, and the like. Clearly they wished the new rules or laws would go away, but since that didn't happen, the employees decided to act as if the annoyances didn't exist. They got the boss and the company into trouble with minorities, unions, government, or the community. In one refinery, for example, the manager simply couldn't resist turning off the pollution control equipment, especially during the night shift when he thought nobody would notice. He produced a giant fine for the company. His justification was "Yeah, but we beat the day shift in production!"

- *Hung on to obsolete ideas.* Although this defect is more likely to be found in longtime employees, it caught some young managers, too. They apparently didn't see the necessity of keeping in line with changes introduced by engineering, personnel, purchasing, scheduling or some other staff department. They hung on to the old ways until finally they built up enough critics in staff positions to get them severed from the payroll. In one plant a new union came along but a couple of old-time supervisors acted as if things were the same as before. Even though the company had signed the contract, the two oldtimers wouldn't stick to its clauses, so finally they had to be fired. Even on the way out the door they were muttering about the evils of the changes.

- *Hung on to obsolete ways of doing things.* In one large firm the chief accountant insisted on hanging on to some procedures and forms that had been rendered obsolete by a computerized management information system. He flatly refused to place any reliance on the newfangled methods, and ultimately he had to be separated. Because of his long service he was offered a lower-level job, but he refused and took early retirement instead. He didn't think computers were really serious business.

- *Persistently tore up employer-employee relations.* Some companies reported that they had people who were simply too hard-nosed, even for a company that prided itself on being firm. People were treated unfairly, or the boss used his position to reward his friends and punish his enemies—for example, favoring certain lodge members over nonmembers. This ultimately led to such a boss's dismissal.

- *Didn't know when to stick with policy.* The good supervisor knows when to enforce company rules rigidly and when to temporarily break or bend them in order to prevent serious losses or make a considerable gain. Managers who stick by the rules even when they make no sense in a specific situation ultimately damage the organization. One supervisor was a stickler on overtime rules, and when a longtime employee wanted to get out of working Saturday because her daughter was being married, he insisted that she work overtime that day anyway. When the employee refused, she was reprimanded and a note was put in her personnel file. Because this was one of a series of bureaucratic actions without sense, upon appeal it led to the supervisor's removal. An opposite but related problem can occur when people use the rules to their advantage and the boss lets them get away with it.

- *Couldn't delegate.* Bosses who usurp all the jobs in the department are apt to be in trouble when performance appraisal time comes. Some people insist on looking over everyone's shoulder, giving employees no room to work, harassing them, and asking constantly for explanations of what is going on. Explaining the objectives of the job clearly to begin with and then leaving people alone, with only occasional checkups, is better than overly close supervision.

- *Couldn't communicate.* People who can't read, write, speak, listen, and run decent meetings are an endangered species in today's management. These skills can be studied, practiced, and developed in evening courses, correspondence courses, or company training programs, if necessary. They are part of a manager's basic competency, and if someone doesn't acquire them, his or her days are numbered.

- *Wasn't tough enough.* People who wither and fade when the pressure is on aren't likely to last. Either they haven't the will to face tough situations and recalcitrant people, or they can't take the pressures of extra hours, ambiguity, or conflicting opinions. They get despondent, go into a rage, or run away. They often don't show up when tough or gutsy decisions are needed. If they're missing at crucial times too often, they may find themselves on the outside looking in.

- *Lacked a sense of timing.* People who haven't learned that there is a time to speak up and a time to be quiet, a time to push and a time to hold back, or a hundred other kinds of timing decisions end up with a bad reputation. This can combine with other flaws to produce a termination when it becomes serious. A sense of timing grows from experience and practice. A good manager keeps eyes and ears open, senses the lie of the land, and moves quickly or slowly as needed for a particular action. The late labor leader John L. Lewis used to recite this little rhyme to his union leaders:

> "When you are an anvil,
> stand you very still.

> When you are a hammer,
>
> strike with all your will."

- *Didn't anticipate.* The good manager is a planner who thinks ahead many days, weeks, months, or years. Anticipation means seeing where threats, risks, and opportunities lie and how to avoid undesirable side effects of present behavior.

Four Problems that Did Not Cause Firings. When I read over the personnel managers' responses, I noted the absence of certain reasons for firing that might have been expected to appear. I questioned the same managers further, and they responded that nobody had been fired for any of the following reasons:

- *Lack of technical knowledge of the business.* Apparently this facet was well checked out during job interviews or selection processes. In the case of one quality control director of a very large plant, for example, the man's boss said, "Bill knew the technical aspects of the product, and he understood quality control and inspection methods very well. It was his lack of interpersonal skills that cost him his job."
- *Showing too much initiative.* Every personnel manager felt that people would assume responsibility, take charge, and initiate actions rather than wait for orders if they were worth their salt. Weak managers were the ones who didn't initiate any changes or improvements and didn't act promptly to solve problems when they developed.
- *Deficiencies in educational background.* It is true that college graduates seem to have a distinct advantage in the initial selection process, but once on the job, it is results that count. People were not fired because of too little education if their job performance was good. Falsifying educational records was a reason for discharge in most firms, however.
- *Personal dislikes unrelated to job performance.* People can't be fired at will. Laws in some states directly prohibit "at-will" firing and provide that discharge must be "for cause." The cause must be clearly defined, and the individual must be informed of the rule or standard to be fulfilled, allowed time to amend his or her ways, and given exact reasons for the discharge when

it finally occurs. If the person to be fired falls into a "protected" category such as black, Latino, American Indian, Asian, female, handicapped, gay, or over forty years old, the burden of proving that the firing was not discriminatory falls on the employer. An ample "paper trail" of documentation must accompany every firing or disciplinary action that involves a member of one of these groups.

How to Avoid or Remedy Poor Performance

The good manager can usually prevent poor performance of subordinates altogether or else remedy such performance problems long before they become a firing matter. The first step in preventing or curing performance problems is identifying each problem's cause or causes.

Preventing Manager-Caused Performance Problems. Although many managers have trouble realizing it, poor performance of subordinates is often at least as much the fault of the boss as it is of the workers who actually make the mistakes. The wise manager will take the following steps to keep performance problems from occurring among those under him or her.

Specify performance standards clearly in advance. Evidence shows that the average manager and subordinate are not in agreement on what is expected of the subordinate. Unless the two have met and systematically discussed those expectations in the form of objectives, standards, action required, and criteria for success, the subordinate may fail simply for lack of information. Many employees have been discharged for failing to do something that they didn't know they were supposed to do. My survey of personnel managers indicated that the reasons why someone might be fired generally were not adequately explained in the hiring interview, and the specific reasons for an employee's firing often weren't made known to the person until the exit interview.

The poor manager, having failed in a basic managerial task— defining objectives for subordinates—may focus on the subordinate's failure instead of his or her own and blame the victim. The wise manager, on the other hand, prevents the problem by making certain that subordinates know in advance what is expected, what help and resources are available, and what conditions will exist if the job is well or poorly done. The very fact of finding out exactly what is expected will usually improve the performance of subordinates (Latham and Yukl, 1975).

Remove obstacles to success. The good manager is supportive of subordinates, for a supportive manager is more likely to produce successful performance in those under his or her command. This supportiveness is more than a benign tolerance of whatever happens; it extends to the active removal of interfering forces that could stop the subordinate from succeeding. It includes provision of ample and suitable tools, equipment, and other resources needed for the work. It also includes elimination of contradictory instructions, distractions, and competing tasks that may overload the subordinate. The supportive manager asks himself or herself, "What could I do, do differently, or refrain from doing that would help my subordinates succeed?" In such a climate, if performance failure does occur, it is viewed as a failure for both parties.

Provide access to necessary training. Many engineers complain that they are thrown into projects and assignments without being given the training, education, or skill development needed to do the work properly. Robert Mager (1972) suggests that before work on a new project begins, the supervisor should ask the question, "Could this person do this job if his or her life depended on it?" If the answer is no, then provision of training is a necessary part of the supportive action required of the boss.

One firm was plagued with a government contracts division that consistently lost money. It responded with a repetitive hiring and firing of general managers. Many of the managers had been very successful in other divisions, but none had the special knowledge needed to direct and develop strategies for a government contract operation. When, almost by accident, an administrator experienced in government-business interaction was assigned to the job, the division turned around. This administrator was able to use his experience to train those under him.

Promotion to a higher position may also require additional training. John De Lorean served with considerable success in the Pontiac, Buick, and Chevrolet divisions of General Motors, but when thrust into a higher post he became out of his element and ultimately quit. "Sink-or-swim" promotions may work if the promoted individual has already been self-taught, in very adaptive and learns quickly, or has been systematically trained for the position. When the individual is not properly prepared, however, performance failure is likely.

Provide favorable consequences for doing right. The explanation for many performance failures lies in the kinds of consequences an individual experiences as a result of behaving right or behaving wrong in terms of job performance. If doing the right thing produces unfavorable consequences, then wrong behavior will ensue and performance failure is predictable.

The president of a small college was made to understand by the college's board of trustees that a major part of his responsibility was fund raising for the college. Yet every time he was absent from the campus, faculty groups complained about their "absentee president." As a result of these complaints, the board called the president in and politely informed him that he was expected to "run this college" and not be "gallivanting around the country." More or less confined to the campus, he unsurprisingly failed to produce large sums of money from foundations and philanthropists who were located hundreds of miles away. Since the consequences for doing the right thing were unfavorable, the unfortunate president failed and was charged with being "too small for the high rank" he held.

Provide feedback. One of the most traumatic shocks an unsuccessful performer can suffer is the discovery that, after proceeding on a day-to-day basis with the assumption that he or she was doing well, he or she has been regarded as doing poorly all along. People need to know two kinds of things about their performance. First, they need to know how well they are doing in their work while they are doing it. This means continuous feedback, not simply a year-end or even quarterly performance appraisal.

Secondly, at the end of a defined period, workers need a summary review of the whole period. All goals set for the period and the progress made toward each should be reviewed for the purpose of revising and setting new goals. This is the point at which performance records are filed. Such records should include full explanatory statements, not only of actual goals and results, but of any extenuating circumstances that could explain less than satisfactory performance.

Encourage self-control. The most perfect form of control over performance is self-control. When the requirements and expectations of the job have been clearly spelled out, with standards of performance, constraints, and definitions of success and failure set forth in advance, a responsible subordinate can become a self-punisher or self-rewarder. Every job should contain methods for measuring one's own performance so that one is not obliged to await the verdict of a remote judge after the fact. Peter Drucker's classic description of MBO was "Management-by-Objectives and self-control." While MBO in many organizations is quite clear in defining outputs expected at the end of a given period, it is often less clear in defining standards by which individuals may apply self-control. However, management information systems, at their best, provide timely, accurate, frequent, and specific knowledge of results to every member of an organization.

Remedying Personal Causes of Poor Performance. Sometimes a manager has done all he or she can to prevent poor performance, yet performance failure still occurs. In such cases the search for causes of poor performance naturally turns to the individual who has failed. If personal causes for failure can be identified, counselling and coaching may be of considerable help to the troubled individual. Whatever the cause of poor performance proves to be, it is the responsibility of the supervisor to supervise, to confront the problem without delay, and to apply discipline or correction as needed.

Some of the most common personal problems that can contribute to poor job performance are listed on the following pages and in Table 3. Some ways to remedy each problem or mitigate its effects on performance are also suggested. These methods have been used successfully by many businesses.

Health problems. The state of an employee's physical health can have an important impact on his or her job performance. As the Age Discrimination in Employment Act lengthens people's work life, more health problems among employees can be anticipated because more employees will be older. This problem, which Mark Lipton (1979) describes as the "unmentionable personnel problem,"

Table 3. Sources of and Responses to Poor Job Performance Caused by Personal Problems.

Source of Poor Performance	Possible Company Response
1. Health problems	1. Medical exams Fitness programs New assignments
2. Stress and emotional problems	2. Counselling Stress training Referral to professionals
3. Off-the-job problems	3. Employee assistance programs Financial counselling Family counselling
4. Work habits	4. Supervision Direction Counselling Progressive discipline Coaching

grows out of the simple facts shown in actuarial statistics. If employees are permitted to work through age seventy, a larger number will become infirm or even die while still on the payroll. Cancer, heart disease, and similar maladies wreak their effects most heavily upon people in their later years. A new definition of handicapped employee may therefore emerge during the nineties as the work force ages, and laws to protect the handicapped will in all likelihood be broadened to cover older people.

Mandatory annual medical exams for all employees, especially managers, will almost surely become part of the human resources management practices of the future. Preventive medicine will also be important. A majority of large corporations already have programs to improve cardiovascular fitness in employees (Pyle, 1979). Obesity and other physical conditions that may adversely affect work performance will be of increasing concern to the managers of a company's human resources portfolio.

Stress and emotional problems. Studies of high-potential people reveal that many of them are so-called Type A personalities; that is, they are compulsive workers, engaged in nonstop activity even to the point where it produces unfavorable effects on their emotional and physical health. The supervisor of problem employees with high potential whose performance has declined should look for Type A behavior and seek professional advice in dealing with subordinates who show this pattern.

Stress often produces undesired behavior in employees. Stressed employees may appear fatigued, overworked, or compulsive in their actions. They may also begin to abuse alcohol or other substances. Stress management courses and groups under company sponsorship are now common, and referral of problem employees to such courses or groups is often useful. Alcoholism is legally considered a disease in some states, and company medical plans are required to provide treatment for the alcoholic employee.

Off-the-job problems. Many problem employees and even some deadwood in a company's human portfolio may be overwhelmed by off-the-job problems. Employee Assistance Programs (EAP), a relatively new development in human resources, place such people under the guidance of a director of assistance programs. The programs deal with such things as personal financial mismanagement, family or marital problems, the effects of alcohol and drug abuse, and stress and other emotional problems.

Work habits. Some poor performance is attributable mainly to the ways that employees go about doing their jobs. They may disdain company procedures, use company equipment for personal gain, or fail in part of their job due to carelessness or inefficiency. The responsibility for providing coaching and counselling to improve such people's work habits lies with their supervisor. Full collaboration of the employee, including agreement about the size of the problem and mutual examination of remedial options, is required for this process.

In addition to managerial and personal causes, poor job performance can be caused by obsolescence of skills. This problem will be discussed in Chapters Eleven and Twelve.

Two Policies for Handling Poor Performance

Douglas McGregor's book, *The Human Side of Enterprise,* is one of those most widely quoted by managers. Published in 1961, it is still regarded as a guidepost for determining what is right and wrong in supervisory and management styles. McGregor did not cite esoteric research studies or present any statistical analysis of managerial behavior. He simply divided all managers into two groups according to their beliefs about people.

There are, McGregor proposed, two kinds of managers: Theory X managers and Theory Y managers. *Theory X* managers believe that people dislike work and avoid it when they can. They thus feel that workers must be dominated, intimidated, coerced, or controlled in order to get them to do their jobs. *Theory Y* managers, on the other hand, believe that most people find work as natural and pleasant as rest or play. Therefore, they say, workers can be relied on to exercise self-control and to be productive and creative if they are given reasons to do so.

While purists in the design of experimental research might raise an eyebrow at these rough classifications, they nonetheless state the most extreme policies that are possible for managers to make. Clearly, the Theory Y manager is the one who is classified with the Good Guys in modern management. Endless research reports strive to demonstrate that favorable assumptions about people will become self-fulfilling prophecies, just as more dour attitudes toward people will produce poor performers.

In handling the various elements of the human resources portfolio, managers must make a crucial decision that is bound to reflect their beliefs about people: what to do about employees who fail to perform. Should such people be fired if they have failed, given an ultimatum to shape up, or treated in some more humanistic way?

You may recall from Chapter Three that two groups of people occupy undesirable classifications in the human resources portfolio. *Deadwood* is the category for people who have little potential and whose job performance is also unsatisfactory. Without either present contributions or hope of future improvement to justify their existence, they are likely to be targeted for removal. *Problem employees* are people who have been shown by a clear and systematic assessment to have a high achievement potential but whose present job performance is unsatisfactory. If their difficulties cannot be remedied within a reasonable time, they, too, should be removed from the organization or at least from their present positions.

Theory X or Theory Y? McGregor's distinction between Theory X and Theory Y managers becomes most useful when a general policy for the management of ineffective performance is being set up. Such policies will inevitably fall into either the Theory X or the Theory Y category. One could say that, just as there are Theory X and Theory Y managers, there are also Theory X and Theory Y companies.

Many firms today have deliberately adopted a Theory X attitude in their policies for dealing with failure. The business press, represented by journals such as *Fortune, Forbes,* and *Business Week,* seems to have a penchant for giving national publicity to "tough guys" at the top of organizations. A few years ago *Fortune* published an admiring list of the "ten toughest managers" and made it clear that in these presidents' organizations short shrift was given to subordinates who failed to get the job done. Other firms have a more benign and generous policy toward people who fail. To date there have been few rigorous studies that compare the business effectiveness of the two policies at a corporate level, although there have been numerous studies comparing their effects at the lower supervisory level.

Table 4 shows the general assumptions and effects of these two company policies in relation to the two categories of performance failure defined in our portfolio system. The situations can be described this way:

- If you fall into the deadwood category and work in a hard-nosed or Theory X company, you will probably be fired. This may be done with due observations of amenities such as outplacement, references, and solid preparation of a case before the firing, but still, being found to be deadwood almost surely means an end to your career in that firm. At the very least it will mean demotion or placement in some isolated shelf-sitting position.
- If you are deadwood in a Theory Y company, a considerable amount of time, money, and other resources will probably be devoted to your rehabilitation or the alleviation of your situation. Your employer will start with the assumption that your failure is most likely situational rather than personal and that changing

Table 4. Assumptions and Actions of Two Policies for Management of Performance Failure.

Policy	*Performance Failure Category*	
	Deadwood (people rated as having low performance and no potential for further growth)	*Problem Employees (people whose performance is low but whose potential is considered high)*
Theory X	1. Performance failure is the fault of the employee. 2. Discharge is preferable, if done with due regard to laws and amenities. 3. If discharge is not feasible, the person should be demoted or shelved in Siberia.	1. Ultimatums, time deadlines, and standards should be set. 2. If ultimatums are not met, the person, who is probably lazy or dishonest, should be discharged.
Theory Y	1. Performance failure is largely due to the situation, not the individual. 2. Individual failure calls for remedial, therapeutic, or corrective actions. 3. Discharge or demotion is a last resort.	1. High potential should never be wasted. 2. The environment, boss, or other circumstances should be changed to permit natural potential to emerge. 3. Firing is evidence of management failure, not worker failure.

environmental or situational factors, training, coaching, counselling, or therapy will bring you up to snuff. Firing will be done only as a last resort and with exquisite attention to the amenities of a decent departure.

- If you are a problem employee in a Theory X company, you may be fired quickly—even abruptly. If you are not fired, you will be given an ultimatum that describes a date by which self-correction must occur and a general statement that performance failure must not be repeated. Don't expect situational analysis, training, therapy, or counselling. If you don't meet the ultimatum within the time limit, you will be separated, with varying degrees of amenity.
- If you are a problem employee in a Theory Y company, considerable remedial effort is likely to be spent on you. Again,

your trouble will be presumed to be situational until facts prove otherwise. Changes in assignment, unreasonable performance expectations, task inteference, inadequacy of prior job training, and lack of knowledge of results will all be investigated as possible causes. If physical, mental, or emotional limitations prove to be at the root of your problem, they will be attacked through counselling, therapy, and endless advice. The company realizes that firing high-potential people is expensive in terms of lost future contributions, and such firing is done only as a last resort. If it does occur, it will be a gentle process of easing out.

The effects of choosing a Theory X or a Theory Y company policy will show in many areas, including rules for discipline, coaching and development, pay, and leadership. A Theory X policy can be called a punitive policy, while a Theory Y policy can be described as a developmental policy. If the top management of a firm holds that punitive policy is best, they will be hostile, exacting, judgmental, and harsh in the face of poor performance. If, on the other hand, they believe that developmental policy is best, they will respond in ways that are analytic, developmental, therapeutic, situational, and caring. This is not to say that punitive policies are always bad; some situations, and some kinds of people, require them. But modern trends point in a developmental direction, and most rules for personnel management today are based on this more positive approach.

10

How to Discipline
Employees Effectively:
New and Traditional
Approaches

We are in bondage to the law in order that we may
be free.   —*Cicero*

In all business organizations there are kinds of behavior that cannot
be permitted because they keep the organization from going toward
its objectives or interfere with the work or personal rights of its
members. If such behavior occurs, some kind of disciplinary action
must be taken. But what kind should it be, and how should it
be applied?

Assumptions Behind Traditional and Developmental Discipline

Two major approaches to discipline can be found in the
business world and in society at large. The *traditional* approach
focuses on punishment for offending behaviors. This approach is
most likely to be taken by companies or managers who follow the
Theory X policy concerning poor performance that was described
in Chapter Nine. The *developmental* approach, on the other hand,

regards discipline as a shaper of behavior. It is the more common approach in business today and is the kind normally found in companies with a Theory Y policy.

Traditional Discipline. The old-fashioned approach to discipline was that of the Old Testament dictum, "An eye for an eye and a tooth for a tooth." The purpose of such discipline was to exact punishment for sins, maintain conformity to customs, and sustain the authority of the old over the young. Traditional rules for retributive justice were based on what was seen as almost a natural law: Certain actions were forbidden to certain classes of persons, and when an offense occurred and was proven, the guilty party was quite properly subjected to the punishment that had been designated for that crime. In some countries in the Middle East, theft is punishable by amputation of a hand; in the American west theft of a horse was punishable by hanging; and so on. Aboard the old British navy sailing ships the punishment was generally the lash, with a specified number of strokes for each kind of offense. More serious crimes, including murder, mutiny, and combat cowardice, merited hanging.

While it is conceivable that this kind of system originally had some behavior change objectives, over time such precisely prescribed punishments acquired a character quite apart from their effects on behavior. They came to be regarded as an almost divinely inspired system of cause and effect, as if the crime itself produced the punishment.

In those few companies that still use this traditional approach to discipline, there seems to be little difference between the pattern of their rules and regulations and those applied to the work force of the pharaohs. The rules were different in ancient Egypt, and the punishments were certainly more severe, but the basic design of the disciplinary system was similar: List the crimes, note the punishments for each, promulgate the rules, and apply the punishments as needed. This old-fashioned approach to discipline is based on several basic assumptions that can be listed as follows:

- Discipline is applied by superiors to subordinates—never the reverse.
- The past is the proper arbiter of present and future action.

- Discipline is punishment for forbidden actions, and the severity of the punishment should be as nearly proportional as possible to the severity of the offense.
- The purpose of punishment is deterrence of those who have not sinned by the example of the suffering of those who have sinned and have been caught and punished.
- Punishment for sins against "principles" should be more severe than punishment for other undesirable acts.
- If the prevalence of a wrong behavior increases in a group, it may be necessary to increase the severity of punishment for the next wrongdoer in order to set an especially impressive example for the others.
- When no single individual can be made to admit responsibility for a violation, the entire group should be punished. This will both strike the guilty individual's conscience and motivate the group to turn in the violator or punish the person themselves.
- Absolute consistency in punishment should be maintained at all times. If this is not done, the disciplined group will protest that injustice is being done and will seek ways of circumventing the disciplinary system.
- The severity of punishment for a second offense should always be much greater than for the first offense, even if the two offenses are identical.
- Announcement and administration of punishment should be given maximum exposure in order to maximize the deterrent effect.

Developmental Discipline. New concepts of industrial discipline emerged during the sixties and seventies. Starting with unionized workers, who established grievance and arbitration procedures to judge the fairness of disciplinary actions, changes in the "rules of the road" for discipline systems have occurred for all levels of employees.

Discipline systems have been forced to meet a number of new requirements. Modern values have tended to turn away from physical punishment. The decline of capital punishment in many states and foreign nations is matched by declining levels of physical punishment for lesser offenses. There is greater protection of the rights of the accused than ever before. The belief that it is better to allow many guilty persons to escape than to punish one innocent person prevails in American society at large, in our courts and police system, and in industrial and business discipline as well.

There has also been a movement away from arbitrary individual judgments and toward group judgments of guilt or innocence. The rights to trial by a jury of one's peers, to counsel, to confront accusers, to cross-examine witnesses, and to see evidence used in systematic fashion are guaranteed in most circumstances. The right to protest unilateral judgments in business disciplinary cases is also increasingly enforced. Even where no labor union exists, some kind of arbitration system with grievance procedures and the right to appeal decisions is found in most businesses. This is true even at management levels.

Modern discipline is viewed not as punishment but as a shaper of behavior. It requires that rules be reviewed periodically against objectives to see if they are still productive, and it allows the exceptional performer who is achieving exceptional results to be treated with exceptional tolerance. It differs from traditional discipline in a number of other respects as well. This more modern and humanistic view of discipline is often called developmental discipline. It may also be called "discipline by objectives."

Developmental discipline, like traditional discipline, theoretically can be applied to any group. Discipline in the workplace, however, has some special features that are not characteristic of discipline elsewhere. These differences center around the particular objectives and purposes of the business firm. The assumptions underlying developmental discipline or discipline by objectives in the work environment can be listed as follows:

- *Discipline at work is for the most part voluntarily accepted; if not voluntarily accepted, it is not legitimate.* The ferocious standards of discipline to which the recruit aboard a whaler out of New Bedford in the early 1800s was subjected could be considered to be voluntarily accepted if the seaman signed the articles and was fully aware of what they entailed. However, if he was shanghaied aboard, beguiled by lies from a recruiter, or forced into accepting the job because he was starving ashore, he could hardly be called a volunteer. In such a case, discipline was simply a harsh penalty for trying to escape a trap into which the victim had unwittingly stepped.

Today's company discipline, however, must be explained and voluntarily accepted by the employee at the time of hiring. Even those who accept may later change their minds or regret their bargain, to be sure. The young accountant who is warned during the hiring interview that his new position will entail extensive travel and long hours at certain times of year may not fully realize the impact this will have on his family life, for example. But after his employer has spent time and money to train him, he cannot expect to break his bargain without incurring some kind of penalty.

- *Discipline is not a punishment system but a shaper of behavior.* Like the operant conditioning of B. F. Skinner, disciplinary action in a modern corporation should serve to provide favorable consequences for the right behavior and unfavorable consequences for the wrong kind of behavior. This means that all the elements in the system that can be conveniently arranged to produce the desired behavior will be employed, not merely the traditional system of accused, prosecutor, judge, crime, and punishment.

On a military base it was noted that young soldiers were slipping over the fence after hours in violation of regulations. Some officers proposed court martials with stiff sentences for violators. Others proposed issuing live ammunition to sentries. The wise commanding officer, however, discovered that most of the offenders were visiting local bars. He ordered that beer be sold in the PX throughout the entire evening. The rate of fence jumping dropped considerably.

The point here is that the commanding officer found the causes of the undesirable behavior and arranged the situation so that it didn't need to occur. Nobody was punished, for that was not the objective. The objective was to keep the soldiers in camp. The officer avoided upholding "principles" and concentrated on behavior and results instead.

- *The past provides useful experience in finding ways to change behavior, but it is not an infallible guide to right and wrong.*

The fact that something has been done consistently in the past is no assurance that it is the best behavior for the present. The greatest use of precedents is in positions where danger, high cost, or excessive losses could result from failure to use the right principle the first time. The boss who suggests, "Do it my way the first time; then, after thinking about it, introduce improvements if you can" is pointing out the importance of experience and encouraging innovation at the same time. He or she is using experience as a base upon which improvements can be built.

- *Contribution to objectives should determine when to depart from rules and regulations.* When a subordinate is aware of his or her own objectives and those of the unit, knowing when to vary rules and regulations becomes a part of his or her professional or occupational skill. The engineer who knows when to depart from rules and when not to is a better engineer than the one who adheres slavishly to every rule simply because it is a rule. When the breaking of a rule is counterproductive and carries an employee or organization away from desired objectives, it should be the subject of unfavorable attention from the employee's superior; but so should the behavior of an employee who adheres so strictly to regulations that the organization is served poorly and its movement toward its objectives is impeded or halted.

  Some organizations are activity-centered or input-centered rather than output-centered. Such organizations use rigid rule systems to prevent nonconforming use of inputs and to keep all activities under control. The control of expense accounts is a common application of an input-centered system of discipline. In such a system, the manager who makes a trip to New York City, where meals and lodging are expensive, will be bound by exactly the same expense account regulations as one going to Dodge City, Kansas, where costs are much lower. No attention will be paid to the fact that the potential gain that is the objective of the New York City trip may be far greater than the potential gain for the trip to Dodge City.

  The traditional office manager might say, "But we simply can't have people setting their own expense rates! We would be sure to be victimized by excessive expenditures." A more modern view might be, "We expect everyone to set and achieve his or her own objectives and to use appropriate means to do so. This is the way to produce innovations that can carry us to new heights of organizational achievement."

Similarly, shortcutting or rule breaking to reach a goal can be constructive for one person and destructive for another. The determination of whether the breaking of a rule requires disciplinary action depends both on the result of the particular action and on the general performance of the rule breaker. It is reported that Alfred P. Sloan, for twenty-eight years chief executive officer of General Motors, in response to complaints that individuals had varied from customary practices or rules on the job, simply asked, "Did he get the job done?" Similarly, Abraham Lincoln, when told that General Ulysses S. Grant drank whiskey regularly in large amounts, is reported to have replied, "Tell me what kind he drinks; I should like to buy a case for my other generals. I can't spare this man. He fights!"

The point is clear. The star performer who is achieving exceptional results should be treated with greater tolerance than the average employee when it comes to violation of rules and regulations. Workhorses, however, should adhere to the rules unless there is a very good reason not to.

- *Rules and regulations should be reviewed periodically to see if they are still productive in achieving current organization objectives.* Rules that apparently have no reason for existence can be a continuing source of discontent, especially among young employees. Such rules, made for purposes long forgotten, continue to be enforced without regard for the fact that their objectives are no longer relevant.

In organizations where the system of management by objectives is used, sound disciplinary policy requires that the personnel department initiate and maintain a review of all rules of conduct to prevent counterproductive behavior from being forced on employees. Such a review should state two things with regard to each rule: the rule as it now exists and the contribution it makes to the organization's objectives. If the rule makes a contribution, or prevents something from happening that could diminish contribution, it stays. If it doesn't do one of these things, it should go.

The following are examples of legitimate contributions that a rule might make:

Avoids sexual harassment charges

Prevents line shutdown

Prevents customer complaints about quality

Enhances safety of fellow workers

Enhances safety of the employee

Improves yield of line

Prevents tool breakage

Prevents overexpenditure for small tools

Prevents computer ripoffs

By contrast, rules for which only the following responses can be found should be eliminated unless further study shows that they make a real contribution to objectives:

It's generally a good thing.

We've always done it that way.

It's our policy.

That rule was made on the basis of many, many years of experience.

The boss (now retired) installed that one.

Because I want it that way, dammit!

Some rules may be absolutely necessary in one location or department but less important or even irrelevant in another. Smoking certainly cannot be allowed in a plant where volatile liquids are used, for example, but it might be allowed in the office.

Creative development and selective application of rules is evidence of good management. There is no inherent virtue to consistency. However, consistency of application among all employees covered by the same rule is necessary to avoid charges of injustice and disputes between employees. A manager might, for example, suspend attendance rules for engineers—but it should be done for all engineers. The manager shouldn't single out Jim and make a new rule for him alone, unless perhaps he is the company's resident genius.

Applying Developmental Discipline

To make discipline into a process of teaching and behavior change, some conditions must be met.

- Rules and regulations should be made known to all employees.
- When an apparent violation has occurred, disciplinary action should occur as close to the time of the violation as possible. Holding off discussions of behavioral lapses until the "annual performance review" or some similar future time will lessen the behavior change effect.
- The accused person should be presented with facts and the source of those facts: For example, "Mr. Smith of the Eliot Store called this morning and stated that you have not taken inventory in his store for two months."
- If a specific rule is broken, the rule should be stated. In the preceding case, for example, the supervisor might say, "As you know, our rules call for an on-site inventory every two weeks and turning in of a signed report certifying the inventory."
- The reason for the rule should be given. For example, "There are three good reasons for this rule. First, the company could lose money without an accurate inventory because it puts goods in stores on consignment, and the store could go out of business and leave us with a big bad debt. Second, store managers like to have accurate billings that are based on inventory, not on estimates. Third, we need accurate inventories in order to schedule our production for the month ahead."
- The apparent offender should be asked if he or she agrees with the facts as stated. If the answer is yes, the employee should be asked what his or her objective was in carrying out the undesirable behavior. Unlike asking for an "excuse" or "alibi," which places the offender on the defensive and can quickly lead to a fight, asking the person's objectives opens the door to future improvement.
- Corrective action should be discussed in positive and forward-looking terms: "How might you meet your objective of covering more stores in the territory and at the same time meet my three objectives for getting inventory taken?"

Figure 11. The Steps in Progressive Discipline.

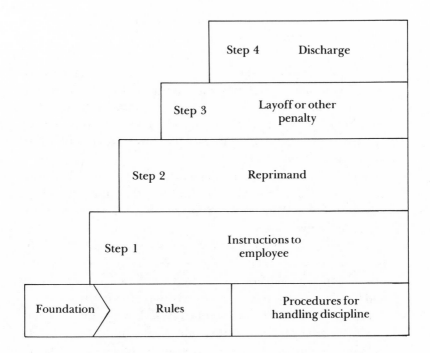

Using Progressive Discipline. For certain kinds of offenses, such as criminal violence, major thefts, serious and deliberate damage to company property and the like, the first offense is the last, since it is a cause for immediate discharge. In the case of lesser offenses, however, progressive discipline should apply.

As shown in Figure 11, progressive discipline means that an offending employee is subjected to several stages of correction. Each stage moves closer to separation but is also designed to effect a behavior change. Progressive discipline systems are used in many firms, including General Motors, Ford, and Chrysler. They have proven successful in correcting undesired behavior and are also regarded as fair to employees.

The steps in a progressive discipline system generally include the following:

Step 1: First offense. Instruct the employee in the desired method of performance, explain the rule and its reasons, and describe the measures that will be taken if there is a recurrence of the offense. Note the incident in the employee's personnel file.

Step 2: Second offense. This could be a repeat of the first, or it could be a different offense of a similar magnitude. If the second offense is a repeat of the first, summarize the instructions and the reasons for them, remind the individual that this is a second offense, and state that this is a reprimand and that the next step will be a temporary layoff without pay. If the second offense is of a similar magnitude but different in detail from the first one, instruct the employee in the proper method and warn of the discipline that will follow a third offense. In either case, write an account of the incident in the personnel record.

Step 3: Third offense. Consult with your superior and the personnel department at this stage, since the issue might become grounds for arbitration. Once you have verified that the need for disciplinary action is clear, instruct the individual and direct a layoff of two to five days without pay, with the warning that a repeat of any similar offense will be cause for discharge. Write the incident in the personnel record.

Step 4: Fourth offense. After getting approval from your superior and the personnel department, tell the offender that he or she is discharged. Write this fact in the personnel record, along with recommendations for rehiring or not rehiring.

Throughout the discipline process you should bear in mind that each move may be subsequently subjected to the close scrutiny of an arbitrator, a review board, a top manager, or a civil court of law. However, progressive discipline has been used successfully by both government and unionized employers, and discharges made under it have been upheld.

Rules for Disciplinary Procedures. Certain "umbrella rules" apply to all stages of the progressive discipline process. Failure to follow any of them could result in the disciplinary action being reversed.

- Be certain that the rule you are enforcing exists, is clear, and is known to employees.
- Have a statute of limitations rule for keeping a record of disciplinary incidents. If a person breaks a rule and this is entered

in the personnel record, remove the account from the file and clear his or her slate if six months of good performance pass without further incidents. Do not carry minor incidents over from year to year. Layoff reports might be kept for two to three years, however.

- Avoid behavior that creates further incidents. Using profanity or personal degradation in disciplinary proceedings (even when it is the ordinary language of the shop) or physically touching the person invites anger, physical responses, and possible sex harassment charges.
- Don't apply the disciplinary procedure inconsistently or make punishments for the same stage different for different individuals unless the facts of a case strongly warrant special treatment.
- Listen carefully to what the accused person says at all times. Note the substance of these remarks in the record.
- Be certain of your facts before making your decision. Wrong perceptions, garbled information, and errors in fact can easily occur. Dig as deeply as necessary to get all relevant facts before taking action.
- Don't skip stages for less than discharge offenses because of emotional pressures. This is the most likely cause of reversal by an arbitrator or a judge, who will reduce the penalty to the level appropriate for the offense. To discharge for spoiling work twice would probably result in the employee being reinstated with full pay, since ordinary practice would call for only a reprimand for a second offense.
- When an employee who has been laid off for disciplinary reasons returns to work, don't continue the punishment. Treat him or her like any employee; don't spend unusual amounts of time checking up. Be businesslike, neither clubby nor aloof.
- Avoid entrapment. Setting snares to encourage employees to violate rules so that you will have an excuse to administer discipline is bad business. It breeds inequity and injustice in the whole system.

The manager who follows these common-sense rules for disciplinary procedures should seldom have his or her decisions successfully challenged. More important, if the rules are used in conjunction with a fair, consistent system of developmental discipline, changes from undesirable to desirable behavior should be maximized.

11

―――――――――――――⚓―――――――――――――

Why High Performers
Become Low Performers:
The Nature
of Employee
Obsolescence

To you O Goddess of efficiency
Your Happy Vassals bend the reverent knee.
                                    —Samuel Hoffenstein

Once identified as a star, the high-potential person often receives a number of insurance policies against future failure. Access to the best managers and top decision makers is smoothed. Assignments are chosen to afford opportunities for growth in personal competence and provide developmental experiences. Such people are not allowed to remain in a single position very long; career-switching procedures assure that they will avoid routine jobs that stay the same for years on end.

Most other employees are not so fortunate. In large corporations where human resources are not treated as assets, the possibility of being locked into a specific function or specialty is high. If the company does not have a policy of posting jobs across divisions or using company-wide searches for higher-level jobs, the person who starts in the claims department of a large insurance firm, for example, may end his or her career there. Perhaps he or she will be higher up the ladder inside the claims group, but the chance of becoming recognized as a corporate star or moving to underwriting, actuarial, or agency departments is minuscule.

This sort of inequity, which dooms many people to labor at levels that don't exploit their full potential, tends to create a self-fulfilling prophecy. The individual who is marked as a "comer" will almost surely come along. The person labelled early on as a workhorse will just as certainly not. Worse still, this situation means that the workhorse's chances of becoming deadwood some time during a life of work are quite high. The immobility of permanent assignments creates the risk of obsolescence, which in turn often results in demotion, assignment to work that is even more wasteful of talent, or, finally, early retirement or a graceful discharge. The manager who implements these final solutions was seldom around at the beginning of the workhorse's career, when the situation might have been averted: old Joe, once a respected contributor but now worthless to the firm, took a long time to arrive at that sad position.

Obsolescence can take many forms. The gist of the problem lies in the ability—or lack of ability—of people and organizations to manage change. What Eric Hoffer (1951) called "the ordeal of change" often makes misfits of those who cannot keep up with it. Such people may even become passionate about their refusal to change, engaging in acts that harm their organizations and getting themselves classified as problem employees. This tendency for even reliable and potentially talented people to become obsolescent is a glaring illustration of the fact that most people work at far less than their full potential. This wasted potential is a loss not only to the individual but to the organization that employs him or her and to society as a whole.

Changes that Produce Employee Obsolescence

Three kinds of change can cause an employee to become obsolescent in the eyes of an employing firm. *Technological change* occurs constantly and irreversibly. It is often accompanied by *social and cultural change.* Sometimes a negative *individual change* occurs. The sum of these forces of change produces changes in economic worth, so that the human asset that was previously undervalued becomes overvalued, its potential is eroded, and its contribution is diminished until finally it must be removed in order to preserve the economic health of the organization.

The effects of these changes on different elements in the human resources portfolio are shown in Table 5. Let's look at each of these kinds of change and its effects in more detail.

Technological Change. Technology is usually defined as the application of science, especially application to meet a social or business need. Westrum and others (1977) state that two sources of technological change are invention and innovation. Invention is the combining of old knowledge in new and different ways. Innovation is the introduction of new knowledge or technology.

Historians of science conclude that invention is not a single act of genius but a steady chain of parallel instances. Often four or more individual inventors working independently, all drawing on preexisting knowledge, arrive at the same breakthrough at about the same time.

Innovation, which is another way of saying "the rate of introduction of invention," is likewise influenced by many factors, most of which are social. Inventions are not adopted by society until they are seen as socially beneficial. Where the institution of slavery flourished, for example, it was unnecessary to fully accept the invention of the steam engine. The demise of slavery, however, made the steam engine useful. Innovation may be resisted for a wide variety of reasons, including natural conservatism, vested interest in old ways, uncertainty about the effects of change, and provincialism. As Westrum puts it, "Innovation does not simply mean . . . changing from one technique to another. It means changing the social order."

Joseph Schumpeter (1937) stated that innovation is the basic source of profit because it provides an important advantage to the innovative firm during the time when the innovation gives the firm a leadership position. Most major firms recognize this and therefore spend a percentage of their revenues for research and development in products and markets, processes, and human resources.

Table 5. The Effects of Technology and Social Change on Human Resource Portfolios.

Type of Change	Examples of Change	Unfavorable Effects	Favorable Effects
Technological Change	• Automation • Computers • New inventions • New techniques	• Requires new technical skills • Requires new social skills • Makes some skills obsolete	• Once-obsolete skills become needed once again • Innovations bring stardom to inventors
Social and Cultural Change	• New employment laws • Changed work force • Conservative/liberal shifts • Change in size of ownership of firm	• Requires changes of attitude • Requires learning new rules	• Different interpersonal and technical skills may become in demand

Technological development, suggests Schmookler (1966), aims at producing either monopolies and unique market advantages or cost reduction. Both of these can give competitive advantages to the firm that successfully employs technology as a tool. Innovations in technology tend to make present products, markets, and processes obsolete. Unfortunately, they can also create human obsolescence among employees who do not grow and change along with their firm.

Technological change can turn workhorses into deadwood. Skills that stood them in good stead in performing their daily tasks cease to be useful when whole new repertoires of behavior are needed. For example, the accounting clerk whose desk calculator is replaced by a data processing system with giant computers probably will not be able to handle the problems of programming and operating the new technology without retraining. The machinist who is skilled in setting up a lathe or milling machine manually may be helpless when confronted by numerically controlled machine tools operated by a computer. The assembly line worker who is replaced by a robot or transfer machine is likely to be made totally useless unless he or she receives the extensive training needed to learn how to set up, adjust, or repair a robot.

Even stars can be reduced to problem employees or deadwood by technological change, despite a sound earlier education. As new principles of science and engineering are discovered, the engineering school graduate of twenty years ago is likely to find that today's graduate knows things he or she never learned. The accountant who learned thirty years ago about debits and credits, ledgers and spreadsheets may find that knowledge of little use in a modern firm that has computerized all of its financial reporting in a Management Information System (MIS).

Technological change can also cause obsolescence by requiring the learning of new social skills. For example, changes in technology sometimes call for changes in the site where the work is to be done. Rather than operating in a small office as an individual professional contributor, the star may have to adapt to being a member of a complex team or project group. This can call for skills in interpersonal cooperation that he or she may not possess.

In addition to these negative effects, technological change can produce favorable changes in the valuation of some individuals. Previous problem employees may become stars, as happened in the case of the maverick in a large firm who kept insisting that a certain new technology had great promise. He was scoffed at by the majority, but later events proved him to be right. In such cases, eccentricity may suddenly be seen as genius, and the fortunes of the newly discovered star will rise accordingly. Even people previously classified as deadwood may find that their obsolete skills have become sought after once more. As a result of the OPEC oil crisis, 40 percent of the homes in northern New England turned to wood fires and wood-burning stoves for home heating within seven years. Suddenly wood stove designers, stove repairers, wood choppers, and chimney sweeps—previously regarded as practitioners of almost lost arts— were very much in demand. Unfortunately, technological change is more likely to produce a fall than a rise in the value of most human assets.

Social and Cultural Change. Laws, values, and customs also change, both in specific organizations and in society at large. Like technological change, cultural and social change can produce obsolescence in those who cannot adapt to it.

Laws are the codified form of the will of society as expressed through the institution of government, specifically the legislatures and the courts. Laws change, sometimes slowly and at other times rapidly. In the past twenty years, there have been radical changes in laws concerning business activities and employment relations. For example, it is now illegal to discriminate against certain protected groups in hiring, pay, housing, or promotion. Further-more, these new laws, unlike some older anti-discrimination laws, are strictly enforced. Similarly, new laws against pollution of the environment are strictly enforced and thus have become important to the business community.

Managerial stars can be turned into problem employees by their unwillingness or inability to live with new and stricter laws. For example, police officers trained under an earlier code of conduct who refuse to read suspects their rights become problem employees and ultimately deadwood in their departments. Forest rangers who resist new environmental practices are likely to be in the same kind of trouble. Standards of job performance are partly shaped by outside influences and those who cannot keep up with these standards fail just as surely as those who fail the firm's own standards.

Moral standards also change and people who previously were stars may become problem employees or deadwood because they cannot or will not adapt to the new moral patterns required of them. Sheriffs and other law enforcement officials who use racial epithets in addressing prisoners have become embarrassing liabilities to their organizations, even though such verbal behavior was formerly considered acceptable in many places. The bribing of foreign governments by corporate leaders to obtain business formerly was not illegal, but when revelations of such bribery burst forth in the 1970s, it was considered morally offensive, and antibribery laws were soon passed. Similarly, antitrust laws have been fairly commonplace for over eighty years (Sufrin, 1983), but society's opinion of the morality of forming large combinations of firms has varied considerably.

Social changes within a firm, likewise, can turn stars into problem employees or deadwood. The tiny firm that exalted the skills of the entrepreneur often grows beyond the ability of its founder or founders to control. The demands of bureaucratic management, the increasingly complex structure of the firm, and the need for teamwork are often incompatible with the independent, freewheeling style of such people, and they may become misfits in their own companies. Mergers and acquisitions, too, often leave the heads of the acquired firms, who were top stars in their own companies, as obsolete as dinosaurs in the newly created organization.

As once-radical ideas become orthodoxy, the basis for evaluating performance can change sharply. The radical political liberal of the thirties is apt to seem quite tame today. In technology, the radical ideas of nuclear physics have become orthodoxy in the nuclear age. In 1954, when the Atomic Energy Act for the Peaceful Use of the Atom was passed, the nuclear engineer was regarded as a star. By 1980, however, antinuclear groups had gained such sway that nuclear engineers were seen as misfits or problem employees. Conversely, the antinuclear movement turned the activist, certainly regarded as a problem during the fifties, into the star of the current decade. The renewal of old customs may turn even deadwood into stars once more as their formerly denigrated skills become in great demand.

Individual Change. Sometimes faithful workhorses or even stars become less competent than they once were. As Saul Gellerman (1968, p. 146) puts it, "Competence is like the hair on the top of a man's head, in the sense that it is not necessarily there to stay." This loss of competence may be attributable to the work situation, lack of motivation, physical or emotional problems, or other causes. Gellerman cautions that we know very little about competence loss and that it can happen to workers of any age. He adds that, in his opinion, it is usually preventable.

The Activity Trap: A Special Kind of Obsolescence. Some people become economically obsolete, not because they do their work poorly, but because they do it too well. They are masters of skills and behaviors that they have used very effectively for a long time. When the objective of their job changes, they continue to behave exactly as before. Thorstein Veblen (1899) called this problem "occupational psychosis." I call it the Activity Trap. It ensnares professionals just as easily—perhaps more easily—than it does hourly workers who are accustomed to being ordered to do things differently, stop doing them, or do them at a different pace and in a different way.

Whole corporations, even the largest and most affluent, can be caught in this insidious trap. So can governments, schools, hospitals, churches, and even families. Unless they are alert to its dangers, the Activity Trap will ensnare even the wisest, most experienced old hands.

People or organizations caught in the Activity Trap start out for what was once an important and clear goal but then become so enmeshed in the activity of getting there that they forget where they are going—or why. Even business starts out to achieve some objective, usually an increasing profit. Resources are assembled from stockholders, loans, or savings and poured into the enterprise. Then everyone gets busy, engaging in activity designed to carry the organization toward its objectives. In time, the business's original goals evolve into different ones. The activity, however, often remains the same and becomes an end in itself—a false goal. This false goal becomes a criterion for making decisions, and the resulting decisions get progressively worse.

Each job or profession in a business has its own version of the Activity Trap. Quality control directors act as if the enterprise were created so they could shut it down and hold up everything produced yesterday. Accountants act as if the business were created so they could keep books on it. The sales manager acts as if there were no problems that couldn't be solved by more volume. Production managers get tonnage out the back gate by shipping junk or using wrong labels and faulty addresses, then ride the backs of the help to get more junk out tomorrow. Personnel managers behave as if hiring all those people, providing them with tools and equipment, and building a plant were done just so the personnel department could make them happy. Labor relations directors act as if the company were formed to give them an excuse to fight with union officers. Meanwhile, the stockholders and the president sit atop the mess, wondering where all the profit went.

The Activity Trap becomes a self-feeding mechanism if it isn't stopped. Everybody in the company becomes emotionally attached to some irrelevancy. Even the president finally loses sight of why he's in business and demands more and more activity rather than results. Layers of professionals help to keep the busywork multiplying. Large corporations have acres of lawyers, each outstripping the other in preventing anybody from producing anything. When profits decline, the president adds a battery of accountants. So what happens? Considerable accounting is produced, but costs go up. Engineers fight engineering problems by hiring more engineers, each with a technical opinion designed to prevent something from happening someplace else in the firm. Many professionals spend their entire working lives taking in each other's administrative laundry, creating jobs and hierarchies to generate more activity that is increasingly unrelated to the purpose of the company's existence. All this activity eats up resources, money, space, and human energy like a mammoth tapeworm.

The Activity Trap is not limited to business. In the same way, churches may become enmeshed with covered dish suppers and basketball leagues—activities generating little besides indigestion and flat feet. Families may get so entangled in the details of living that they forget what families were started for. There's the story of the perfect housewife whose kid got up at night to go to the bathroom; by the time he came back, she had made his bed.

One sign of the Activity Trap is disagreement between manager and subordinate concerning what the subordinate is expected to produce—though the two may agree reasonably well on the activities to be conducted. My research shows that the average boss and subordinate caught in the Activity Trap will fail to agree on 25 percent of the employee's responsibilities. They will disagree on about 50 percent of the subordinate's major problems. Worst of all, they will be in about 90 percent disagreement on how the subordinate's performance should be improved.

As a result of being obsessed with means rather than ends, nothing really changes in the way things are done. The environment changes, the customers' tastes change, the values of the employees change, but the methods remain static and the organization is made obsolescent by the outdated acts of its own employees.

The Activity Trap does more than cut profit. It makes employees *shrink*, both personally and professionally. They nod their heads when the boss chastises them, but they sense that they have been cheated. They are stabbed daily in duels they didn't know were under way. Trees fall on them, and then somebody yells "Timber!" Their only defense? Keep active.

Employees in this situation may be chastised or even fired for doing something wrong when they never knew what "right" was. They run a race without knowing how long the track is. They can't guess when to spring for the wire because they don't know whether they're running a 100-yard dash or the Boston Marathon.

The effects of the Activity Trap are cumulative. Because employees don't know the ordinary objectives of their jobs, they are punished for failures that grow out of not knowing what spells success. This produces a reluctance to look for problems, for the problems they discover may be attributed to their own shortcomings. Suggesting something new in such an environment is risky. Everyone concludes that it is better to stick with the old activity, and looking busy becomes safer than being productive.

Effects of Employee Obsolescence

Clearly, being declared obsolete can have a devastating effect on the individual employee. When large numbers of workers become obsolete, there are major effects on society as well.

Who Is Truly Obsolete? Labelling someone as economically useless is a damning and final kind of judgment to make. It implies that even a person's best efforts are not good enough. Classifying an employee as deadwood—totally useless to the organization— therefore should not be done lightly. For such a classification to be valid, the following conditions must exist:

- Whatever skills the individual possesses must be useless to the organization. This obsolescence may have been caused by technological changes, social changes, or both.
- The skills needed to bring the person out of obsolescence cannot be implanted through remedial training, new experience, or other administrative or motivational action, or else such reme-

dial efforts cost more than the employer is willing or able to spend. The company may prefer to find another person whose skills, learning capacity, and future stream of income are greater. This is particularly likely to occur if there is reason to think that training attempts would be fruitless because of an individual's resistance to learning and change.

- Problem employees, like deadwood, may resist retraining, but their resistance is more likely to come from emotional causes than from sheer lack of ability. The resistance may grow out of a sense of professional pride, for example, or standards that are no longer relevant. Jealousy or resentment of new people with higher skills may also call forth a resistance to the new. For example, admirals who clung to the battleship when the prevailing mass of professional opinion stated that it was unfit for an age of nuclear warfare may have done so out of suspicions of intrigue on the part of those surrounding them, love of tradition, loyalty to old comrades, or simply failure of imagination.

- The individual's skills must be unlikely to be needed again in the foreseeable future. Occupations classified as obsolete or economically impractical do sometimes make a comeback, though not often. The rise in the cost of oil made many occupations based on cheap oil obsolescent, for example, but it raised others previously considered economically impractical to a new level of importance. When American television manufacture became uneconomical because of foreign competition, the television design engineer came to be regarded as obsolete, but technical breakthroughs in some domestic firms have restored their inventors to stardom. In the eighties, the rapid rate of technological and social change may raise and lower and raise again the economic value of many occupations.

Both deadwood and problem employees are as much the result of failure of the institutions that produced them—families, schools, and employers—as they are of personal inadequacy. They may also be the victims of misjudgments made by others. One reason for hesitating to call people obsolete is that in the process of classifying them as failures, we may find out more than we care to know about who made them that way.

Social Effects of Obsolescence. Being economically obsolete in America is not as dire a fate as it might be, but the social and financial costs of dealing with employee obsolescence are high. Obsolescence has been made less of a burden to many in our society because of public assistance and income maintenance programs. Government programs such as welfare and Aid to Families with Dependent Children have made it possible for the economically redundant to survive and maintain their income at minimal levels. Transfer payments, occasionally in cash but more often "in kind"— food stamps, housing, medical aid, and the like—reach millions of people whose income has been cut off by unemployment, lack of useful skills, old age, physical disability, or other obsolescence-creating forces.

For some people, government support becomes a way of life. Morton Pagland of Portland State University cited a rise in end transfer payments from $1 billion in 1970 to over $14 billion in 1980, and the sum continues to increase. The poverty level is presently calculated on the basis of cash income, but Pagland suggests that if the total of "in kind" payments were added in, the current official figure of over 30 percent of Americans living below the poverty level would be reduced to less than 5 percent.

These statistics have an important bearing on the supply of workers available for jobs at the lower end of the wage scale. Because it is often possible to bring in almost as much income from welfare and transfer payments as one could earn from being employed at the minimum wage, many people have found it uneconomical to take jobs at low wage levels. As economist Milton Friedman pointed out on a national public television panel in 1979, it is foolish for a person to work forty hours a week for the same level of income that could be obtained by avoiding work and living in the transfer payment culture. The result has been that many menial service jobs have difficulty in attracting applicants. In one large eastern bank during a white collar unionization drive, a young woman teller stated to an interviewer, "I work at minimum wage, and when I applied for a credit card at the same bank that pays me that low wage, they turned me down because my pay was below their minimum level of credit acceptance." Small wonder then that potential workers might prefer welfare to work.

This lack of applicants has created a vacuum that, in turn, has produced a strong demand for immigrant labor. The Simpson-Mazzoli Immigration Act of 1983, which takes a more tolerant view of immigration than past laws, had the silent support of many employers who were eager to staff low-paying positions with the sort of willing workers that they could not find at home. Immigrants from Vietnam, Cuba, Central America, and Mexico proved equally eager to fill this employment gap—legally or otherwise. The amount they could earn at even the lowest-paying jobs in the United States was often greater than the median wage in their homelands. A barber who gets 50¢ for giving a haircut in Mexico City will receive $6.50 for the same haircut in Southern California. Domestic workers earn $40.00 a month in Mexico and usually have to live in miserable slums, whereas they may receive $600.00 a month in California and at the same time enjoy social benefits such as free education of their children, health care, and comparatively high buying power.

The social change of immigration produces other changes. The surge of immigration from Spanish-speaking nations to the south, for example, has resulted in a great infusion of Spanish-speaking people into the work force. Professor Clark Reynolds of Stanford University cites a figure of 5 million undocumented aliens in this country today, mainly occupying menial jobs, and the number may well rise to a range of 15 to 30 million by the year 2000. For employers this may comprise a welcome addition to the lower-level work force of the nation. Many of these undocumented aliens are Hispanics. Currently, the average age of the Spanish-surname population in the United States is estimated to be below twenty years, and this population is growing faster than the Anglo population. This is likely to lead to an increase in bilingualism and in the prevalence of Hispanic culture. Future supervisors thus may be required to be bilingual and may have to deal with subordinates whose motivations and values differ from the ones they are used to. Supervisors who cannot adapt to these changes may themselves become obsolete. Thus, human obsolescence creates social problems that may produce further obsolescence in their turn.

12

---◆---

Avoiding and Overcoming Employee Obsolescence

If you are not made straight when you are green, you
will not be made straight when you are dry.
                                        —*African proverb*

There is no question that at any given time certain employees
in an organization will fit in the human resources portfolio category
we have called deadwood. Certain unemployed members of society,
too, may seem to possess such a low level of skills that they would
automatically become deadwood if they were hired; that is, they
appear to be unemployable. How is management to handle these
people? Even more important, how can workers be removed from
the deadwood category, and how can new workers be prevented
from entering it?

   The first thing to keep in mind is caution in classifying
an employee as deadwood. Aging, for example, is by no means
always accompanied by a decline in the power to do useful work,
although some changes in the work environment may be required
to allow full use of the older worker's powers.

   Second, if the deadwood classification does seem to be valid
in a given case, the cause of the decline should be established as
clearly as possible so that appropriate remedial action can be taken.
If illness or deterioration of physical capacity has played a part
in the decline of abilities, for example, the physical problem should

be treated before psychological therapy or remedial training is considered. If the main problem appears to be a deficiency in learning ability resulting from unfavorable past learning experiences, then "learning how to learn" may be the first step in appropriate remedial action.

According to modern management thinking, very few people in the deadwood category are so hopeless that they must be separated. Human capacity is so much underutilized that even when it declines from prior levels, enough usually remains so that if the person is properly assigned, trained, and motivated, he or she can still perform many workhorse-level assignments. The wise manager should remember that over time, the costs of separation and supporting a former worker on welfare are always higher than the cost of remedial training, even though training costs are not small.

In other words, deadwood doesn't necessarily have to stay dead. In recent years many programs, sponsored by both government and private industry, have grown up around the belief that human obsolescence is both a preventable and a curable state. Instead of being written off as losers, people can be taught how to win.

Programs to Fight Obsolescence

Attacks on human obsolescence during the last forty years have centered on two areas: (1) reforms in education of the young and (2) remedial programs for people who are already classified as obsolescent or unemployable.

Each of these approaches has its advantages and disadvantages. Better education is an obvious way to prevent future human obsolescence, but formal education faces an important difficulty in preparing people for a successful future: We can't be sure what the future will be like. Thus, education in specific technical skills is useful only to people who will graduate soon after the completion of their schooling and immediately take jobs that will use those skills. However, education can implant more basic human skills, such as logical thinking, reading, writing, and speaking. In 1983 a national commission on educational excellence reported that American schools do not do an adequate job of teaching such basics, with the result that "a wave of mediocrity" may engulf us in the future. The report called for longer school hours, more days of class, better trained teachers, rewards for superior teachers, and similar reforms.

As we noted in Chapter One, people's education has a major bearing on how well they will perform for the rest of their lives. It also sorts them into categories in which they often remain throughout their lives. For example, the child designated as a deficient student is usually routed through a slower and less taxing path in the school system and therefore gains less from his or her education. This lower educational level, in turn, leads to less taxing career paths, until finally the adult becomes a workhorse at best and deadwood in far too many instances. Thus, reforms in education of the young are vital in preventing the development of future deadwood.

Dealing with the deadwood of today, however, is equally important. Confronted by the socially undesirable effects of too much economic deadwood, government and the business community during the 1960s and 1970s created numerous programs that sought to remedy the effects of past failure in the educational system and consequent present failure in the world of work. These "manpower programs" were aimed mainly at persons considered unemployable for a variety of reasons. Their intent was to make such people employable and then to place them successfully in jobs, thus providing them with both income and status. Some programs were also designed to enhance the competence of people who were already employed at low-level jobs, in order to bring them greater success in the labor market.

The following are some of the major government programs that have been aimed at preventing or curing human obsolescence during the second half of this century.

The GI Bill. Enacted in 1944, this bill provided four years of college or its equivalent to any of the 16.5 million men and women then in the armed forces who wished it. Of that group, 7.8 million enrolled in the program: 2.2 million went to colleges and universities, 3.5 million went to other schools, 1.4 million received on-the-job training, and 750,000 were trained on farms. The program, which cost $14 billion, boosted each graduate's income by an average of $1,800 a year. This produced a return of over a billion dollars a year in federal taxes and also brought about something of a social revolution in human resources investment. Another $4.5 billion was paid for education of 2.4 million veterans of later wars.

The GI Bill was the sole direct investment by government in human resources and employment for some fifteen years following World War II. Then during the late fifties a number of influences, including high unemployment of youth and an apparent shortage of engineers highlighted by the need for talented people to compete against the Russians in the new space race, created a demand for programs aimed at producing full employment and a more remedial national manpower policy.

The Manpower Development and Training Act (MDTA). The rise to power of a liberal Democratic administration upon the election of John F. Kennedy to the Presidency in 1960 saw a rebirth of interest in public expenditure for employment training. A product of the Area Redevelopment Act, the MDTA of 1962 was intended to retrain mature, experienced family heads who had been displaced by technological and economic change, giving them income while they were in training. Some saw the program as a defense against automation. Others viewed it as a means of giving unemployed workers a chance to qualify for apparently plentiful job opportunities, for serious worker shortages existed in the sixties in many occupations. Still others, inspired by the reported successes of the GI Bill, saw the new program as a further investment in human resources.

Title I of the act instructed the Secretary of Labor to "improve the adequacy of the nation's manpower development efforts." It also required an annual manpower report from the President, akin to his annual economic report. Title II authorized a small-scale, federally financed, state-operated training program, mainly for unemployed but experienced adult workers. Local offices of the U.S. Employment Service were required to provide estimates of the likelihood of employment for those trained, and local school systems involved in the training were reimbursed at rates equal to the unemployment compensation then being paid.

Later amendments provided for youth training, and the program was further embellished by the Vocational Education Act of 1963. In the application of MDTA to youth it was discovered that often these people's most serious problem was illiteracy, which in turn was rooted in deep motivational problems. Having acquired an early aversion to learning, they showed a similar distaste for it later in life, which made retraining difficult.

The War on Poverty. When Lyndon Johnson became President in 1964, he launched an antipoverty campaign that had, among other components, a host of bills aimed at eliminating unemployment of the obsolescent. The Equal Opportunity Act and others provided remedial education, training, and work experience. The Head Start programs, the only preventive element in the package, gave special educational help to the very young in low socioeconomic classes in the hope of off-setting later educational deficiencies they might encounter. Job Corps, Neighborhood Youth Corps, Youth Conservation Corps, and Job Corps Conservation Centers were mainly job creation programs for youth, although they also had a vocational training element, but not placement.

These manpower development programs had little real effect on the labor market, since only about 250,000 people enrolled in them out of a labor force of 75 million. The state of the economy at a given time was far more important. Every time a burst of prosperity came along, it was discovered that most of the "unemployables" really weren't, and they disappeared into the regular work force. Meanwhile, a small "hard-core" group proved to be resistant to every effort to train them or find them work. Support for outright dole, public employment, or public payments to private employers who would hire such workers grew during the sixties.

Office of Economic Opportunity and Department of Labor programs such as Concentrated Opportunity, JOBS, and the Work Incentive Program added to the war on poverty. The number of federal vocational rehabilitation and vocational education plans grew from five in 1961 to sixteen in 1969. The total cost of the 1969 programs was $2.5 billion. It was clear that remedial and helping programs for the deadwood of society were now a major matter of public policy.

Public Aid to Education. During the sixties a further attempt to help the obsolescent or potentially obsolescent get into the mainstream came through dramatically increased aid to education.

The Higher Education Act of 1965 and the Elementary and Second-dary Education Act of the same year provided some $2.4 billion in federal funds to schools in poverty-stricken areas. There was also increased federal support for vocational education, and the definition of "handicapped" was enlarged to include impairment due to "vocational, cultural, social, environmental, or other factors." The purpose of the U.S. Employment Service was reversed, from "screening out" people being referred for jobs to "screening in" people. The new programs were accompanied by a maze of reg-ulations that fixed eligibility, duration, conditions of training or work, and pay to participants. While the motives of these programs were laudable, their effects were often disappointing, and they were subjected to considerable criticism not only from conservatives concerned with cutting costs but also from professionals involved in the programs themselves.

Comprehensive Employment and Training Act (CETA) and Other Seventies Programs. During the seventies, the flow of Vietnam veterans enlarged the programs under the GI Bill. Other federal funds went to the colleges to provide scholarships, grants, and loans to stu-dents. CETA programs, successors to the other job creation programs of 1968, provided public service jobs with training purposes. Other programs provided medical care, food stamps, housing assistance, rehabilitation, and numerous other kinds of remedial, preventive, or compensatory help for those whom society had classified as dead-wood. The tax bill for all of this mounted steadily.

The change in national administration in the seventies was accompanied by a change in strategies for handling the hard-core unemployed as EDA, MDTA, and similar programs disappeared and were replaced by CETA. Whereas under Johnson remedial training had been an important, if not the central, thrust of the strategy, the emphasis now was on ameliorating the effects rather than preventing or remedying the causes of unemployability. No-tions such as "negative income tax" were bruited about, and payments for welfare, Medicare, food stamps, housing assistance for the elderly, and similar amenities took up most of the social services budget. Elimination of discrimination, protection of the environment, and occupational safety replaced job training as concerns of the hour. As the "reverse baby boom" began affecting the lower grades of public schools, budgets for education were slashed to decrease the burden on payers of property tax. State legislatures, often dominated by rural and farm elements, also began to cut back on higher education budgets. The one important exception to this decreased emphasis on training was vocational education through community colleges, which grew rapidly during the seventies.

Programs of the Eighties. The Reagan administration has made drastic cutbacks in all federal training and development expenditures. CETA programs were abolished, although new training initiatives began under the Jobs Partnership Act. When Congress appropriated $24 million for retraining those who had lost their jobs because of foreign competition, the administration in Washington refused to provide the money to the states during fiscal 1982. It was only after Federal District Court Judge Joyce Greene directed the Labor Department to release the impounded funds in mid-1983 that even this relatively small sum could be used. Attempts to train and upgrade society's deadwood, it now appeared, were to be left to the private sector or the affected workers.

Modern Approaches to Overcoming Obsolescence

One provocative conclusion suggested by the success of many modern employee training programs is that deadwood as a portfolio classification may be momentarily valid but perhaps could be eliminated entirely by appropriate training. Let's look at some of the approaches to training that have worked best.

Some Model Programs. In 1967 in San Francisco, a remarkable demonstration project caused a new look to be taken at the definition of "unemployable." Sponsored by the U.S. Department of Labor, the program aimed to place hard-core unemployed in mainstream positions in the civil service. Despite a shortage of funds, the project gave about 500 "unqualified people," mostly blacks, temporary assignments in the post office. These people were informed that within one year they must qualify for their jobs by passing minimal civil service exams. Then, while they continued to work, they were placed in training courses to prepare them for the tests. In January, only 13 of the 500 could pass the exam. One month after the start of classes, however, 273 took the exam again and 92 passed. In total, 513 took the classes, 416 took the exam at one time or another, and 263 passed. In addition, 230 of the original employees found other employment, at least in part as a result of the training and experience they had received in the post office training program. The turnover rate, sick leave usage, and annual leave usage of those who continued in jobs were lower than average for merit system employees (Mangum and Glenn, 1969).

The assumptions behind this project were remarkably different from traditional assumptions about obsolescent or "unemployable" people. The project claimed that if the employer would assume that the workers would succeed and would take remedial action to assist them, they would no longer be failures. Rather than "screen, then hire," the project's approach was "hire, then qualify." It appeared to be a resounding success.

Earlier, inside IBM, Walter McNamara (1963) reported a similar experiment in which the upgrading training in electromechanical skills was offered to a group of employees who would normally have been considered poor risks for such programs. IBM conducted the classes on a stretched-out time schedule, allowing the employees 25 percent more time to complete the learning than was usually given for such classes. It also provided preliminary grounding in arithmetic basics and electricity to bring the learners up to the same educational starting line as the regular fast-learner class. Two thirds of the employees in the experimental group completed the course satisfactorily.

The IBM program points up one important characteristic of successful remedial training: timing. The learning-impaired take more time to learn than others do, and the steps in learning must be smaller. This calls for patience and tighter organization on the part of instructors. Emphasis on hands-on or practical experience rather than on theoretical, textbook, or conceptual learning also seems to work better for slow learners.

On a more basic level, the success of the IBM experiment, like that of the San Francisco program, seems to stem from the assumption that workers' employability could be brought to a higher level by proper training. It suggests that, given sufficient time, investment, and motivation, even seemingly unpromising people can be upgraded to handle relatively complex work. It also suggests that workers become deadwood and fail to adapt mainly because they are not given the proper adaptive tools.

Similarly, observers of migrant laborers from Sicily, Spain, Greece, and Turkey who were working in Germany noted that the majority of these workers not only were incapable of speaking German but were illiterate in their native tongue as well. Most would have been labelled "hard-core unemployable" in American personnel offices. Still, they were trained to do complex jobs in the steel, pharmaceuticals, chemical, and electronics industries. The fact that German firms had no alternative source of workers in the face of drastic labor shortages apparently was a powerful motivator for them to devise successful training programs for even these unlikely employees.

Fitting workers to jobs can sometimes be assisted by rewriting task descriptions to bring them down to the level of newly trained workers. The requirements for jobs have often been overstated by management, thereby creating an artificial barrier to the employability of many workers. Insisting that all municipal workers—even those who merely plow snow or cut brush—must be high school graduates, that all police officers be college graduates, or that all supervisors have MBAs creates deadwood where it need not exist.

The Importance of Diagnosis: A Case History. In one large state university it was discovered that the failure rate in introductory accounting, a course required of all business majors and many other students, ran at 30 percent. The teacher therefore slowed down the pace in the course, with the result that the best students suffered while the worst ones still flunked and had to repeat the course. Considerable teacher time was used up in handling the repeaters. But if a student protested that things were going too fast, the standard reply was, "Don't worry, you'll get it next semester."

A study to seek out the causes of the failure uncovered basic arithmetic deficiencies. Many students could not add, subtract, multiply, or divide. They had graduated from accredited high schools, but they couldn't pass a simple arithmetic test, let alone add the columns of figures and do the simple ratio calculations required for introductory accounting. The number of students who failed the diagnostic test proved to be almost exactly equal to the number who were presently failing introductory accounting.

The test, incidentally, was open-book, with no time limit. The students could bring any book they wanted and even use handheld calculators. Even so, a third of them failed.

The remedial solution chosen for this problem was a long weekend of cram math prior to regular classes. The cram course was taught by specially trained teaching assistants who drilled each student in the specific skills that the test had shown him or her to lack. On Sunday evening the students took the diagnostic exam again. Those who passed began the accounting course on schedule. Those who failed were enrolled in a semester of remedial math and arithmetic courses. At the end of the remedial courses they took the diagnostic test yet again. If they passed, they entered the accounting course. Those who persistently repeated the remedial course and failed the arithmetic test were advised to change their major to one that did not require accounting.

As a result of this combination of diagnosis and remedial training, failures in the accounting course dropped to less than 2 percent. About 8 percent of those taking the remedial course were rejected and transferred to other majors.

The economic gains from the new approach were clear. Before the remedial program was begun, 30 percent of all teacher time in the accounting course was spent on repeaters, thus tying up over $100,000 worth of teaching salary each semester—not to mention the time of an expert in a field where teachers are in short supply. The cost of the diagnosis and remedial coursework was less than a tenth of that loss. Furthermore, under the new system, the already qualified students in the course were no longer held back by the failures. As a side benefit, the diagnostic testing uncovered several cases of dyslexia, some reading deficiencies, a few cases of "math phobia" induced by bad teaching at an early age, and some apparent psychological problems in addition to the math skill deficiencies. The point here—and it has been demonstrated in many other educational programs as well—is that successful remediation must be based on diagnosis.

Diagnosis is also vital in helping employees classed as present or potential deadwood. First, jobs should be analyzed to determine what skills each really requires. Then diagnostic tests or other ways of measuring those skills should be prepared. Finally, applicants should be tested and given remedial work as needed.

A Model for Remedial Training of Obsolescent People. The full use of human capital requires that we adopt a model for treatment of seemingly obsolescent people. Such a model is pictured in Figure 12. The examples cited in this chapter suggest that this kind of approach has a good chance of paying off for the individual worker, the employer, and society. The steps in the model can be described as follows:

1. At the point of entry into the system a screening diagnosis should be applied: Does the individual have the knowledge, skills, attitudes, motivations, and habits needed to do the job or to learn its requirements? If the answer is affirmative, the person enters the job, is trained in its performance, and hopefully proceeds to become a solid performer, perhaps even a star.

2. Those who are found by the screening to lack necessary skills, motivations, knowledge, or habits are routed into remedial training. This training is paced to suit the slow learner and probably includes some preparatory work before the main course begins. If the trained employees can now pass the entry-level diagnosis, they enter the original job and proceed through job training to ordinary worker status. If an employee fails a second time, further diagnosis attempts to pinpoint the part of the remedial work that must be redone or done differently, and the person is routed back into additional remedial programs.

3. Those whose repeated remedial work fails to bring them up to the level of Job A, the higher-level job, may still display enough learning ability to qualify them for the less demanding work of Jobs B, C, or D.

4. Only those whose remedial progress is so low that there is no conceivable position within the organization to which their skills might apply should be considered unemployable by the firm.

Figure 12. A Model for Remedial Training of Obsolescent People.

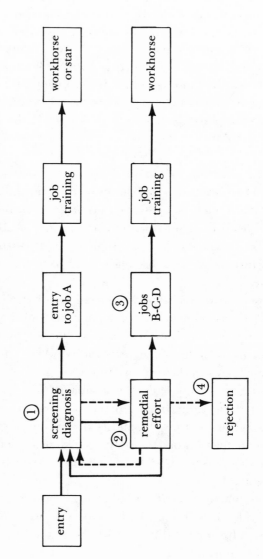

Applying a model like this to a firm's deadwood should be highly beneficial to the firm as well as to the individual workers. The costs of remedial training are usually far less than the expected stream of income from individuals whose abilities have been given close and accurate assessment prior to job entry. At present, many people with hidden deficiencies slip into jobs, and the training needed to maximize their utilization is not defined.

Remedial training must avoid the stigma of being a "dumbbell class." Rather, it should be presented as part of a more precise placement effort. Remedial work may be needed at any level, including technical, managerial, and professional. The accountant who joins a firm knowing IBM computers and BASIC will need remedial education if the firm uses DEC Equipment with FORTRAN.

Breaking Out of the Activity Trap. In the previous chapter I described the special kind of obsolescence caused by the Activity Trap. This form of obsolescence also can be prevented or cured if an organization is willing to take steps to combat it.

The key person in determining whether an organization will escape the Activity Trap is the top manager. He or she must decide that the organization will be managed by objectives and results, not activity, and determine corporate objectives and strategic goals. Subordinate managers then define operational objectives that fit these top-level goals and strategies.

Nonbusiness organizations benefit from explicit objectives, too. Families with defined objectives can permit relatively wide variations in behavior as long as their objectives are met. Service clubs find that definite objectives attract more resources and workers to their cause.

An attack on the Activity Trap may well be the best place for a corporation to begin its attempts to prevent or cure employee obsolescence. Five steps are needed to break out of the Activity Trap:

1. At the beginning of every period, each boss and subordinate must sit down face-to-face and talk out the objectives of the subordinate's work, his or her responsibilities, and the standards of performance by which he or she will be judged. The main points of the discussion should be confirmed in a memo.

Now, when the curtain goes up, both actors will have the same script; this usually improves the quality of the acting considerably.

2. Boss and subordinate must agree upon the resources and help needed to reach the objectives.

3. The subordinate must thereafter be freed of any harassment, interference, or unduly close supervision that might hamper or prevent progress toward the agreed-on goals.

4. Ongoing information and feedback must be available so that the subordinate will know how well he or she is doing the work while he or she is doing it.

5. Summary appraisals must be given at the end of the period, when the whole process will start anew.

Part Four

Implementing Portfolio Management Strategies

We write well when we expose frauds and hypocrites.
We are great at counting warts and blemishes and
weighing feet of clay. In expressing love we belong
among the underdeveloped countries.   —*Saul Bellow*

13

Strengthening
Performance Appraisal
Systems

I prefer an executive to visualize a business as a
succession of balance sheets.   —*H. Ronald Kibel*

The job of chief industrial engineer in a major plant in a large
firm became vacant, and the vice-president of engineering for the
corporation was responsible for choosing a replacement. After
consultation with the personnel manager, he called a conference
of engineering managers to review the personnel folders of the
possible candidates. "I want a strong engineer with some solid
experience who is a thinker and a doer," he had told the personnel
department. Accordingly, the folder for every engineer between ages
thirty-five and fifty who had no major black marks in his folder
was produced. (There were no women in this category.) Each file
was found to contain the following:

- A resumé submitted at the time of hiring, including references
  provided by the applicant, usually professors or past employers.
- Salary progress year by year, recorded to the penny.
- A wide variety of appraisal forms that had been in existence
  in the firm or its various divisions over the years. Some were
  based on personality trait lists. Others were based on master

lists of skills, described in rather general terms such as "good organizer," "cost minded," and the like. A small number had rudimentary statements of results compared against objectives. Since the corporation as a whole had no uniform appraisal system, the standards against which the different people had been appraised were not the same. The judgments of the raters varied from very severe to positively euphoric.

As the folders were passed from hand to hand, the committee made notes on each one. After an hour of this the chairman called for their comments. Almost all the comments were centered on "knock-out factors":

"Jim looks okay, but I see that he was a bit weak in math in college. C average."

"Ted shows very little exposure to manufacturing management."

"Harry is at a very low salary level for his grade. He must have been viewed as ineffective by his managers over the years."

"I see Bill turned down a transfer from Indianola back in '80."

"I gather from this record that George can't move unless we find a suitable job for his wife, an accountant."

The committee finally concluded that there were no really strong people to take over the job and that the firm should therefore start an outside search. A placement firm was hired, a national search was conducted, and three candidates were interviewed. One of them, a tall, prepossessing-looking man with a resumé packed with glittering achievements, was finally hired. He lasted one year before he quit and went to a higher-level job in a competing firm.

Incidents like the one in this true story are unfortunately all too common in large firms. The point of the story is that most appraisal systems aren't very useful in revealing different levels of performance or helping to identify promotable people. As a result, few corporations have a clear picture of the quality of their human assets. An excessive number of employees end up being confined to the workhorse category, and opportunity for the best people is diminished.

While there certainly may be occasions when it is necessary to go outside the firm to hire a replacement or fill a newly created position, it usually isn't the best way. A policy of promotion from within the company is a morale builder, an attractant to the most ambitious and competent youngsters, and an aid in using fully the portfolio of assets that an organization already has in its possession. Such a policy demands a good appraisal system.

The chore of completing an annual performance appraisal, which is usually done by an employee's immediate supervisor and reviewed by some higher-level third party, is not popular. As one government executive stated to this writer, "I don't sleep the night before I have to do one of those performance reviews on my people." (Presumably the people being reviewed don't sleep the night *after* the review.) The appraisal of performance is apt to be difficult for line managers unless they have had specific training in the understanding of human behavior and in the techniques of listening, coaching, and holding discussions with subordinates. Many find it easier to follow the practice of one old navy chief petty officer, who told me, "If they do okay, they don't hear from me. If they screw up, they hear from me loud and clear." In other words, some people are willing to do the job of appraisal only when they get mad. Conversely, those who are more mild-mannered are willing to do the job only if they can say good things to the person being appraised.

Why Accurate Performance Appraisal Is Important

The two major dimensions of the human resources portfolio, you will recall, are potential and performance. We discussed the assessment of potential in earlier chapters. Performance is just as important as potential in determining who shall be classified as stars, workhorses, problem employees, or deadwood.

All employees should have their performance and contribution to the organization appraised at least annually. Such a practice makes possible a system of coaching and development of people's abilities that turns the human resources portfolio from a static to a dynamic thing. (There is no special advantage to holding the review annually, as opposed to any other time period, except that such a pattern corresponds with the many other business activities that are done annually.

Management Concerns Affected by Performance Appraisal. There are many reasons why performance appraisals should be done systematically, regularly, and periodically. They relate to concerns that are chronic and recurring for anyone who must manage others, especially those who must manage managers. These concerns include the following:

- *Pay raises.* Should the pay of a subordinate be increased, decreased, or left the same? How should salary increase funds be allocated among subordinates?
- *Bonuses.* Upon what basis should available funds for bonuses be distributed? How can this distribution be made so as to reflect actual contribution to the surplus that created the bonus? How can windfalls be prevented? How can hard luck be taken into consideration?
- *Promotability.* What elements in present performance can be used to predict success or failure if a person is promoted to a higher-level job? How good is the individual's performance in those areas?
- *Performance records.* What entries about achievements and failures to achieve during the past period should be made in a person's record?
- *Coaching and improvement counseling.* What aspects of recent performance should be discussed with the subordinate? What areas need improvement? In what areas is the subordinate doing an exceptionally fine job?
- *Management training and development.* Is there any kind of formal education or training that might improve the subordinate's performance or potential? Should the person attend a course or seminar, join an association or be given assignments to enlarge experience?
- *Future assignments.* Should any changes be made in the tasks included in the subordinate's job? Should new responsibility be delegated?
- *Legal requirements.* Does management of this subordinate comply with all Equal Employment Opportunity (EEO) laws concerning race, sex, age or other discrimination?

All these areas of concern require discriminatory judgment about a person's performance, as measured against expectations, and his or her professional capacity.

Lack of a reliable performance appraisal plan can cause a number of problems for a firm and its managers. Without an appraisal plan that lets people know what is expected of them, how well they are doing, and how well they have done, a manager may not be able to fire deadwood and make it stick. Without such a plan, stars may be overlooked because they work for a boss who doesn't like them. Without sound appraisal, a manager may never realize how a problem employee could be brought back on stream and be turned into a winner—indeed, many never even identify the employee as a problem, let alone find out the problem's causes. Without appraisal, a manager may not know when workhorses need further motivation or might benefit from coaching and counselling. Finally, without sound performance appraisal, differences in salaries may become sources of rivalries that seriously damage employee morale. In summary, it is simply impossible to manage a human resources portfolio properly without a valid performance appraisal system.

Why Accurate Performance Appraisal Is Difficult

A number of factors make accurate performance appraisal hard to accomplish. For one thing, in large, decentralized companies the managers may be rated by a remote boss who sees them once a month at most. Similarly, with company growth and job transfers occurring at today's high rate, a substantial portion of managers or other employees being appraised are likely to be working for bosses who haven't observed them long enough to make good judgments about their performance. Many ratings will have to be made on the basis of indirect information or insufficient observation, and a distortion of the valuation of important assets may accordingly occur.

Even—perhaps especially—when a boss knows a subordinate well, attempts to rate performance accurately may come into conflict with the human fallibilities of the manager who cannot put subjectivity aside. Managerial biases, conscious or unconscious, tend to fall into two major categories, which we might call the *halo effect* and the hypercritical or *"horns" effect.*

The Halo Effect. The halo effect is the tendency of a boss to place an excessively positive aura or halo over the rating of a subordinate. This may happen for a variety of reasons, including the following:

- *Past record.* Because the subordinate has done good work in the distant past, his or her performance is assumed to be OK in the immediate past, too. Good work tends to carry over into the current period.
- *Compatibility.* There's a tendency to rate people whom we find pleasing of manner and personality higher than they deserve. Those who agree with us, nod their heads when we talk, or even make notes of our words may get better ratings than their performance justifies.
- *Recent high performance.* An outstanding job done recently can offset a mediocre performance over the rest of the year, especially if the act occurs just before the annual review.
- *Irrelevant attributes.* The glib talker, the person with an impressive appearance, the one who has advanced degrees, or the graduate of the boss's own alma mater may get a more favorable rating than the subordinate who lacks these often irrelevant attributes.
- *Blind spot.* The boss may not notice certain types of defects in others because they are too much like his or her own. The boss who is a big thinker may be unable to recognize that a subordinate likewise has no eye for detail, for example.
- *Paper tiger.* The boss judges the subordinate by how well the person looks on the paper records, not by what he or she has done for the organization.
- *No news is good news.* If a subordinate has no complaints, the boss assumes everything is terrific. The subordinate who speaks up about problems but gets the job done may be rated lower than the person who both says nothing and does nothing.

The Horns Effect. The reverse of the halo effect is the hypercritical or "horns" effect—the tendency to rate people lower than their performance actually justifies. The following are some specific causes of the horns effect:

- *Perfectionist boss.* Because the boss's expectations are so high, he or she is often disappointed and rates people lower than they deserve.
- *Contrary subordinate.* The boss pays back a subordinate's tendency to argue too often by giving him or her a low rating.
- *Oddball subordinate.* Despite the lip-service paid to people's right to nonconformity, it all too seldom finds its way into practice when appraisal time comes around. The oddball, the maverick, the nonconformist often get low ratings simply because they are different.
- *Membership in a weak team.* A good player on a weak team may end up with lower ratings than he or she would have had while playing on a winning one.
- *Guilt by association.* The person who isn't really known will often be judged by the company he or she keeps. If someone hangs out with a frivolous crowd or works for the wrong boss, he or she may suffer reductions in rating.
- *Recent failure.* A recent goof can wipe out the effect of years of good work and produce a low rating on the latest appraisal.
- *Undesirable personality traits.* The subordinate who is too cocky, too loud, too meek, or has some other personality trait the boss dislikes may suffer in rating. So may the subordinate who lacks a trait that the boss considers "good."
- *Self-comparison.* The person who doesn't do the job as the boss remembers doing it when he or she held that position may suffer more than those whose jobs the boss is not too familiar with.

In short, subjective ratings, founded as they are on human perception and judgment, must necessarily be inaccurate. Even in industrial engineering, where relatively great precision can be attained, accurate judgment is held to be impossible for differences in rate of effort of less than 15 percent. How much more imprecise, then, must be judgments on the performance of staff managers, supervisors, office employees, and executives?

Problems Arising from the Halo and Horns Effects. The valuation of a firm's human resources portfolio can be grossly distorted by the widespread presence of either horns or halos in performance ratings. When the horns effect predominates, there are no stars. No mortal could possibly earn the highest performance rating, and those who might have been impelled to the heights of top management are constantly chopped down. Potential stars become downgraded to workhorses, and the slightest evidence of originality or variance from norms further reduces them to problem employees in the eyes of the assessor. Workhorses are mistaken for deadwood, and employees who persistently advocate change may end up in this category as well.

The halo effect has the reverse impact, for the rater who is adorned with such rose-colored glasses sees everyone in a light of idealism and optimism that is unwarranted by the facts. The good steady workhorse may be praised as a star without really having the potential to justify that status. The problem employee, too, is glamorized into a star. Deadwood employees are frantically scanned for any evidence of merit and classified as workhorses whenever possible: "Jim is slow but steady, and if things got rough we could count on him." (Translation: When Jim is sober, he's all right.)

With a subjective rating system, negative effects arising from differences in rater attitudes are virtually unavoidable. The only realistic antidote to the halo and horns effects is to define very specific standards and methods of measurement, train all raters in applying those standards (and retrain them from time to time to prevent slippage), and have a third party review all ratings for undue rater bias.

Legal Constraints on Performance Appraisal

The most important danger of subjective performance appraisal systems is their tendency to run afoul of new legal standards concerning the management of human resources. Title VII of the Equal Employment Opportunity Act of 1964 and the subsequent guidelines of the Equal Employment Opportunity Commission (EEOC) have broadened discrimination rulings to cover not only the initial hiring decision but promotion decisions as well. The Office of Federal Contract Compliance (OFCC) issued an Order on Testing and other selection procedures which, like the EEOC's guidelines, the courts quickly interpreted as applying to promotion as well as hiring. Such rulings have radically altered performance appraisal practices.

The courts currently require that an employer, in appraising job performance, have very clear measures of whatever performance is expected. This effectively torpedoes appraisal systems that rely on subjective supervisory ratings of performance. Employers are now required to demonstrate that their standards are related to job performance and do in fact reflect such performance. In *Griggs versus Duke Power*, for example, the court ruled that the skills required by an employer must actually be used on the job. Tests could be used only if they measured skills required on the job. The company's requirement of a high school diploma for employment was thrown out, since that requirement didn't have "a manifest relation" to the jobs in question.

In other decisions the courts have focused on the specific content of performance appraisal forms. They have rejected overly general criteria of appraisals, including subjective rating by supervisors of qualities such as "leadership, public acceptance, attitude toward people, appearance and grooming, outlook on life, ethical habits, resourcefulness, capacity for growth, mental alertness, and loyalty to organization" *(Wade versus Mississippi Cooperative Service)*. In another case the court threw out performance reviews of workers as being possibly discriminatory against certain protected groups when "judgments are based upon judgments and opinions" and ruled that objective tests of performance, administered and scored under controlled and standardized conditions, are required *(Row versus General Motors Corporation)*.

In other words, the courts are deeply interested in performance appraisal forms, controls, and scoring systems. They insist that performance appraisals be formal, standardized, and objective. They must also be job related, characterized by formal job analysis, administered by trained evaluators, and rated by people who have constant contact with the employee. Each criterion must be weighted, job opportunities must be posted, and more than one level of supervisor must review the results (Lubben, Thompson, and Klasson, 1980).

Laws Against Discrimination. Much of the dilemma in trying to establish valid performance rating systems lies in the managerial desire to play God. As Jones (1983) summarized this attitude, humanistic management assumes that numbers cannot capture the essence of human beings. This view doesn't deny that numbers must sometimes be used in judgments, but it insists that judgments go beyond the numeric. Human relations are not linear, it points out, and the treatment of people in numerical terms results in a static concept of their nature.

The courts have pointed out, however, that this preference for subjectivity can permit partiality, bias, favoritism, and the "spoils" system to operate freely. With an adjectival trait rating system as the only criterion for judging subordinates, bosses are free to reward friends and punish enemies or to reward people like themselves and discriminate against those who are different. The victims of this "humanistic" approach to performance appraisal are likely to be those groups that have traditionally been regarded as less desirable by the mainstream of corporate society. These "different" people may include any of the following, all of whom do now or are likely in the near future to fall into legally protected categories.

- *Racial minorities.* Blacks, Indians, and Spanish-speakers have traditionally found less opportunity to gain high-level ranks than whites. These were the original protected groups, and they remain the largest protected category.
- *Women.* Women were included in the category of protected workers under the original EEOC laws and regulations, and the courts have given harsh judgments against employers who failed to provide equal opportunity to women in matters of jobs, promotions, and pay. Women have won numerous lawsuits, including some multimillion dollar judgments, against employers found guilty of discrimination. Women today are also protected against sexual harassment, such as the demand by supervisors for sexual favors in return for job opportunity.
- *Older workers.* In the early eighties the rising number of successful lawsuits under the provisions of the Age Discrimina-

tion in Employment Act (ADEA) of 1979 focused the attention of employers on those workers who might be released prematurely from their jobs because of age. The law provided that workers must not be discriminated against solely because of their age but instead must be judged by job-related performance criteria. Numerous judgments in the multimillion dollar range were made against employers who failed to comply with this law.

• *Handicapped people.* Laws prohibiting discrimination against handicapped people were broadened and became a matter of management concern with the passing of the Rehabilitation Act of 1973 and subsequent court decisions. The definition of handicap was extended to include a wide range of physical and mental limitations. Employers were required to make "reasonable accommodation" to allow handicapped employees full access to the work place and to jobs and promotions. While there are still many unresolved issues in dealing with this protected group, state laws as well as federal regulations make it clear that some form of protection of the rights of such persons will be required in the appraisal process in the eighties and nineties.

Homosexuals. Laws protecting gay rights were just emerging at the time of this book's writing. The U.S. House of Representatives narrowly defeated national legislation to protect persons from discrimination in jobs and housing based on their sexual preference. Laws barring such discrimination already exist in some states, however. This further requires job-related performance appraisals by employers.

Other Legal Constraints. In addition to laws protecting specific groups of people, other laws have been passed that protect all workers' rights in certain ways. Employment at will laws have appeared in a dozen or so states and seem to be becoming more common. Under this kind of law, the employer loses some traditional rights to discharge people at will and may be required to defend some firings in the courts. Performance appraisal is an important element of proof in such cases.

Constraints on discipline now appear to be increasing as well, based on rulings by the EEOC, ADEA, and the like. These rulings suggest that the procedure of demoting may fall under the same kinds of regulations and judgments that apply to promotion. An employer may not be able to demote a worker without documented evidence of job failure that is founded on systematic performance appraisal, using clear standards and explicit measures that are both job related and objective.

Comparable worth refers to the right of employers to apply different pay rates to newly hired employees than to those who do the same work but have been employed longer. Based on the Equal Pay Act (EPA) of 1963 and other rulings, arguments are mounting in the courts that "equal pay for work of comparable worth" must be observed to prevent discrimination against protected groups. This trend, like the others described, provides an important reason for improving the quality of performance appraisal systems.

The Four Kinds of Performance Appraisal System

Studies reveal that there are four major kinds of performance appraisal system in use in most organizations today (Schneir and Beatty, 1979; Odiorne, 1969). The four can be described as follows:

Personality-based systems. In such systems the appraisal form consists of a list of personality traits that presumably are significant in the jobs of the individuals being appraised. Such traits as initiative, drive, intelligence, ingenuity, creativity, loyalty, and trustworthiness appear on most such lists. They may be accompanied by brief explanations, but often they are simply left to the imagination or opinion of the rater to define in terms of behavior and job results. When this occurs, the construct validity (definition of meaning) of the terms is missing, and they become subject to individual subjective interpretation by the supervisor doing the rating.

Generalized descriptive systems. Similar to the trait appraisal in form, they differ in the type of descriptive term used. Often they include qualities or actions of presumed good managers: "organizes, plans, controls, motivates others, delegates, communicates, makes things happen," and so on. Such a system, like the trait system, might be useful if meticulous care were taken to define the meaning of each term in regard to actual results, but in ordinary use it tends to permit subjectivity and bias on the part of the supervisor and have been rejected by the courts as not meeting legal antidiscrimination standards.

Behavioral description systems. Such systems feature detailed job analysis and job descriptions, including specific statements of the actual behaviors required of workers for success. A typical example is the system known as BARS (Behaviorally Anchored Rating Scales). These systems work well on lower-level jobs, where the job requirements are known, specific, and often repetitive, but they are less viable for evaluating professional, technical, and managerial positions, where independent behavior by the employee is required.

Results-centered systems. These appraisal systems are very job related. They require that boss and subordinate sit down at the start of each work evaluation period and negotiate agreements on the work to be done in all areas of responsibility and the specific standards of performance to be used in each area. These agreements then become the basis for judging the results produced by the subordinate on the job. Typically, these are known as MBO systems. Because they deal with outputs rather than activities or personal qualities, they have a good record of proving defensible in court challenges of appraisals.

How the Four Systems Meet Appraisal Objectives. Earlier in this chapter we listed eight areas of concern in managing human resources. The limitations and strengths of the four appraisal systems just described in regard to each of these areas of concern are shown in Table 6.

In addition, certain general statements about these appraisal systems can be made.

- Results-based appraisal systems work best for high-level jobs, whereas BARS-type or behaviorally based scales are sound for lower-level jobs. Neither of the other two forms ties closely to performance; they are more subjective in operation.
- Systems that pay for success according to the rating on a personality trait or general description scale don't relate pay

Table 6. Type of Appraisal System.

Area of Management Concern	Personality Trait	General Description	Behavioral Description (BARS)	MBO or Other Results-Based System
1. Pay Raises	Fails to reward achievement.	Overly subjective, needs definition of terms.	Very useful for lower-level jobs.	Rewards results leading to goals.
2. Bonuses	Could lead to internal dissension.	Opens possibility of subjective judgments.	Can be useful in worker incentive plans.	Tough but fair—easily understood.
3. Promotability	Widely used but specious.	Can be a useful general description.	Limited value for executive-level work.	Important element but not complete decision-making tool.
4. Performance Records	Simple to design and use.	Simple to design and use.	Difficult to design and use.	Difficult to design and use.
5. Coaching and Counselling	Not within the scope of most untrained people.	Creates boss domination without behavior change.	Easy to teach on lower-level, simple tasks.	Excellent; deals with specifics, facts, results.
6. Management Training and Development	Invades privacy, could lead to psychological damage.	Produces verbal behavior more than job performance.	Skill training will be improved.	Moves development out of class onto the job.
7. Future Assignments	Fails to maximize use of talent.	Useful if the descriptive terms really relate to future needs.	Useful only if future behavior is predictable.	Only useful to the extent that job objectives of the future are known.
8. Legal Requirements (EEOC)	Has been found discriminatory in many case.	Has been rejected by courts.	Job-related and hence defensible.	Defensible as being job related.

to results. Results-centered appraisals and behaviorally anchored rating scales, however, do this very well.

- Assignment of bonuses, which are usually limited to officer and major manager levels, could get into trouble if it is based on personality or descriptive ratings. Managerial work isn't easily described by specific behaviors and is best measured by overall results. Thus the results-centered appraisal system is both the best and the most prevalent one used in bonus plans. Conference Board surveys indicate that results-based appraisal for bonus calculation is now almost universal.

- Promotability in practice is very often based on personality factors and general descriptions rather than on specific behaviors or results. MBO appraisal systems are only partly useful in determining promotability. If traits or other descriptive terms are used, however, they must be clearly defined.

- The simplest way of collecting and maintaining records is found in the two forms that are the least valuable. The more complex systems are difficult to devise and to use, but their results are more useful. MBO is probably the most complex system to train people in, to devise procedures for, and to standardize, but it is worth the effort entailed in outcome.

- Training and management development programs based on appraisals are most valuable when they are results centered and require mentoring and coaching as part of their procedure. This is found only in MBO and similar results-centered systems. Personality-based management development courses often probe into personal matters better left untouched. They can produce unwanted side effects, including psychiatric damage.

 Proven performance is the best basis for predicting success in future assignments: If you want to get a job done well, give it to someone who has performed well in the past. General trait or skill descriptions have a poor track record in predicting success on specific assignments. BARS ratings are the best predictor of success where the job involved is lower level and the specific behaviors required in the assignment are clearly defined.

- In court challenges, MBO and other results-based appraisal systems have stood the tests of job relatedness, closeness of supervision, and systematic application when the supervisors involved were trained in goal setting and performance review methods. Without such training, these systems become weaker. BARS appraisal programs are clearly defensible and measurable for lower-level jobs where specific behavior can be defined. Descriptive trait and skill systems have been held by the courts to open the door to partiality and bias.

In summary, MBO for higher-level jobs and BARS for lower-level jobs appear to be the preferable choices for an appraisal system. In managing the human resources portfolio, where performance is one of the two major dimensions to be appraised, a well-developed MBO plan would appear to have the highest value. In the following chapter we'll show in detail how management by objectives can be applied to performance appraisal.

14

Setting and Achieving Performance Standards

> If you do not know where you are going, then any
> road will take you there.   —*The Koran*

As described in the previous chapter, the best standards for appraising employee performance are those that measure results against goals or objectives set for the organization as a whole or for some portion of it. Such standards grow out of the management strategy called management by objectives (MBO). Particularly in the case of lower-level jobs that require specific behaviors as well as defined outputs, Behaviorally Anchored Rating Scales (BARS) provide a good supplement to performance standards established through MBO.

In brief, the system of management by objectives can be described as a process whereby the superior and subordinate managers of an organization jointly identify its common goals, define each individual's major areas of responsibility in terms of results expected, and use these measures as guides for operating each unit and assessing the contribution of each of its members. MBO ties the strategic goals of the whole company and the operational goals of the various parts into a single, coherent structure. Because it focuses on basic goals and allows a wide latitude in approaches to achieving those goals, MBO is an ideal system for guiding and appraising performance at managerial levels.

The logical beginning point for MBO is at the top of the organization. Yet management by objectives is not entirely a top-down process, in which long-term plans are made rigidly by top management without room for accommodation to the operational experience of lower levels. At the same time, MBO is not a bottom-up process, in which various departments' short-run goals are added together to make the long-term plan. Rather, MBO provides that yearly goal setting and budgeting will be melded with long-run plans through dialogue and discussion.

The strategy of MBO implies that certain conditions exist over the whole matrix of an organization's management. First, the business must be stable and under control. Deviations from standards must be dealt with by responsible, committed persons to restore normality when objectives are not being met. Furthermore, innovation and improvement in regular operations, as well as strategic improvements that affect the character of the whole organization, must be highly valued and rewarded. Finally, the results of commitments made by people in manufacturing, selling, and staff positions must be used for decisions and action in managing managers and determining future goals.

Setting Strategic Objectives

Strategic objectives are long-term objectives that usually apply to the organization as a whole. In MBO they are most commonly embodied in a five-year plan that is revised yearly, with the previous year being dropped and a new fifth year being added each time. The plan becomes a rudimentary calendar of events expected or desired to occur in the organization during the five-year period. It provides a realistic connection between long-range planning and immediate operational goals, making them different dimensions of the same process.

The Five-Year Plan. The first step in preparing the annual edition of the five-year plan is to define the ordinary calendar of events that must occur in the organization. This entails the listing of some events that occur prior to the beginning of the target year (the first year of the five-year plan being prepared) and some events that will occur during the target year.

For a company with a fiscal year starting in January, the close-off date for the annual five-year plan would probably be July 1 of the previous year, or about three months in advance of budget submission. This timing allows budgetary planning that can move resources to new uses, seek new funding if necessary, and make decisions about the launching or abandonment of programs or plans. In addition to preparation of the annual plan, there should be quarterly reviews of results and interim adjustments of activities to keep them aligned with the year's objectives. A basic MBO strategic planning cycle is shown in Exhibit 1.

An annual five-year plan should be prepared for each major area of responsibility within the organization. Thus there should be an annual five-year personnel plan, financial plan, technical plan, and so on. These goal-setting actions on the part of staff departments allow what is called "management by anticipation."

The five-year plans should be based on audit information, which includes program audits and overall reviews of the major strengths and weaknesses of each staff department. This information should be reviewed to provide a basis for finding major opportunities and problems that may occur in the years ahead.

Once audit information is reviewed and the annual edition of the five-year plan is written and circulated, allocation of resources can occur as the third step in management by anticipation. This timing permits more rational commitment of resources, including the use of zero-based budgeting for support services and of cost-effectiveness studies of possible facility and program decisions.

How to Formulate Strategic Objectives. A suggested format for annual strategic objectives statements, showing the major concerns to be addressed by such statements, is shown in Exhibit 2. In formulating strategic objectives, the following points should be considered:

- Strategic objectives should be stated in advance of budgetary decisions.
- Strategic objectives should define strengths, weaknesses, problems, threats, risks, and opportunities.
- Strategic objectives should note trends and missions and should define options, including the consequences of each option.

**Exhibit 1. A Rudimentary MBO Strategic Planning Cycle for an
Organization Operating on a Calendar Year Basis.**

Date	Event	Comments
July 1	Completion of annual edition of the five-year plan and review of previous year's five-year plan.	Lists responsibility of the top manager and all major functional (staff) heads, assembled by planning department.
October 1	Submission of budget for the following year to decision group.	Moves upward from all units, starting with sales forecast, cost estimates, and profit forecast, to budget committee.
	Review, revision and approval of final budget figures.	Handled by Executive Committee.
January 1	Start of new budget year; release of resources.	Issue detailed, approved financial targets in final form.
January 15 to February 1	Completion of individual operational objectives at all levels.	Sets standards for managerial performance for the year.
	Annual goals conference by managers of departments.	Purpose: to share goals and improve teamwork.
	Annual message of the president.	Purpose: to give a challenge.
April-July 1 October 1	Quarterly reviews of individual results against goals, with adjustments as required.	Involves all managers at all levels.
April 15	Audits, including program audits.	Involves staff departments.
Monthly	Meetings of the executive and finance committees to note exceptions and make corrective moves.	
Passim	Preparation of position papers for circulation and discussion and policy committee actions as major issues are noted.	Done by staff experts or any responsible manager or professional or functional group.
July 1	Repetition of process.	

Exhibit 2. Format for Annual Strategic Objectives Statements.

Annual strategic objectives statements:

1. Should be prepared three months in advance of budgeting decisions.
2. Should come up from below as proposed alternative strategies.
3. Should be prepared annually at *half-year*.

OUTLINE   COMMENTS

I.   Present condition: describe statistically and ver-
     bally *(add your professional opinion):*

     1. Internally: Strengths, weaknesses, problems?
     2. Externally: What threats, risks, and opportun-
                    ities do you see?

II. Trends: If we didn't do anything differently in
     this area, where would we be in 1-2-5 years? *(Do
     you like this possible outcome?)*

III. Major missions: Why are we in business? Who
     are our clients? What is our product? What
     should it be?

| I V . What are some optional | What would the consequences be? | | |
| strategies? | Contribution | Cost | Feasibility |

1. Do nothing differently.
2. _____
3. _____
4. _____
5. _____
6. _____

(Press for multiple options)

Recommend Action Plan: To be turned into OBJECTIVES

- Strategic objectives call for indicators or criteria by which success or failure in achieving the objectives may be measured. These are the overall guides, such as ROI, by which company performance may be appraised.
- Strategic objectives should answer the question, "Are we doing the right things?"
- Strategic objectives need not necessarily be measurable, but they should use both words and numbers with clarity. An example of a strategic objective statement might be, "Apex Corporation will become the leading seller of solid-state monitoring devices by 1985."
- Strategic objectives for each staff department and major business unit should address certain key questions. These questions are shown in Exhibit 3.

Setting Operational Objectives: Management by Commitment. Sound strategic objectives should be established before operational objectives are chosen. Without strategic objectives stated in advance, operational objectives may not be valid. The result may be simply a well-run bankruptcy.

Operational objectives are established in meetings between managers and subordinate managers. Unlike strategic objectives, which answer the question, "Are we doing the right things?" operational objectives answer the question, "How do we do things right?" A major function of operational objectives is the management of managers. Objectives agreed upon between boss and subordinate become the criteria for pay, bonus, promotion, coaching, training, and selection for future assignments.

At the beginning of the operational year, each manager and subordinate manager sit down and conduct a dialogue regarding the specific operational objectives for the subordinate for the coming year. Prior to the discussion, each should review the present situation, the results of the previous year, and some of the more likely requirements for change. Each thus comes to the discussion prepared to arrive at commitments and to assume and delegate responsibilities. The boss should be armed with information about budget limitations, strategic goals that have been agreed upon by top management, and results obtained during the previous pe-

Exhibit 3. Some Key Strategy Questions to Be Answered in Defining Strategic Objectives.

1. **Market orientation.** Are we market centered or technology centered? Do we make things for the sales department to sell, or do we find market opportunities and invent things to fit?

2. **Service.** How completely do we wish to follow up our product?

3. **Top down or bottom up?** Do we have the top management (board, etc.) come up with the numbers for sales and growth and work back from the numbers at lower levels? Or do we collect the bottom-up goals and cumulate them to find the corporate goals?

4. **Indicators.** What is the best indicator (or indicators) of total organization success? Dollar profit? Percent profit? Earnings per share? Return on investment? Return on gross assets? Market share?

5. **Pricing.** Are we a market skimmer? A price cutter? Are we in price competition or nonprice competition?

6. **Ethics.** Are we a "straight arrow" company, or do we consider ourselves "rough and tough" in dealing with competitors, suppliers, employees, customers?

7. **Systems.** Do we rely more on experience and personal knowhow of managers or on systems such as computers and analytical models?

8. **Incentives.** Do we aim at sharing our profits and successes widely with employees, with just a few managers, or not at all?

9. **Employee growth.** Do we spend resources to grow our own people, or do we let them take care of that themselves and hire others from outside when a new demand for talent crops up?

10. **Technology.** Are we a basic inventor and exploiter of our own research, or do we wait for others and assume a second-bite-of-the-apple approach to new technology?

11. **Products.** Are we a cadillac, a medium-price, or a low-price product company, or perhaps all of them?

12. **Compensation.** Where do we wish to stand on employee compensation with respect to the community and competitive firms? Higher, the same, or lower?

13. **Community relations.** Are we a community leader, a middle-of-the-road citizen, or low profile and silent?

14. **Government relations.** Do we respond when required, do we permit some affirmative actions toward government, or do we assume positive leadership and work to affect government?

riod. The subordinate should come with some expectations and knowledge of his or her own performance strengths, weaknesses, and problems as well as potential external threats, risks, and opportunities.

Operational management by objectives adds a new dimension to management by anticipation. This dimension is a face-to-face relationship with the superior and, through that superior, with the organization itself. This fourth dimension could be called "management by commitment." The key to management by commitment is that the hard bargaining about what constitutes excellence of performance is done up front before the period begins— not after a year or so of effort.

Commitment means that a person makes promises to somebody else whose opinion is important to him or her. This commitment is specific, explicit, measurable, and worthwhile. *Responsibility* means that the person accepts full accountability for the outcomes produced during the commitment period, without excuses or explanations. This doesn't guarantee that a person can't fail for reasons beyond his or her control, but it implies adult behavior, professional effort, and mature self-control in engaging in one's work.

In this system the superior as well as the subordinate is committed. If the superior agrees in advance that the proposed operating goals are meritorious, those objectives are agreed to be the criteria for judging performance at the end of the period. Rewards for good or excellent performance could include salary adjustments, merit pay recommendations, bonus awards, high appraisal, promotability notations, and the like. After accepting objectives as criteria in the beginning, the superior cannot legitimately apply capricious or *ex post facto* judgments later.

For the subordinate, the objectives discussion should answer these five questions:

- What will be expected of me during the coming period?
- What help and resources will be available to me in my work?
- How much freedom may I expect, and what reporting times and form should I use?

- How can I tell how well I am doing in my work while I am doing it?
- Upon what performance bases will rewards be issued?

Operational Objectives and Their Indicators. As shown in Figure 13, operational performance objectives should be written in three categories, constituting an ascending scale of excellence. These categories can be defined as follows:

Category I   :   *regular responsibilities* of the position. These are the ongoing, recurring, repetitive, and measurable objectives of the job, such as dollar volume of sales or units per shift.

Category II :   *major problems* that should be attacked and solved in the job during the coming period. A problem is a deviation from a standard that persists and causes trouble or that somebody important wants to have fixed.

Category III: *innovations* to be attempted. These are proactive goals—improvements that will cause the unit under the subordinate's control to operate better, cheaper, faster, safer, at higher quality, or with greater dignity to people.

Exhibit 4 shows some sample regular objectives for a division general manager. It highlights some important features of regular operational objectives. First, such objectives are stated as *outputs for a time period.* Statements of activities are not objectives but means.

Second, the numbers listed in the objectives are stated as *ranges.* Superior and subordinate should define the middle or "normal/realistic" figure first. This figure should be based on history, estimates, industrial engineering studies, or sales forecasts. The subordinate should then set the optimistic or stretch objective. Finally, the superior should choose the pessimistic figure. This is the exception point at which the subordinate should notify the superior that things are not going according to plan. At that point the subordinate should know why the deviation has occurred and

Figure 13. Relating Operational Performance Objectives to Human
Resources Portfolio Valuation.

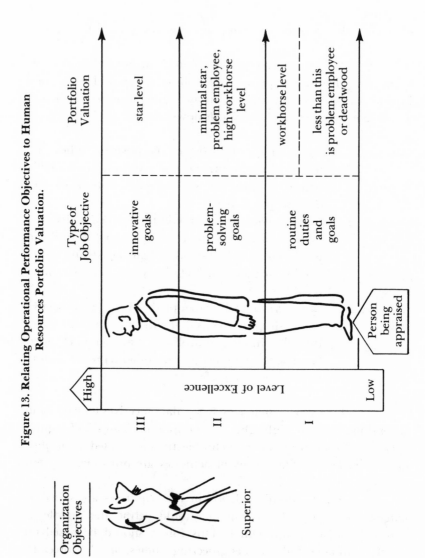

Exhibit 4. General Manager Regular-Basic Indicator Objectives.

Responsibility		Level of Result Sought		
Output Indicator	Time Period	Pessimistic	Normal Realistic	Optimistic
1. $ Volume of revenue per mo......	Qtr.			
2. Profit: R O I .... $ volume per mo.....................	Qtr. Qtr.			
3. Cash at mo. end $.......................	Qtr.			
4. Receivables: $ mo. end.............. Days.......................................	Qtr. Qtr.			
5. Inventory: mo. end $................ Turnover days......................	Qtr. Qtr.			
6. Capital budget % deviation........	Qtr.			
7. Labor problems—Step 4 Grievances	Qtr.			
8. Share of market %......................	Qtr.			
9. (Other) _____ _____ _____ _____				

Target No.	Results Scope Sheet				
	1st Qtr.	2nd Qtr.	3rd Qtr.	4th Qtr.	Total
1					
2					
3					
4					
5					
6					
7					
8					
9					

should have taken whatever corrective action seemed possible. If the subordinate is achieving in the middle range or better, he or she should be left alone to operate without interference.

Third, regular operational objectives should be stated in terms of key indicators. Indicators found to be common among the objectives of a sample of fifty general managers included the following:

- dollar volume of revenue per month
- return on investment per quarter
- cash on hand at quarter's end
- receivables, average age in days per quarter inventory, average dollar level over the quarter
- budget deviations as percent of capital budgets, growth in dollar volume per quarter, labor stoppages per year.

The pattern of regular operational objectives and indicators proceeds downward through the organizational hierarchy. The general manager's objectives must be supplemented by objectives for each of the key subordinates reporting to him or her. The manufacturing manager, for example, might have regular objectives stated in terms of these indicators:

- average daily output per month
- units per shift per month
- indirect labor as a percent of direct per month
- factory overhead as a percent of total per month
- average quality reject rate per month
- warranty and policy costs per month
- step four grievances per quarter
- overtime hours per week per quarter
- hours of supervisory training per quarter

Regular objectives for the sales manager, on the other hand, might be stated in terms of these indicators:

- dollar volume per month per quarter
- costs of producing the revenue per month per quarter

- new products introduced
- dollar level of bad debts per quarter
- days of sales training conducted per quarter
- new customers added per quarter
- lost accounts per quarter

The regular objectives for each person reporting to the general manager would be stated in terms of indicators relevant to that particular position, but all would follow a similar format.

Problem-solving objectives and innovation objectives would also be established for each position. Each statement of a problem-solving objective would define the present condition or situation, the condition that will exist if the problem is solved, and the time needed to solve the problem, stated as a range (pessimistic, realistic, optimistic). Similarly, the statement of an innovation objective would include the present condition or situation, the innovation to be attempted, the condition that will exist if the innovation works well, and the range of time that might be needed to implement the innovation.

Auditing and Reviewing Operational Objectives. Two forms of review and audit are important in MBO. The first is the periodic audit. One important kind of periodic audit is the comprehensive financial audit, which can be done by professional internal auditors or by an outside audit group such as a CPA firm. Program audits should also be performed periodically. For example, personnel audits and manpower audits for such matters as affirmative action, replacements of key persons, compliance with company or organizational personnel policy, and labor relations should be included in periodic audits. Safety audits against OSHA standards should also be included to prevent unfavorable audits by OSHA or other outside enforcement agencies. Other useful forms of periodic program audit might include technical audits, community relations audits, public responsibility audits, purchasing practices audits, and legal compliance audits for antitrust or patent protection.

In addition to these periodic audits, every manager should make ongoing reviews of his or her own performance. These reviews entail observations and notation of actual results and comparison of the results with the objectives to which the manager is committed.

Supervisory management may ask for daily, weekly, monthly, or quarterly reports of outputs.

One of the major advantages of MBO is that it permits self-measurement of results by the manager against objectives agreed upon in advance. Self-monitoring has powerful motivational effects, for the tightest and most perfect form of control is self-control. Commitment as a means of motivation is considerably enhanced when self-correction is built into the system.

As shown at the bottom of Exhibit 4, the manager should be able to post actual outcomes on the original objectives sheet and send a copy to his or her superior. The superior should respond with help and resources when these are requested or when he or she is notified that problems are present.

Finally, at the end of each operational year, superior and subordinate pull out the list of objectives prepared in advance and compare actual results against each objective. This is a preface to defining new objectives for the coming year. Such discussions should be treated as important events and should be done free from distraction. They should deal with objectives, results, problems, deviations, and improvements needed. They should avoid personal denigration or a manner that is exacting, hostile, judgmental, or punitive.

With the comparison of results against objectives in hand, the superior can make the personnel decisions that are required for portfolio analysis.

Using Operational Objectives for Portfolio Analysis. As the boss defines the three categories of objectives jointly with the subordinate, he or she is also establishing an ascending scale of performance excellence on which the subordinate can be evaluated. Since goals are produced jointly through discussion and dialogue, a higher level of commitment is likely to be present than there would be if they were simply dictated from above or dispatched in written memos. At the end of the period the boss can judge the performance results of each subordinate, using the agreed-on objectives as standards. The judgments can be expressed in portfolio management terms, as shown in Figure 13.

Deadwood are those employees who fail to perform the ordinary, routine, and regular responsibilities of their jobs. If the person is a learner, then patience, coaching, and experience may bring him or her up to minimal levels. For the experienced employee, however, failure to accomplish routine objectives is evidence of unsatisfactory performance.

Falling into the deadwood category shouldn't imply immediate discharge, certainly not the first time a person drops into this classification. A determination of whether the failure is due to "can do" or "will do" factors is necessary. That is, is the failure due to some lack of training in skills needed to do the job? If so, remedial training may be the answer. If, on the other hand, the problem is a "will do" deficiency, the implication is that the person *could* do the job but doesn't want to for some reason. Finding that reason and applying coaching, counselling, or motivational aids may solve this kind of problem.

Problem employees, unlike deadwood, have been identified as having high potential, but they share with deadwood a habit of performance failure. The performance review of a problem employee may show mixed results that meet some but not all of the job's objectives. For example, a brilliant engineer may be superior in certain kinds of innovative work but may fail to see and solve everyday problems or may be weak in routine and administrative tasks such as report preparation. Other problem employees may suffer from the "George Patton" effect. That feisty tank commander of World War II was superb under battle conditions, but in the routines of civilian affairs, public relations, and regular garrison duty, he got into trouble constantly. "Patton"-type employees respond admirably to problems during emergencies, but when things settle down and only routine work is required, they fail to perform.

Still other problem employees may have great skills in one type of work but may have been assigned to the wrong job and are not performing well there. A last type of problem employee might be a person who does some special duty with distinction but has personal habits or nonconforming behavior that disrupts the rest of the unit, wiping out the positive effects of his or her own good performance by the difficulties created for colleagues.

In the performance scale shown in Figure 13, the problem employee shows variations in levels. Since the scale of three categories comprises an *ascending* scale of excellence, missing any of them comprises a lesser level of performance.

Workhorses do all of their routine duties without fail and can usually solve everyday problems as well. They understand the procedures for doing things right, and they also understand the best responses to deviations from normality, including early notification of supervisors and effective use of supporting staff and services when major problems appear. They produce few, if any, unpleasant surprises for their bosses.

Stars, like workhorses, will fulfill all the ordinary requirements of their job and will be able to solve common problems. Two other kinds of results will also be evident in their performance appraisal. They will anticipate major and unusual problems that could change the character and direction of the organization, and they will produce imaginative and creative solutions. The unique quality of stars is that they are innovative. Peter Drucker has stated that the executive job isn't a matter of problem solving or of routine duties but of "exploiting opportunities." Thus, stars—future executives—must display evidence of being able to make things happen rather than simply watching what goes on and responding to pressures that come to them. They must be deciders, not merely drifters.

Stars create and fulfill special goals that would not even have been considered without their innovative skills. Their innovations may occur in any area of the business. As technical experts on the way up, stars demonstrate technical innovation. As staff middle managers, they form new ideas for creative staff work. As middle managers of line departments, they shape and improve the departments entrusted to them. They sense the need for changes, translate those changes into specific objectives, and then turn the objectives into reality. Lawrence Appley, longtime president of the American Management Association, suggests that the best top managers are people who see possibilities that ordinary managers do not see. They may envision something that doesn't exist at present, such as a new plant, a new product, or a new organization form. They then transmit that dream to others and enroll them in the effort of turning the vision into a reality. Warren Bennis lists this visionary quality as the most important one for successful top managers.

Peters and Waterman, in *In Search of Excellence* (1982), likewise cite vision of what might be as characteristic of the top management of excellent firms.

In performance appraisal this quality of innovation is likely to appear first in the kinds of goals that stars establish and sell to their superiors. This habitual approach to their work shows up from the earliest days of their careers. If they start in sales, for example, they add new details to their duties that produce higher levels of sales than others achieve in similar positions. Yet the risks they take are reasonable; they also do the regular things well and confront problems promptly. They move steadily upward by making changes within the framework of company practices and cultural norms. It has been said that presidents are often those who have taken unorthodox approaches to every job they have held. This should reveal itself in the MBO appraisal process as higher levels of achievement, new goals, and improvements along with good performance of ordinary duties.

Behaviorally Anchored Rating Scales (BARS) as Performance Appraisal

MBO, according to several surveys, appears to be the dominant form of performance appraisal used today, especially for managers, and it is used almost universally for bonus calculations. Yet there is some concern that when the emphasis is on results alone, the jobholder might in the process of producing those results engage in actions that could ultimately produce undesired side effects or even total disaster. Because MBO stresses outputs and results and is usually indifferent to the means by which goals are achieved, it may produce excessive attention to the short run, with long-run results that are less than desirable. Guidelines concerning the *behaviors* needed to achieve an MBO-type goal are seldom provided. This can be remedied by a system that defines and appraises means as well as goals.

Many jobs, even for managers and professionals, require that specific procedures be followed or avoided. In industries like banking or insurance, management is responsible for the safety of other people's money, and security procedures must be included in objectives. In pharmaceutical and chemical businesses there are safety and health procedures that must be followed and controlled without fail. In certain office jobs such as tax preparation or public accounting, conventional accounting practices are essential parts of the job objectives. Methods of taking inventory can have an important bearing upon working capital management, so the desired method becomes part of the job objectives. In instances such as these, when measurement of results against objectives must be accompanied by means tests, BARS is a rigorous and scientific approach that can make a valuable contribution to performance appraisal.

Most BARS statements use a standard format (Schneir and Beatty, 1979). It includes the job title and a statement of the dimensions of the job, anchors for good performance, anchors for fair performance, and anchors for poor performance. *Anchors* are specific statements of behavior that illustrate performance at each level of excellence.

For example, a sales manager might have some responsibility for credit losses realized from sales orders. As an MBO objective, this would merely require an overall end result or output. Over time the sales manager, under pressure to achieve sales volume goals, might begin to take risks, cut corners, and fail to make required checks on the credit rating of customers before accepting their orders. The result could be a serious bad debt loss. A BARS statement for the credit area of the sales manager's job might include the following behavioral descriptions as anchors for good performance:

- Prior to the acceptance of an order from a new and unknown customer, the sales department will report the order and its size to the credit department.
- The sales department will await a report from the credit department on the potential customer's credit rating and suggested limits of credit before accepting an order.
- The sales department will direct rejection or acceptance of orders based on the recommendations in the credit report.
- Any new information that might affect a customer's credit rating will be reported to the credit department within one week of its receipt.

Note that all the anchors focus on verbs, such as *report, await,* and *direct.* They are descriptions of *actions* or *behavior.* Anchors for poor performance would probably include failures to perform the preceding actions and might also include such statements as "accepting new business without checking." BARS anchors deal only with activities that can be seen, measured, counted, or pictured—not with psychological processes.

Coupled with MBO, BARS provides an excellent standard for measuring job performance. While it is clearly most applicable to lower- or middle-level jobs—typical workhorse positions—BARS may be an important element in performance appraisal for many kinds of jobs. The disadvantage of BARS lies in the detailed attention that must be paid to each job when preparing the anchors—a time-consuming and often difficult task. Since the BARS anchors often apply to more than one job, it is useful to use group discussion in shaping the anchors. This will improve their reliability and enhance the motivation of people to stick with the anchors produced.

Pressures of time may keep BARS from being feasible for some companies, but if an organization is determined to do performance appraisal thoroughly and with full cognizance of the ways in which performance appraisal systems will be scrutinized in the future, BARS is a worthwhile investment.

BARS to Help Problem Employees. One worthwhile application of BARS is in the case of the employee who is recognized as having high potential over the long run but whose immediate job performance is deficient. Going through a BARS exercise may define the specific behaviors that are missing from the employee's performance and allow full exploitation of his or her potential. Teaching the details of asking for an order or making sales presentations can often make the difference between a successful salesperson and a loser, for example. Results produced by people who have fallen into ineffective work habits may be improved by doing a careful study of their jobs and preparing BARS anchors for the areas where improvement is needed. BARS is especially useful as a coaching device because it deals with specifics. Coaching that is based only on generalities ("Are you hitting the ball, Harry?") often does more harm than good.

Figure 14. The Key Elements in Performance Appraisal.

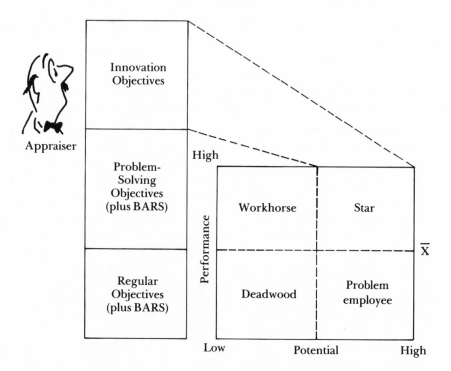

BARS may be the key to devising a specific improvement program for a subordinate whose performance has been lower than expected or hoped for. Statements of the type, "You said you would produce 10,000 widgets a week and you missed it" do give comparison of results against goals, but unless the subordinate knows what went wrong and how to improve, the performance review will be merely a punishing experience. By means of the anchors, BARS defines *where* the performance went wrong and what specific action is needed to remedy performance in the future.

BARS is valuable not only during the goal-setting process but also at the end of the evaluation period and in feedback given during the period. If a workhorse or deadwood is failing, exhortations and reprimands won't convey the knowledge of what went wrong and what must be done to improve results. BARS has this capacity.

In summary, performance is a key element in assessing the worth of assets in the human resources portfolio. Performance appraisal for all job categories should center around the results sought. As shown in Figure 14, the vertical line of measurement in the portfolio includes objectives of the job in terms of output for a period of time, broken down into the three categories of routine, problem solving, and innovation, plus BARS anchors for those jobs where specific behavior is part of the objectives of the job.

15

Strategic Human Resource Planning

A little leaven leaveneth the whole lump.
—*1 Corinthians*

The decade of the seventies saw significant changes in the role of the personnel department. For one thing, its name changed. "Human resources" replaced industrial relations, employee relations, or personnel department as the label most often attached to this staff function. The switch to "Human resources" is, in fact, more than a name change; it implies a departure from the traditional paths that have guided this department since the first formal personnel departments sprang into existence following World War I. This new outlook has raised the sights of its professional practitioners and changed the kinds of people who succeed at its tasks. Dale Yoder, a pioneer in personnel theory, predicted some thirty years ago that personnel departments would evolve into "human resources management," and this prediction came true during the seventies. Two features of the change stand out: (1) human resources departments became more central to the purposes of their firms, and (2) this new role centered around strategic considerations rather than operations details. The human resources

284

staff has become a leaven that raises the whole loaf of organization life.

The Changing Role of Staff

The first step in understanding the new role of the human resources staff is to understand the changing role of staff in general. The role of staff departments has grown in all areas of the business universe. Marketing, engineering, traffic, legal, purchasing, finance, public affairs, and other staff departments rose in size and importance as the hourly wage work force declined. Staff departments tended to be made up of more highly educated people than formerly, and the management of these high-talent human assets assumed a higher level of significance to the future of the firm.

Yet many firms today find their corporate staff departments to be sources of considerable discontent. Although the cost of staff employees is rising as professional salaries leap, this increasing expenditure often is not accompanied by commensurate increases in output. Furthermore, many staff members are becoming increasingly dissatisfied, reporting that they feel powerless, baffled, and irrelevant in their specialists' role. This leads to what consultant Clark Caskey (1968) has called the "mess in middle management."

Much of this professional discontent can be attributed to the traditional, often outmoded, views of staff functions—views rooted in the "staff-serves-the-line" philosophy—that reduce most corporate staff positions to the status of elegant flunky jobs. With the possible exception of controllers and a few engineers, staff people cannot look forward to general executive responsibility. At best they will have an ascending career within their department, leading to an ultimate dead end. Many staff members have slowly realized that they have but one thing in common with the company president: neither can expect to go any further in the organization.

Attempts to resolve the problems of staff discontent by applying orthodox MBO plans, which work quite well in manufacturing and selling situations, have had a dismal record because staff work often takes years to show results. Furthermore, outputs are frequently not under the control of the accountable staff person. Since the outputs are intangible, they can seldom be measured in the same way that the results of plant or sales managers' efforts can be measured.

Joseph Juran (1961), a New York management consultant, has stated that staff departments of large corporations are actually makers of "software" (intangible products) that they sell to internal management. These products fall into four major categories: advice, service, information, and new knowledge. Today some corporate staff departments are assuming new and significant roles in management by adding a fifth product line: strategic planning.

This "new product line" benefits everyone concerned. Putting staff professionals' knowledge and experience to work in problem-solving and planning functions is an efficient and cost-effective use of human resources. Furthermore, where staff people in areas such as personnel, public relations, employment, engineering, accounting, and data processing are encouraged to make innovative contributions to strategic planning, their motivation, zeal, and creative responses are greatly increased.

Analyzing Staff Output. The first step in turning a staff into strategic planners is to analyze their present functions by breaking down total staff time into percentages devoted to producing different kinds of outputs—the "intangible products" mentioned previously. Each staff department, in collaboration with its supervising officer, should prepare a statement dividing its outputs into the five major categories of advice, service, information, new knowledge, and strategic statements, as shown in Exhibit 5. This process should start with the subgroups within each staff area being studied. The human resources department, for example, should require this two-column estimate from the supervisor of each subdepartment as well as preparing a final summary of the entire department for discussion with the administrative officer over that department.

Some practical hints for completion of this analytic tool would include the following:

- The total of all outputs from the five major classes should equal 100 percent. Most staff department efforts, resources, time, and results can be forced into one or more of these categories without undue stretching of definitions.

Exhibit 5. Staff Department Output Analysis Chart.

Area of effort, activity, or output	Present percentage for year ___	Target for ___
1. *Advice.* In this category show what percentage of staff effort goes to producing advice, counsel, opinions, specific recommendations (legal, technical, personnel, etc.).		
2. *Service.* This includes things done for other line or staff departments that they probably can't do for themselves. It may be technical, administrative, or human resource services. It is usually stated in terms of units produced (people hired, units repaired, service complaints processed, etc.).		
3. *Information.* This means data, facts, reports produced. They may be routine, special, response, for internal users, for government agencies, for customers or suppliers. Would be characteristic of accounting, data processing, and similar staff departments.		
4. *New knowledge.* This means invention, research-data analysis, market research, and the like.		
5. *Strategic statements.* This means outputs and activities that deal with future outcomes, hoped for conditions, new ideas to be implemented in the future, or analysis for strategic planning.		

Note: This analysis is intended to determine the posture and general objectives of specific staff departments and subdepartments. The first step is to determine the mix of objectives and strategic areas for each subdepartment; then a summary will be prepared for the entire staff department. Thus the personnel department report should be a cumulation from the reports of substaffs such as training, labor relations, compensations, benefits, employment, and so on.

- Usually it is safe to assume that one of the five functions will account for about 80 percent of the work of a given staff department. For example, the accounting department will ordinarily be about 80 percent information (category 3), while the employment department or customer-services department will ordinarily be 80 percent service (category 2) and corporate counsel will put about 80 percent of its effort into producing advice (category 1). Research labs should be devoting as much as 80 percent of their efforts to producing new knowledge (category 4), with the remainder being spent on advice and technical service.

- The two columns should be filled in separately. The first column, "present percentage," should be as factual as the best estimates of the staff members involved can make it. After column 1 has been filled in and studied, then column 2, the target mixture of products from the staff department, can be determined. A research lab, for example, might find that it is engaged in too much technical service and not enough research. The lab might then devise a plan to (1) increase its knowledge output, and (2) reduce its technical-service function by dispersing this work to other departments. This determination of targets is the key to improving the effectiveness of staff departments. The targets also provide a model for discussion of each department's objectives.

Staff as Strategic Planners. The department that finds itself doing little, if any, strategic planning for its own areas of concern is probably not contributing to the long-run effectiveness of the firm. Strategic planning in staff departments allows better bottom-up management of staff talent, more effective use of zero-based budgets, and more appropriate shifts in resources to suit the future needs of the organization.

As they develop strategic plans for their departments, staff members learn that strategic management:

- Entails thinking of new concepts and rethinking old systems and ideas.

- Often contains an element of surprise for somebody—perhaps the management of the firm, maybe the customer, and most certainly the competition.
- Answers the question "Are we doing the right things?" rather than "Are we doing things right?"
- Requires that each staff department be prepared to submit the best fruits of its expertise for inclusion in the firm's multiyear business plans rather than simply responding to overtures initiated by management.

Once staff members assume the role of strategic planners, they must begin to think like strategic planners. They must not concern themselves so much with operational objectives—those short-term goals that are easily measured, tough perhaps but realistically attainable within a relatively short time period. These remain the domain of the line manager, the plant manager, the sales manager, and the service manager.

How will staff members know whether their objectives are really strategic? Here are ten characteristics of good strategic objectives:

- They almost always take more than one year to execute—perhaps five or ten years or even more.
- They change the character and direction of the business and often require something wholly new and surprising.
- They require that a view of outside influences, such as government, competition, or tastes and values of society, be incorporated in the form of assumptions or projections.
- They are more than forecasts; they are inventive and creative, not simply projective.
- They call for consideration of the resources that will be required over the long haul and the returns that will be achieved by expending those resources. When they relate to budgets, the budgets in question are multiyear financial forecasts.
- They involve making decisions in the face of uncertainty and imperfect information, in an imperfect world, with imperfect people. Therefore they are not nearly as precise in their first form as are operational objectives.

- They extend well into the future but are revised annually on a rolling basis, like the movement of a sand dune. Each time a year is completed, a new edition of the five-year or ten-year plan is prepared.
- They are based on detailed analysis and study, not on impulse or wishful thinking.
- They employ numbers as much as possible, but their most important characteristic is incorporating experienced judgment of senior management.

Creative Goal Setting. To aid staff members in their new roles as strategic planners and stir their imaginations, creative goal setting using MBO may be applied. The purpose of these goals should be improvement. Anything can be done better, faster, cheaper, easier, more safely, and with greater dignity to people if people are committed to changing the status quo. If a critical mass of people in an organization starts with the assumption that things can be improved, things are sure to get better.

Creative goal setting can be divided into two categories. The first, extrinsic creativity, comes from introducing new ideas from another source. Applying existing technology to new situations requires that the initiator take three logical steps:

1. Master the technology and become an expert in its theory and applications by study, investigation, and questioning.
2. Do a feasibility study to determine whether it will fit the proposed new use and what changes and modifications will be required to make it work in its new home.
3. Install the new method, with due recognition of its experimental nature and willingness to hang on through the debugging period.

The second kind of creative goal setting is intrinsic creativity, which is finding the germ of a new method within a present method. This is the basic idea of work-simplification programs. One starts by studying the present system exhaustively, listing every detail fully. One then questions every part of the present method: Why is this necessary? What is its purpose? Where should it be done? How should it be done? When should it be done? Who should do it? One should even ask whether the whole thing should be done at all. (That's the ultimate in work simplification—eliminating the job altogether.) From this, one often comes up with a better way of doing things. Inside every job, every process, every product is something new crying out to be discovered and released by an observing analysis.

If you believe that something can be improved, you will be sure to discover the way to improve it. The great barrier to innovative goal setting isn't in technical incapacity but in the human attitude that things are okay, or perfect, or beyond improvement. The fact that something has been improved recently doesn't mean that it can't be improved again.

Creative goal setting will work only if an organization's management follows these five steps to encourage change:

1. Ask corporate staff for innovation and expect to get it.
2. Train people in methods of creativity and innovation in ongoing educational programs.
3. Get commitments to innovation from both individuals and teams.
4. Let people know that the status quo is not good enough and that standing still will not be rewarded.
5. Reward innovation and creativity in tangible ways such as pay increases, bonuses, awards, or promotions. Do not promote stodgy, antiinnovative people.

Endorsement and support of creativity and innovation in policy, supervision, and recognition will lift some of the natural bureaucratic barriers to innovation that organizations tend to establish.

The Importance of Explicit Planning. People doing strategic planning must accustom themselves to deferred gratification rather than to the immediate pleasure of achievement so often sought in today's business world. It is often difficult, therefore, to find people who have the patience to define strategic objectives and work successfully at them. Deferred gratification is not something most Americans of today are comfortable with.

We also seem to like implicit better than explicit planning. Most corporations still hang on to a heavy dose of nineteenth-century mentality when it comes to planning. Their frontier or cowboy mentality assumes that luck, hard work, grit, and a pell-mell approach to the unknown will make things work out okay (implicit planning). It sees such things as detailed planning and careful forecasts (explicit planning) as parts of a plot by pointy-headed intellectuals to strap down human ingenuity and initiative.

The nineteenth-century American tended to believe that if things didn't work out on this plot of land, one could always pack up, move over to the next mountain, and start again. The west was developed by people who didn't have an office of management and budgets to make rulings on such things as the cost-effectiveness of the Louisiana Purchase or the acquisition of Alaska. The only problem with such thinking is that we have run out of old-style frontiers and have as yet failed to develop new ones.

It is true that Andrew Carnegie became the first billionaire without having a single Harvard Business School graduate on his payroll or a single professor as a consultant. Daniel Boone and Davy Crockett didn't have specific, detailed objectives when they mounted their horses and rode west. But times have changed. Most of the west is overdeveloped, and the side effects of uncontrolled mining, forestry, and superhighways have come home to haunt us.

What is the best way to implant a strategic objectives outlook in the minds of the implicit planners—one could say the anti-planners—on one's staff? First, training in the benefits of explicit planning and goal setting helps make such techniques familiar and eases the suspicion about setting goals. Second, developing skills in actual goal setting can make the transition to explicit planning more comfortable. Third, rewards should be reserved for people who can define good strategic goals and then make them happen. These three elements are within the control of management and should be part of the top agenda for staff leaders.

In summary, explicit strategic planning is a vital activity in today's better-managed companies. It points out areas that companies can begin working in and methods they can use to better prepare themselves for the many challenges and changes coming in the 1980s and 1990s.

Strategic Planning for Human Resources

In view of the general increased emphasis on strategic planning, it is not surprising that human resources administrators have been pressed to do more strategic planning and have responded seriously to this demand. Some recent trends in strategic planning and strategic management for corporations at large would fit the human resources strategic planning process quite comfortably. One such idea is that of finding a paramount strategy or central theme of strategic management for the firm. Tregoe and Zimmerman (1980) call this *strategic drive,*—the driving strategy that characterizes the company's forward look. While the idea that a company is "technology driven" or "market driven" has appeared in the literature before, it has not previously been applied to managing human resources.

Driving Forces and Human Resources Strategy. Often the human resources (personnel) strategy of a firm is derived from the driving strategy of the business as a whole. That is, if the firm is "technology driven," then the recruiting, hiring, placement, and compensation of engineers and scientists with specialties in needed areas will be the driving strategy of the human resources people in the firm.

Amway, Avon, and Stanley Home Products have as their driving strategic force a method of distribution. They sell only door-to-door, and their sales representatives are usually part-timers, often without prior experience. They rely on a high level of motivation, enthusiasm, and spirited persistence to produce gains in sales and profits. They offer little in terms of technical breakthroughs, sticking to fundamental health, beauty aid, proprietary drug and kitchen products. The delivery of the product into the home, with sales occurring on the doorstep or in the living room, by part-time salespersons who are mostly women, defines a whole set of human resources strategies that have become paramount to the success of these firms. Recruiting part-timers and amateurs and training them is vital. The compensation system is mainly commission based. Except for a small corps of people who perform sales support, product development, manufacturing, and other staff jobs, there is no provision for high employee benefits, job security, or similar personnel policies that characterize most other firms.

McDonald's and similar fast food firms, on the other hand, use a different method of distribution as a driving strategy: standardized local franchise facilities that prepare standardized menu items to exacting criteria in precise and often tightly choreographed fashion. The extreme standardization allows them to offer lower prices than would be possible in more personalized restaurants. The paramount personnel strategy in such firms is to hire mostly youthful workers, often high school or college students, who learn the necessary procedures under tight organization, detailed training, and close supervision and carry them out with the precise timing of a professional football team. These firms also make occasional forays into employment of immigrants from Cuba and Mexico or other persons who occupy the lowest levels of the labor market.

In each organization and each business unit within a larger corporation, the human resources strategy must fit the corporate or business driving strategy. The driving force of the business will determine the best mix for its human resources portfolio. Certainly it will determine who is likely to become a company star. It is unlikely that a nonaviator will go far in the Strategic Air Command, nor a nonchemist or chemical engineer in a firm such as Dow, for example. Table 7 gives examples of firms with different driving forces and the occupations that are most important in each.

Elements of Human Resources Strategy. Three major elements must be considered in defining a business's paramount strategy for dealing with human resources. They may be described as follows:

Demand strategy. The shape and direction of a business and its central themes create the demand for the kinds of people it will require. Personnel and human resources departments that misread their company's driving strategy will be likely to fall into wrong policies, programs, procedures, and organization. The firm that operates through a method of distribution centering on small local units, like Pizza Hut, Manpower Incorporated, or Kentucky Fried Chicken will have little or no use for MBA stars from Harvard or Stanford. A corporate drive to control natural resources will create a demand for metallurgists, chemical engineers, and other people willing to go to wild places to explore for oil, operate paper mills, or mine for copper. Personnel policies intended to meet the needs

Table 7. The Driving Forces and Their Effects
on Human Resources Strategy.

Driving Force for Organization	Sample Organizations	Predominant Human Resource Needs
1. Resource	Anaconda, Gulf	metallurgist, geologist, contract officer
2. Technology	Texas Instruments, Hewlett-Packard	engineer, physicist
3. Product	Pratt & Whitney, General Motors	production expert, designer
4. Market need	Gillette, Colgate, General Mills	marketer, product manager, ad manager
5. Method of sale	Avon, Amway, Stanhome, Tupperware	house-to-house salesperson
6. Method of delivery	Consolidated Edison, local phone companies, Strategic Air Command	rate negotiator, craftsperson
7. Growth	I.T.T., United Technologies, Allied Corp.	mergers expert, general manager, staff head
8. Earnings	General Electric, IBM, Marriott	group executive, general manager
9. Finance	Citibank, Prudential, Merrill Lynch	lending officer, group vice-president

of such people will be different from those of a large insurance company whose stars are actuaries working in opulent offices in New York or Hartford.

Supply Strategy. The driving strategy of the firm narrows down the kinds of labor supply that are available for its jobs. The chemical production plant in New Jersey employs some lab chemists, but it relies much more heavily upon skilled craftspeople in trades such as pipefitter, carpenter, rigger, millwright, electrician, electronics technician, and instrumentation technician. Often such skilled craftspeople outnumber unskilled workers by more than two to one and outnumber engineers and managers by four to one. Thus the process-centered nature of the plant produces a paramount human resources strategy that is founded on the supply of skilled labor in the workhorse category. It must seek out people with aptitudes for mechanical and technician trades, focus its training efforts on craft skills, generate local community support and increased labor supply through vocational educational programs, and have skilled labor relations negotiators and floor representatives to speedily and competently process grievances with a variety of craft unions.

The efficient human resources portfolio for McDonald's or Burger King, made up mostly of youthful employees, would be worse than useless in such an environment. Thus the supply of labor for the chemical plant is utterly different from that for the fast foods shop. Consciously shaping the best human resources portfolio for each company is the strategic challenge presented to human resources administrators in the eighties.

Pricing Strategy. Price, as rudimentary economics training teaches us, is determined by the confluence of supply and demand. What and how a company should pay its people—whether minimum wage, by commission, at the average going rate for the labor market, or above the maximum—is not a function of the beneficence or parsimoniousness of its management. Rather, it is determined by the paramount human resources strategy as worked out by portfolio analysis, which in turn is derived from the central driving strategy of the business.

For the oil company that bases its future on exploration, high salaries for a strong corps of skilled and experienced geologists are central to its strategy. For the firm that grows by mergers, its accountants, lawyers, and tax people are worthy of the highest salary levels if they succeed in expediting the growth that is central to its driving strategy.

For a food service contractor such as Saga or ARA Services, where hiring local labor, mainly workhorses and even managerial deadwood, to perform relatively unskilled tasks is the central human resources strategy and costs must be kept to a minimum if the company is to provide clients with services at prices lower than they could get for themselves, paying minimum wage is an essential part of the strategy. This in turn generates a whole set of human resources policies, including a willingness to accept high turnover, a protocol for hiring large numbers of people as replacements for those departing, and a supervisory practice that motivates low-paid and unskilled workers through human relations programs, careful diagnosis, and remedial training.

Planning a Human Resources Strategy. Some basic questions arise for those trying to devise a human resources strategic plan.

- Has top management consciously chosen the direction and nature of the business? If so, what is their driving strategy?
- What features of the company's driving strategy could affect human resources strategies?
- Do people in the human resources department know the paramount human resources strategies (supply, demand, and prices)? Can they answer these questions: What labor markets do we hire from? What demand do we have, and what quality of person is demanded?
- Does each of the department's key managers agree on the choice of paramount strategy? If not, why not? Where did they get their ideas? What needs to be done to resolve this disagreement?
- Do the company's staff and line managers understand the strategy, and are they willing to work to implement it? Line and staff participation is essential to effective portfolio analysis.
- Is the strategy clear enough to turn into programs, policies, and procedures in the organization's personnel departments? A portfolio analysis that is not turned into action is useless.
- Will the paramount strategy be used to make future personnel decisions, including what is urged, what is permitted, and what is excluded?
- Are personnel policy manuals reviewed on a regular basis to adapt them to changes in strategy and in content of the human resources portfolio?
- Are the budgetary and financial implications of the present paramount strategy and proposed changes in that strategy worked out? Portfolio analysis must add to profit, value added, and cost-effectiveness, or it will not survive.
- Is information about the environment and about legal constraints and requirements included in strategy estimates? These

factors help to determine measurement of performance and assessment of potential, the two key portfolio dimensions.

- In corporate mergers and acquisitions, are the personnel strategies of the target firm explored to determine how they might affect the success of the acquisition? How is the main company's portfolio impacted by mergers and acquisitions?

- Is all portfolio information up-to-date and relevant to organization goals? Are actual effects of human resources strategy audited and compared against theoretical projections? The portfolio is an annual balance sheet, not a daily task or a monthly performance review. It is the major audit instrument for human resources staff effectiveness.

Choosing the Best Portfolio. Money and people are at the core of all business driving strategies. Despite the often-discussed shortage of capital these days, most worthy programs will find financial support. The human resources dilemma is more complex. A strategic drive that is brilliant from the business, technical, and financial points of view can still fall on its face if the precise human resources portfolio needed to implement it is not available.

A good human resource portfolio strategy has the following characteristics:

- It is tailor made and custom planned for the present and future of the individual firm. There are some general portfolio management principles, but they need drastic modification for different strategic situations.

- The generalized concept of the "good employee" needs to be set aside in favor of a more sophisticated model. The good employee in coal mine probably would not be a good employee in a chain of women's-wear boutiques, nor would the management of the two be likely to be similar.

- Some common articles of faith in personnel management have to be examined and perhaps thrown out in specific situations. For example, there are instances where employee turnover is highly desirable and should be effected by policies that will produce the desired turnover level. There are other situations in which the high cost of turnover is so unthinkable that turnover should be discouraged by every imaginable means.

- The attractiveness of a labor market from which to recruit is not a function of the market itself or of any of its components but rather of the human resources portfolio of the hiring firm.
- The suitability of wage, salary, and benefit plans is not determined solely by labor market surveys and estimates of equity; it is also determined by contribution to the human resources portfolio of the firm. The strategy of some firms demands minimum-wage or commissioned employees while others have a strategy that requires making successful stars very rich.

It quickly becomes apparent that finding a paramount human resources strategy, building a human portfolio to execute it, and managing that portfolio place human resources itself in the central core of management strategy making. This reinforces what many scholars have been noting for years, that the line between general management and human resources management becomes thinner and thinner until it appears that the key to any company's success lies in its ability to build a suitable paramount human resources strategy and execute it in program and practice by means of a properly developed and managed human resources portfolio.

Implementing a Human Resources Portfolio Analysis. Case studies of firms that have implemented human resources portfolio analysis offer some guidelines to the organization that wishes to try portfolio analysis for the first time.

1. *Use portfolio analysis as a strategic tool.* The most important element in beginning is to note that portfolio analysis is not a day-to-day, week-to-week, or month-to-month operating tool. It is not a profit improvement instrument but a balance-sheet instrument that measures the value of certain key assets, the firm's human resources. It is thus a strategic tool. Its major use is in shaping annual editions of the five-year or other multiyear plan of the firm. Its purpose is long-term development of the human resources of the firm through clear identification of the quality of the human capital on hand.

2. *Incorporate human resource planning into the company calendar.* The typical firm has some kind of calendar of managerial

events in its planning process. Often this is a series of closing dates, such as the following:

- Organizational audits and reviews of the most recent year's performance and present condition should be done in the spring of each year, about April 15 through May 1.
- The annual edition of the long-range business plan of the firm is to be submitted about the middle of the previous year, that is, around the first of July.
- Budget requests are to be filed about the first of October if the firm is on a January-December fiscal year.

Human resource portfolio analysis should be planned to fit into the firm's existing calendar. In the example just given, the calendar for human resources portfolio analysis might read like this:

- Between January and April, performance appraisals and assessments of potential submitted by line managers on their subordinates should be collected and analyzed by human resources staff. From these the portfolio itself, which will include everyone in the organization—or at least all technical, managerial, and professional personnel—will be constructed. Computerized human resources information systems can add immensely to the speed and uniformity of this construction.
- Using the best staff advice available as well as the participation of division general managers and key department heads, the portfolio should be reviewed, and multiyear strategic plans for new directions to be taken to improve the balance and upgrade the value of the portfolio should be devised. The Review Board method, described in Chapter Five, offers an excellent vehicle for the review of the portfolio. If used, it should be scheduled in late spring after the staff work is complete. Each division manager and department head should meet with the top management review board to discuss the human assets under his or her charge. Plans for finding challenging assignments for stars, solutions for problem employees, better motivation for workhorses, and remediation or disposition of deadwood should be discussed.

- Human resources department budgets should be set up to reflect decisions made in regard to the human resources strategic plan. If the top management of the firm has agreed on the dimensions of the portfolio and devised the strategies for its upgrading, there will seldom be problems with finding budgetary resources to implement the needed actions.

- Annual operating objectives for the personnel and human resources departments, including those related to salary administration, benefits, bonus administration, training and management development programs, hiring plans, and other chronic concerns, should be set to move in the direction laid out in the strategic human resources plan.

3. *Involve managers widely in the process.* Without general management involvement, human resources portfolio analysis will become merely another pet project of the personnel department. Strong support from the top is required. General management participation includes mandatory filling out of performance appraisals by every manager for every subordinate, an assessment of the potential of every manager, and clear-cut decisions about the respective role and status of every person on the salaried payroll. Extension of portfolio analysis into hourly and clerical ranks should probably be deferred until the most highly talented and therefore the most highly paid employees—the technical, managerial, and professional staff— have been valued.

   The creation of a personnel policy or human resources policy committee is common in many large firms. Often this is merely the management committee of the firm under another name. If a special human resources committee is formed, it should include high-level executives, with the staff assistance of the human resources manager. In many firms this staff chief sits in on the meetings as secretary and is responsible for producing necessary documentation, managing the meeting, disseminating its decisions, and implementing the actions agreed upon.

4. *Build, upgrade, and provide training in use of the two basic measurement instruments.* Two sets of procedures, with neces-

sary forms, instruction manuals, and plans for full training of all managers in their use, are required. The first is a procedure for results-centered performance appraisal, and the second is a procedure for assessment of potential. Appraisal and assessment procedures that imply clear standards, uniformly applied and administered by trained people, increase the defensibility of decisions made about the human resources portfolio.

The exact design of appraisal forms will depend on the needs of the company, but some general rules to keep in mind while constructing such forms might include the following:

- The simpler the form, the better. Many good programs such as MBO have foundered on too much paperwork, which a besieged and overworked management team rejects or executes in a perfunctory or offhand manner.

- The summary goal statements in a results-based appraisal system should be limited to three pages at most. If they deal with outputs rather than activity, this should be possible. Dividing the goals into the three categories of regular, problem solving, and innovation clarifies and simplifies the process.

- The documents that are finally filed with the personnel administrator should be clear summaries of the major conclusions, not extensive reports like case studies filed by a social worker. Facts, not verbiage, should prevail.

The courts have found that where procedures for performance appraisal exist on paper but the people who must make the appraisal decisions have not been trained in their use, the system is not effective. All managers, therefore, must be trained in the use of whatever appraisal and assessment systems the company chooses. The performance appraisal form itself must be used as part of the training course, along with examples and illustrations of its use. If the form is results centered, role play and demonstrations of the best way to conduct goal-setting interviews and postappraisal interviews should also be included. Managers may need to be trained in effective listening, coaching, counselling, and face-to-face communication methods to maximize the quality and acceptance of the appraisal system. This training may be given in a number of forms, including Transactional Analysis (TA), which has many valuable applications to appraisal interviewing.

The assessment of potential may be handled through another form, or it may be accomplished by interviewing managers. As described in Chapter Five, potential assessment may be made through assessment center actions, review board decisions, or staff analysis. It should cover the six basic factors described in that chapter. Where the assessment center method of identifying potential is employed, training for assessors must precede their service on such panels.

5. *Keep portfolio analysis current and modify it.* Periodic review of the many facets of portfolio analysis will help it retain vitality and usefulness. William Streidl, management development director at Tenneco, has found that bringing in behavioral scientists to do rigorous research into the effectiveness of the company's MBO program and other development efforts generates a continued high level of interest in such programs among managers as well as improving the quality of the programs themselves.

16

The Case of the Plains City Millers: An Illustration of Portfolio Management

The Plains City Millers is a baseball team that plays in the major leagues. It has an affiliated farm club, the Big City Batbreakers. The team and its club were acquired by two wealthy businessmen, Bert and Harry, who had long desired to own a baseball team. The men could afford their expensive hobby, but they had no desire to dump endless amounts of money into the team. Indeed, they even had a glimmering hope of being able to make a profit on it or eventually sell it at a capital gain.

In January they hired Professor Smothers, a member of State University's faculty in sports management, to serve as a consultant on the management of their player personnel. Smothers established a system for valuation of the team's human resources portfolio.

Smothers explained to the two owners, "The basic tool we will use for the valuation of the player roster is a portfolio approach, the same technique a mutual fund or investment officer in a bank would use to assess the value of his stock and bond portfolio.

Remember that all of the players are under contract. This recognizes that they may not be around next year—they may quit, be injured, play out their option, or lose their skills for one reason or another. Remember also that we own the affiliated Batbreakers, so when we call up a player from that club we don't pay the going market price.

"In effect, we can classify every player into one of the squares in this portfolio. By the act of classifying we will find an ideal suggested strategy for managing that player," said Professor Smothers as he laid out the portfolio chart before the owners (Figure 15).

"As you can see, we have two dimensions by which to measure the players. The left-hand side measures the actual statistical results they are producing right now—their performance. The horizontal line across the bottom measures or rates their potential for future productivity to the team. In finance you would call this the "expected stream of future income." Bert nodded in understanding.

Figure 15. Plains City Millers Baseball Club, Inc., Player Portfolio.

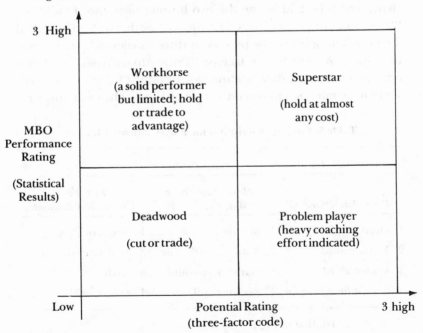

"Let's look at the four categories of players," Smothers went on. "*Stars* are players who have high potential, are playing up to that potential fully, and have a fairly long time left to play. *Workhorses* are your good solid players who do very well, but they may be aging a bit so that their time span for future productivity is short. They should be well paid but not overpaid, and they may be good trading material. *Problem players* are players with a lot of time left and with excellent skills, but whose performance isn't up to par. They need a lot of attention from coaches, trainers, doctors, and the manager to bring them up to their potential. If it can't be done, they should be traded or even cut. *Deadwood* are players who used to be stars or workhorses, but for one reason or another they simply don't contribute any more, and improvement seems unlikely. A trade or cut is indicated clearly for this group.

"Our basic objective is to make a return on your investment," Professor Smothers pointed out. "If we win games and thus draw big gates, we will be more likely to show a high income, but the objective isn't primarily to win games."

Smothers reached into his briefcase again and took out a chart, which he laid before the two businessmen. (See Exhibit 6.) "If you study this roster," he said, "you will see that we have classified the potential of all of the players in three categories." He pointed to column A, which was labeled "Price Attractiveness." "If you refer to the chart called 'coding description' (Table 8), you will see that we rate each player on a scale of 1 to 4. The most attractive

Table 8. Coding Description for Player Potential Rating.

Code A	Code B	Code C
Price Attractiveness	Player Life Cycle Maturity Level	Five-Year Production Estimate
1. Overvalued	1. Mature/decline	1. Negative
2. Fairly valued	2. Rapid growth state	2. Moderate/average
3. Undervalued	3. Start-up/youthful	3. High
4. Exceptional bargain	4. Rookie regular	4. Exceptional

Note: Highest rating is 4, lowest is 1.

Exhibit 6. Human Resources Analysis of Potential—Plains City Millers.

Prepared by: _____ Reviewed by: _____
Date: _____ Date: _____

	Name	Position	*Code A Price Attractiveness	*Code B Maturity	*Code C Five-Year Forecast	Total
1	Aaron, H.	P	2	3	3	8
2	Jones, M.	RP	1	1	1	3
3						
4						
5						
6						
7						
8						

*Refer to coding description for criteria

player is the undervalued player—one who is not being paid up to the league average for a person in his position or with his performance record. The least attractive is the one who is overvalued, being paid a high premium with a high salary and a bonus to boot but not really doing much to earn them. In other words, low pay for high performance and potential is good, and the reverse is bad. But this can't be carried too far—we don't want to lose people we need to keep," he added.

Column B was labelled "Player Life Cycle Maturity Level." "This column is where we rate the players according to their remaining playing life," Smothers explained. "For a major league team like the Millers, the statistics show that the average playing life occurs between twenty-five and thirty-two years of age. Here again we rate each player on a scale of 1 to 4, with 4 being the players with the highest expected stream of income for the club—usually the ones with the longest remaining playing life."

Column C was "Five-Year Production Estimate." "This is an estimate of future productivity made by the coaches, managers, trainers, the statistics office, and the player personnel manager," said Smothers. "It's based on each player's playing statistics to date, history, scouting reports, overall health and physical condition, and motivation."

"And the total is the value of all three columns added up, right?" asked Bert.

"Right. The total is each player's rating of potential."

"But what about the differences between player positions?" Harry asked. "A designated hitter is different from pitcher, and both are different from a shortstop or first baseman."

"Good point," replied Smothers. "You have to construct a separate roster for each of the major categories of player. Make a pitcher roster, a relief pitcher roster, an infield roster, a DH roster, an outfield roster, and so forth. You rate each player against the *objectives* you set for him as a member of the team, and the objectives for a bullpen crew relief pitcher are certainly different from the ones for a second baseman. But the beauty of this potential chart is that it translates these differences into a common potential rating, which helps in trading, pulling people up from the minors, and salary negotiations."

"But doesn't performance on the field count, too?" Harry asked.

"Of course it does. That's the vertical line on the portfolio chart. That is where we use the statistics that every baseball writer and a lot of our fans keep track of. Every kid in Plains City knows who the .300 hitters are and who the twenty-game winners are. We have a lot of other statistics that the managers get regular reports on too. They show how hitters do in night games or against left-handers, what their RBI average is, and a slew of other facts. Somebody once said that baseball was a game for statisticians, and they were probably right. Along the left-hand side of our portfolio we use a management by objectives system to rate the performance of the players."

"Management by what?" said Bert.

"Management by objectives. Every player sits down with the coach for that position or subgroup—the pitching coach, the batting coach, and so forth—and works out a set of objectives for himself for the coming month. These objectives fall into three categories (see Figure 16).

"First, the player and coach and manager define what the regular statistical figures expected of the player should be. This includes percentage of hits, RBIs, slugging average, homers, and substats such as on-the-road, home games, night games, production against lefties, and the like. For the pitchers they set targets for walks, strikeouts, innings pitched per game, saves for relief pitchers, and so on. The figures they choose are based on past records and on coaching plans for improvement. Every player should know his own strengths and weaknesses and have a stretch objective in every area that counts.

"Each player should have an objective or two to solve problems in playing skill," Smothers went on, pointing to Level 2 on his chart. "When a hitter has a problem with lefties, he gets special coaching and extra batting practice against lefthanders. This category of objective focuses on the weaknesses in a player's skills. He should be working on his two or three most serious problems with the coaches at all times. The coaches should use these objectives to focus their time and attention for each player rather than fiddling away their time with general pep talks.

Figure 16. Player Performance Rating Against Objectives.

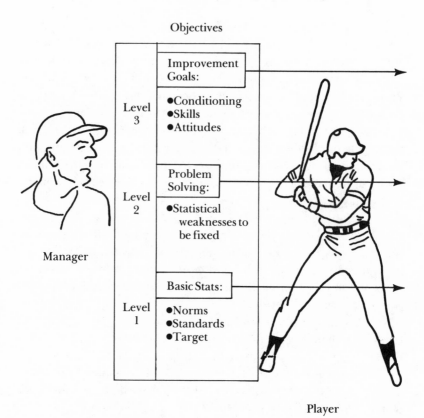

"Finally," Smothers said, "improvement goals are developmental goals to improve the players' skills, conditioning, or attitudes. They make the difference between ordinary workhorse players and stars. Every player at every level should have an improvement goal or two that he has worked out in a discussion with his individual coach or the manager. Fred Lynn spent a year on Nautilus, for example, building his overall strength, and he moved into a star category the following year with the Red Sox. That's achieving an improvement goal.

"Or maybe you have a younger player who is making more money than he ever made before in his life, but he can't handle prosperity. He needs a financial advisor or a good agent. He needs to work on an attitude problem, plus getting some sound financial counsel.

"Now you take the scores from the performance chart and rate the player as a 1, 2, or 3. The lowest rating is for the player who has only average statistics and also has some weaknesses and areas of conditioning, skills, and attitudes that could be improved. A Level 2 is a player who is competent in the stats and who is working hard with the coaches to eliminate some of the weaknesses that opposing teams might spot and take advantage of. The highest level is the player with good stats who has cleaned up most of his weaknesses and has the proper attitude, has highly refined skills, and stays in top condition."

Bert was enthused. "I like this idea! We get players who compile a good stat record one year and show up thirty pounds overweight at training camp the next. We should set some objectives with everybody in each area where they need improvement."

Smothers nodded in agreement. "Now," he said, "we combine the scores from the two charts; the potential rating goes along the horizontal scale, and the performance rating goes on the vertical scale. Then we put each player in one of the four squares of the portfolio. That gives you a good inventory of your human assets—your players."

"What do we do with the portfolio once we get it completed?" asked Harry.

Smothers produced still another chart (see Table 9). "You can use it for coaching, for one thing. Each coach of each subgroup such as pitcher, infielders, and the like can use it to work out his coaching plans with each player. Beyond that, you as owners and the manager, personnel director, and scouts can get together and decide on some *strategic target* for the team for the coming year and the coming five years, and the portfolio can help you achieve it. You can use the portfolio to plan your trades, for example. You build your stars, keep your workhorses happy and motivated, fix your problem players, and trade or cut your deadwood. You see, by the act of classifying each player, you also find a suitable strategy for managing him individually. No more relying on locker room pep talks for the whole team! Each player is managed according to his performance and potential. You can even use these ideas in negotiating new contracts. Pay your stars the limit, or even no limit—but remember that the player the press calls a star may not

Table 9. Aggregate Summary: Human Resources Portfolio Analysis—
Player Management, Hiring/Placement Policy Guide.

Investment Objective	Total Roster Analysis	
	Guideline Limits (low/high)%	Current Level
1. *Workhorse:* Maximize current job performance up to potential.	60–80	
2. *Problem player:* Remedy or cut or trade.	0–10	
3. *Star:* (a) Long-term growth is projected to be greater than current yield.	0–10	
(b) Current yield is predicted to remain high over the long term.	10–30	
(c) Maximize long-term growth by contract and perquisites, special treatment.	0–5	
4. *Deadwood:* Cut from present roster; trade if possible.	0–2	

be a star in your portfolio, because of limited potential. Stars have both performance and potential. Reporters shouldn't decide club strategy! Dig in your heels with workhorses when they get too greedy. The problem players are a special case; they have star potential, but they aren't performing, so you work hard and spend time and money to fix them up."

Harry was excited. "I like it, but I can see some problems. What about the superstar like a Hank Aaron or a Ted Williams as he gets older? Players like that cost us a bundle, you know."

"Sure," Smothers nodded. "They earn their high pay by being stars and drawing crowds at the gate. Their price attractiveness is related to their drawing ability at the turnstile. But if a star is thirty-six years old, his expected stream of income is shorter and his potential is lower than it was when he was younger."

"Won't there be exceptions?" asked Bert.

"Of course. For instance, Carl Yastremski played until he was forty, well beyond the average retirement age, and hit and fielded well right until he quit in 1983. His club got a bonus because Carl stayed in condition and kept improving to adjust for his age. In the end Carl was a beloved workhorse, a former star.

"Management can always allow for exceptions," Smothers went on. "For example, there might be times when you will want to take a chance on a problem player—like when Durocher put Dusty Rhodes into a World Series and he won the pennant with a big hit, even though Dusty was probably a big headache most of the time."

"I see," said Harry. "This is a tool for strategic management of the team as a business, not a simple guide to day-to-day management of game play."

"Right," Smothers answered. "Calling the plays, pulling a pitcher soon enough, or using the bench cleverly are operational and tactical decisions that depend on the baseball know-how of the manager in the dugout. This system is supposed to help you and the coaches build a dynasty, not win tomorrow's double-header. If you have a solid strategic plan, your percentage will improve— and that's how dynasties are built, not by a savvy manager on the bench."

"Would this apply to the front office personnel too?"

"Sure, but it would be harder, because you would have to figure out what performance and potential mean for the accountant, the lawyer, the player personnel director, and the scouting director. The same principles do apply, though. If you evaluate performance and potential for each person on the payroll, you will have a stronger front office."

Bert and Harry were grinning now.

"Professor, I think this system will work, and we want to give it a try," Harry declared happily. "Lots of owners like Tom Yawkey of the old Red Sox and George Steinbrenner of the Yankees seem to think that all you have to do is pay out millions for players and keep firing managers and you will automatically win pennants. I think I can see now what they miss most of the time. By the way, I own a dozen factories. Do you suppose this portfolio system would work with my factory managers or my sales managers?"

"Definitely, if you work at it."

At this point the club statistician, a greying codger who resembled a 185-pound hamster, woke up and began to show some animation.

"I think this is terrific, and I have just the ticket for measuring player performance along that left-hand line on your portfolio chart," be bubbled. "Have you ever head of SABR? That's the Society for American Baseball Research. It was founded by a guy named Bill James, who produces the *Annual Baseball Abstract*. James has the latest thing in statistics for measuring player performance and team performance."

"Tell us about it," said Bert.

"Well, since 1977, Bill James has developed five major sets of performance evaluation tools. One evaluates and analyzes hitters, the second evaluates pitchers, the third evaluates defense, the fourth evaluates player careers, and the fifth evaluates teams as a whole. Take hitters, for example. James has nine measures to evaluate hitters. These include runs created, runs created per game, offensive wins and losses, park adjustments, home/road, left-handed pitching and right-handed pitching breakdowns, isolated power, and the power/speed number."

"Sounds interesting," said Harry.

"Fascinating is the word," replied the hamster. "James added an 'e' to the acronym SABR and tagged 'metrics' on the end and calls his system 'Sabermetrics.' He sits in front of a Kaypro computer and turns out ratings on every player for every team on offense, defense, and pitching. He also rates the teams overall. His ratings provide us with some readymade standards of performance, set up by position."

"So we really don't have to develop all those stats, just records of our own players and team, right?" asked Bert.

"I think that's correct. Game score cards are the basic source. I plug each play into my desk computer—and presto! Performance evaluation!"

"Does Bill James have anything that's the equivalent of Smothers's analysis of potential?" asked Harry.

"Yes. He has what he calls VAM—'Value Approximation Method.' He estimates the life of a player to be twelve years. The age of the player is balanced against his performance-point-score rating. High performance for twelve years is higher potential than for one more year. This is a point scoring scheme that involves individual judgments. For example, a player who hits .250 gets one point, .273 two points, and so on. Similarly, a player gets points for games played, slugging percentage (extra bases), home run percentage, stolen bases, walks, and the like. Defensive players earn points for fielding average and specific defensive skills (double plays, for example). You find the common value of various players by converting them into points."

Smothers was pleased. "Tie his Sabermetrics to my portfolio and you'll have a dynamite management tool," he told Bert and Harry. "But I think my three-part system for rating potential is better than his.

"I agree," said Bert. "Anyway, the two of you make a winning team—and I'm sure you'll make the Millers a winning team, too!"

References

Ackoff, R., and Rivett, P. *A Manager's Guide to Operations Research*. New York: Wiley, 1963.

Adams, J. F., and others. *Labor Markets in the Rural South*. Atlanta: Georgia State University, 1977.

Agnello, R. J., and Hunt, J. W., Jr. "The Impact of a Part-Time Graduate Degree and Early-Career Earnings on Late-Career Earnings." *Journal of Human Resources*, 1976, *11* (2), 209–218.

Albers, A. F. "How (and How Not) to Approach Job Enrichment." *Personnel Journal*, 1979, *58* (12), 837–841.

Albers, A. F. "Making Job Enrichment Pay-Off." *Supervisory Management*, 1982, *27* (1).

Albers, A. F., and Blumbers, M. "Teams Versus Individual Approaches to Job Enrichment." *Personnel*, 1981, *58* (1).

Alfred, R. L. "Socioeconomic Impact of Two-Year Colleges." *Junior College Resource Review*, 1980.

America, R. F., and Anderson, B. E. "Moving Ahead Black Managers in Business." *MBA: Master in Business Administration*, 1979, *12* (9), 40–42.

American College Testing Bureau. *The Effects of College Grades on Career Success.* Iowa City: American College Testing Bureau, 1962.

Anderson, R. C. "Learning in Discussions." Harvard Educational Review, 1959, *29*, 201–214.

Andrew, L. D., and Wellsfry, N. L. "Community College System Pays Its Way." *Community and Junior College Journal,* 1977, *47* (6), 28–31.

Antros, J. R., and Mellow, W. S. "The Youth Labor Market: A Dynamic Overview." In *Employment and Training Administration (DOL).* Washington, D.C.: U.S. Government Printing Office, 1978.

Apodaca, J. "Managing Our Human and Natural Resources: A Challenge for Higher Education." *National Association of Secondary School Principals Journal,* 1978, *29* (10), 17–19.

"At Potlatch, Nothing Happens Without a Plan." *Business Week,* Nov. 10, 1975, pp. 129–134.

Bartol, K. M., Anderson, C. R., and Schneier, C. E. "Sex and Ethnic Effects on Motivation to Manage Among College Business Students." *Journal of Applied Psychology,* 1981, *66* (1), 40–44.

Beaudine, F. R. "Making the Most of Now." *Nation's Business,* 1980, *68* (11).

Beaudine, F. R. "The Falling Superstar." *Nation's Business,* 1981, *69* (9), 64–65.

Becker, S. *Human Capital.* New York: Columbia University Press, 1964.

Beckhard, R. "The Changing Shape of Managing Development." *Journal of Management Development,* 1982, *1* (1), 51–62.

Bellante, D. "Changes in the Migration of Human Capital and the Southern 'Brain Drain.'" *The Journal of Behavioral-Economics,* 1978a, *7* (1), 53–77.

Bellante, D. "Education and Changes in North-South Flow of Human Capital: 1955–70." *Proceedings of American Statistical Association,* August 1978b, pp. 244–249.

Bellows, R., Gilson, R., and Odiorne, G. *Executive Skills.* Englewood Cliffs, N.J.: Prentice-Hall, 1963.

Benford, R. J., and others. "Training for Results." *Personnel,* 1979, *56* (3), 17–24.

Berle, A., and Means, G. *The Modern Corporation and Private Property.* New York: Macmillan, 1932.

Bills, D. B., and others. *Trends in Inequality of Educational Opportunity in Brazil: A Test of Two Competing Theories.* Madison: University of Wisconsin Press, 1978.

Blake, R. R., Mouton, J., and Bidwell, A. "The Managerial Grid: A Comparison of Eight Theories of Management." *Advanced Management Journal,* 1962, *27,* 5.

Blume, M. E. "On the Assessment of Risk." *Journal of Finance,* March 1971.

Bolweg, J. F. "Quality of Work Life: An Industrial Relations Perspective." *Proceedings* (I.R.R.A.), 1980.

Bowen, W., and Feregan, A. *The Economics of Labor Force Participation.* Princeton, N.J.: Princeton University Press, 1969.

Bowles, S., and Gintis, H. "The Problem with Human Capital Theory—A Marxian Critique." *The American Economic Review,* 1975, *65* (2), 74-82.

Bowman, M. J., and others. *Three Essays in the Economics of Education.* Stockholm: National Swedish Board of Universities and Colleges, 1978.

Boylen, M. E. "Career Development Through Employee Training." *Public Relations Journal,* 1980, *36* (3).

Braden, R. "Processing Health Insurance Claims." *Journal of Systems Management,* 1978, *29* (10), 28-33.

Briloff, A. S. *Unaccountable Accounting.* New York: Harper & Row, 1972.

Buckley, S. "Giving Managers New Tools." *New York Times,* August 31, 1983.

Burnham, J. *The Managerial Revolution.* Bloomington: Indiana University Press, 1960.

Butterfield, A. D., and Powell, G. "The Good Manager: Masculine or Androgynous?" Academy of Management Journal, 1979, *22* (2), 395-403.

Carnazza, J. *Succession/Replacement Planning.* New York: Center for Research in Career Development, Columbia University, 1978.

Caskey, C. *Balance in Management.* Ann Arbor, Mich.: Masterco, 1968.

Catsiapis, G., and Robinson, C. "The Theory of the Family and Intergenerational Mobility." *Journal of Human Resources*, 1981, *16* (1), 106-116.

Cavanaugh, H. W. "The Power of Positive Discipline." *Electrical World*, October 1982.

Chandler, A. D. *The Visible Hand: The Managerial Revolution in American Business.* Cambridge: Harvard University, Belknap Press, 1977.

Chiplin, B., and Sloan, P. J. "Sexual Discrimination in the Labor Market." *British Journal of Industrial Relations*, 1974, *12* (3), 371-402.

Cleveland, H. *The Future Executive.* New York: Harper & Row, 1972.

Colberg, M. R. "Age-Human Capital Profiles for Southern Men." *Review of Business and Economics Research*, Winter 1975-76, *11* (2), 63-73.

Connell, J. J. "Managing the Electronic Office." *Nation's Business*, 1982, *70* (2), 59-60.

Conroy, W. G., Jr. "The Valiant 77 Million." *Peabody Journal of Education*, 1980, *58* (1), 7-14.

Cooper, A. C., and Bruno, A. V. "Predicting Performance in New High Technology Firms." *Proceedings of Academy of Management*, August 1975, 426-428.

Correa, H. *The Economics of Human Resources.* Amsterdam: North Holland, 1963.

Cron, R. L. *Assuring Customer Satisfaction.* New York: Van Nostrand Reinhold, 1974.

Crosswell, M. *Basic Human Needs: A Development Planning Approach.* Washington, D.C.: Agency for International Development, 1979.

Cullin, J. G., and others. "Cost Effectiveness: A Model for Assessing the Training Investment." *Training and Development Journal*, 1978, *32* (1), 24-29.

Curtis, T. D., and Campbell, J. M., Jr. "Investment in Graduate Human Capital: An Evaluation of the Rate of Return Approach." *Review of Business and Economic Research*, 1978, *14* (1), 74-89.

Dahl, H. L., Jr. "Measuring the ROI." *Management Review*, 1979, *68* (1), 44-50.

Davis, L. E. *Dictionary of Banking and Finance.* Totowa, N.J.: Rowman & Littlefield, 1978.

Davis, R. C. *Fundamentals of Top Management.* Harper & Row, 1951.

Daymont, T. M. *Pay Premiums for Economic Sector and Race: A Decomposition.* Columbus: Center for Human Resource Research, Ohio State University, 1980.

Deavers, K. L., and Brown, D. L. *Social and Economic Trends in Rural America.* Washington, D.C.: Economics, Statistics, and Cooperatives Service, 1982.

Demetriades, E. I., and Psacharopoulos, G. "Education and Pay Structure in Cyprus." *International Labor Review,* 1979, 118 (1), 103-111.

DeMoura, C. "Vocational Education and the Training of Industrial Labor in Brazil." *International Labor Review,* 1979, *118* (5), 617-629.

Despres, D. "The Management Exercise—A Practical Training Method." *Journal of European Industrial Training,* 1982, *6* (4), 12-15.

DeTray, D. *Child Schooling and Family Size: An Economic Analysis.* Bethesda, Md.: National Institute of Child Health and Human Development, 1981.

"Developing Managers for Improved Performance." In American Management Association Extension Institute, *Management by Objectives* (script for audio cassette course). New York: American Management Association Extension Institute, 1975.

Dittman, D. A., Juris, H. A., and Revsine, L. "On the Existence of Unrecorded Human Assets: An Economic Perspective." *Journal of Accounting Research,* 1976, *14* (1), 49-65.

Donnelly, R. M. "How to Manage the MBA." *SAM Advanced Management Journal,* 1982, *47* (3), 43-51.

Dowdall, G. W. "Intermetropolitan Differences in Family Income Inequality: An Ecological Analysis of Total White and Nonwhite Patterns in 1960." *Sociology and Social Research,* 1977, *61* (2), 178-191.

Dresch, S. P., and Waldenberg, A. L. *Labor Market Incentives, Intellectual Competence and College Attendance.* Washington, D.C.: National Institute of Education, 1978.

Drucker, P. *The New Society.* New York: Harper & Row, 1950.

Drucker, P. *The Practice of Management.* New York: Harper & Row, 1954.

Drucker, P. *Management, Tasks, Responsibilities, Practices.* New York: Harper & Row, 1973.

Dulewicz, V. "The Application of Assessment Centres." *Personnel Management,* 1982, *14* (9), 32–35.

Eddy, B., and Kellow, J. "Training Facilities." *Training and Development Journal,* 1977, *31* (5), 32–36.

Elton, E., and Bruber, M. *Modern Portfolio Theory and Investment Analysis.* New York: Wiley, 1981.

Erikson, E. *Insight and Responsibility.* New York: Norton, 1969.

Fama, E. *Foundations of Finance.* New York: Basic Books, 1976.

Fayol, H. *Industrial and General Administration.* London: Pitman, 1930.

Federal Reserve Bank of Boston. *Introducing Economics.* Medford, Mass.: Tufts University Press, 1979.

Field, H., and Holley, W. "The Relationship of Performance Appraisal Characteristics to Verdicts in Selected Employment Discrimination Cases." *Academy of Management Journal,* 1982, *25* (2), 128.

Filley, A., and House, R. *Managerial Process and Organization Behavior.* Glenview, Ill.: Scott, Foresman, 1971.

Finn, D. *The Corporate Oligarch.* New York: Simon & Schuster, 1969.

Flamholz, E., and Lacey, S. *Personnel, Human Capital Theory, and Human Resources Accounting,* Monograph 27. Los Angeles: University of Southern California, 1981.

Fleischman, E., and Harris, E. *Leadership and Supervision in Industry.* Columbus: Bureau of Educational Research, Ohio State University, 1955.

Fogel, W. "Occupational Earnings: Market and Institutional Influences." *Industrial and Labor Relations Review,* 1979, *33* (1), 24–35.

Franke, A. G., Harris, E. J., and Klein, A. J. "The Role of Personnel in Improving Production." *Personnel Administration,* 1982, *27* (3).

Freeman, R. B. "The Decline in the Economic Rewards to College Education." *Review of Economics and Statistics,* 1977, *59* (1), 18–29.

Freud, S. *The Problem of Anxiety.* New York: Norton, 1936.

Fulbright, J. W. *The Arrogance of Power.* New York: Random House, 1966.

Fulton, O., and others. "Higher Education and Manpower Planning." *Education Policy Bulletin,* 1980, *8* (1), 83–113.

Gaarder, R. "Organizational Development in Tanzania." *Journal of European Industrial Training,* 1982, *6* (1), 18–22.

Gant, C. R. "Economics of On-the-Job Training." In *Annotated Bibliography and Literature Review, 1974–1976.* Lowry Air Force Base, Colo.: 1977.

Garfinkel, I., and Haveman, R. "Earning Capacity, Economic Status, and Poverty." *Journal of Human Resources,* 1977, *12* (1), 49–70.

Gay, R. M., and Albrecht, M. J. "Specialty Training and the Performance of First-Term Enlisted Personnel: A Report." Santa Monica, Calif.: Rand Corp., 1979.

Gellerman, S. *Management by Motivation.* New York: AMACOM, 1968.

Gill, R. W. T. "A Trainability Concept for Management Potential and an Empirical Study of Its Relationship with Intelligence for Two Managerial Skills." *Journal of Occupational Psychology,* 1982, *55* (2), 139–147.

Gilroy, C. L. "Investment in Human Capital and Black-White Unemployment." *Monthly Labor Review,* 1975, *98* (7), 13–21.

Godin, V. B. "The Dollars and Sense of Simulation." *Decision Sciences,* 1976, *7* (2), 331–342.

Goffman, E. *The Presentation of Self in Everyday Life.* New York: Doubleday, 1959.

Gordon, P. J. "Transcend the Current Debate on Administrative Theory." *Academy of Management Journal,* 1963, *6* (4).

Gordon, P. J., and Meredith, P. H. "Creating and Using a Model to Monitor Managerial Talent." *Business Horizons,* 1982, *25* (1), 52–61.

Greenfield, S. *The Human Capital Model and American Youths: The Roles of Schooling, Experience and Functional Literacy.* Austin, Texas: Southwest Educational Development Laboratory, 1980.

Griffin, L. J. *On Estimating the Economic Value of Schooling and Experience: Some Issues in Conceptualization and Measurement.* Washington, D.C.: National Institute of Education, 1977.

Griliches, Z., and Freeman, R. *Econometric Investigations of Determinants and Returns to Schooling, Training, and Experience.* Washington, D.C.: National Institute of Education, 1977.

Hanson, M. C. "Career/Life Planning Workshops: Are They Working?" *Training and Development Journal,* 1982, *36* (2), 78.

Harbison, F., and Myers, C. A. *Education, Manpower and Economic Growth.* New York: McGraw-Hill, 1964.

Hardin, E. "The Applicability of Human Capital Variables to a Specialized and Troublesome Work Force Category." *Proceedings of American Statistical Association,* August 1975, pp. 330–335.

Harris, J. K., and Krogstad, J. L. "A Profile and Index of the CMA Examination." *Accounting Review,* 1976, *51* (3), 637–641.

Haupt, A., and Kane, T. *Population Dynamics.* Washington, D.C.: Population Reference Bureau, 1979.

Hayes, J. "The Secret of Successful Management." *The Director,* 1983, *35* (8), 76.

Hedstrom, J. E. *Selective Bibliography in Economics Resources.* Washington, D.C.: National Institute of Education, 1978.

Henderson, B. *The Experience Curve.* Boston: Boston Consulting Group, 1974.

Hendricks, J. A. "The Impact of Human Resource Accounting Information on Stock Investment Decisions." *Accounting Review,* 1976, *51* (2), 292–301.

Herzberg, F. *Work and the Nature of Man.* Cleveland: Globe, 1966.

Herzberg, F. "Productivity Begins with the Individual." *Industry Week,* 1981, *211* (5).

Hodgson, R. C. "Nothing Seems to Have Taken Hold." *Business Quarterly,* Oct. 1982.

Hoffer, E. *The Ordeal of Change.* New York: Harper & Row, 1951.

Hoffman, F. O. "Is Management Development Doing the Job?" *Training and Development Journal,* 1983, *37* (1), 34–39.

Hollingshead, A. B., and Redlich, F. R. *Social Class and Mental Illness.* New York: Wiley, 1958.

House, R. *Managerial Process and Organization Behavior.* Glenview, Ill.: Scott, Foresman, 1969.

"How Texaco Turns Management Potential into Performance." *Management Review*, 1978, *67* (11), 49-50.

Howard, A., and Wilson, J. A. "Leadership in a Declining Work Ethic." *California Management Review*, 1982, *24* (4), 33-46.

Huffman, W. E. "Black-White Human Capital Differences: Impact on Agricultural Productivity in the U.S. South." *American Economic Review*, 1981, *71* (1), 94-107.

Husband, R. "What Do College Grades Predict?" *Fortune*, June 1957, pp. 157-158.

Jackson, C. "Education Cuts—Economic Consequences." *Forum for the Discussion of New Trends in Education*, 1981, *23* (3), 60-63.

Jaggi, B. "Human Resources Are Assets." *Management Accounting*, 1976, *57* (8), 41-42.

Jennings, E. E. *The Executive in Crisis*. New York: McGraw-Hill, 1965.

Jennings, E. E. *The Mobile Manager*. Ann Arbor: Bureau of Industrial Relations, University of Michigan, 1965.

Jewkes, J., Sawers, D., and Stillerman, R. *The Sources of Invention*. New York: Norton, 1969.

"Job Training Funds Ordered." *New York Times*, August 15, 1983.

Johnson, D. H., Jr. "Mobility in the Virgin Islands: An Introduction to a Microstate Study." Paper presented at Caribbean Studies Association Conference, Virgin Islands, May 1981.

Johnson, T. "Time in School: The Case of the Prudent Patron." *American Economic Review*, 1978, *68* (5), 862-872.

Joint Economic Committee. *Human Resources and Demographics: Characteristics of People and Policy*. Washington, D.C.: Joint Economic Committee, 1981.

Jones, E. B., and Long, J. E. "Part-Week Work and Human Capital Investment by Married Women." *Journal of Human Resources*, 1979, *14* (4), 563-578.

Jones, J. "Humanistic Numbers." In L. Baird (Ed.), *Performance Appraisal Source Book*. Amherst, Mass: Human Resource Development Press, 1983.

Jones, J. R. "Investing in Human Capital." *Vocational Education*, 1981, *56* (1), 60-62.

Journal of the Operational Research Society, 1979, *30* (1), 33-41.

Juran, J. *Managerial Breakthrough*. New York: McGraw-Hill, 1961.

Kafka, V. N. "Every Employee a Winner." *Training and Development Journal*, 1981, *35* (6), 28.

Kastner, H. H., Jr. "Cost/Benefit Analysis of Community College Education." *Community College Review*, 1977, *4* (3), 14–26.

Kaye, B. "Career Development Puts Training in Its Place." *Personnel Journal*, 1983, *62* (2), 55.

Kelly, J. "The Costs of Job Redesign." *Industrial Relations Journal*, 1980, *11* (3).

Kemp, N., Clegg, C., and Wall, T. D. "Job Redesign," *Employee Relations*, 1980, *2* (5).

King, A. G. "A Note on Lucas: A Critique of the Human Capital Model." *Journal of Human Resources*, 1979, *14* (1), 130–135.

King, R. H. *The Labor Market Consequences of Dropping Out of High School*. Washington, D.C.: Employment and Training Administration, 1979.

King, R. H. "Some Further Evidence on the Rate of Return to Schooling and the Business Cycle." *Journal of Human Resources, 1980, 15* (2), 264.

Kocher, J. E., and Fleisher, B. "A Bibliography on Rural Development in Tanzania." East Lansing: Department of Agricultural Economics, Michigan State University, 1979.

Korno, S. "Effect of Human Resources Planning upon Corporate Profitability." Unpublished doctoral dissertation, University of Massachusetts at Amherst, 1983.

Latham, G., and Yukl, G. "A Review of Research on the Application of Goal Setting in Organizations." *Academy of Management Journal*, 1975, *18*, 824–845.

Lazer, R. I., and Wikstrom, W. *Appraising Management Performance*. Washington, D.C.: The Conference Board, 1977.

Lee, L. "How to Achieve and Maintain White Collar Productivity." *Journal of Systems Management*, 1981, *31* (3).

Levin, H. M. *Assessing the Equalization Potential of Education*. Washington, D.C.: National Institute of Education, 1979.

Levinson, H. *The Exceptional Executive*. Cambridge, Mass.: Harvard University Press, 1968.

Lewis, D. *The Public Image of Henry Ford*. Detroit, Mich.: Wayne State University Press, 1976.

Lewis, R., and Stewart, R. *The Managers*. New York: Mentor Books, 1961.

Liberman, J. "Human Capital and the Financial Capital Market." *Journal of Business,* 1980, *53* (2), 165–191.

Liebing, H. E. *The Corporation in the American Economy.* New York: Quadrangle Books, 1970.

Likert, R. *New Patterns in Management.* New York: McGraw-Hill, 1961.

Lindsay, C. M. "More Real Returns to Medical Education." *Journal of Human Resources,* 1976, *11* (1), 127–130.

Link, C. R., and Ratledge, E. C. "Social Returns to Quantity and Quality of Education." *Journal of Human Resources,* 1975, *10* (1), 78–79.

Linthicum, D. S. *Economic Impacts of Maryland Community Colleges: A Closer Look.* Annapolis: Maryland State Board for Community Colleges, 1979.

Lipsett, L. "How to Stop Losing Your Best Workers." *Administrative Management,* 1980, *41* (2), 34.

Lipton, M. "An Unmentionable Personnel Problem." *Personnel,* 1979, *56,* 58–65.

Livingston, J. S. "New Trends in Applied Management Development." *Training and Development Journal,* 1983, *37* (1), 14–16.

Locke, E. "Employee Motivation: A Discussion." *Contemporary Business,* 1982, *11* (2).

Long, J. E. "AMS Foundation Launches Far-Reaching Study." *Management World,* 1982, *11* (6), 19–20.

Lubben, G., Thompson, D., and Klasson, C. "Performance Appraisal, the Legal Implications of Title VIII." *Personnel,* 1980, *57.*

Lucas, R. E. B. "Is There a Human Capital Approach to Income Inequality?" *Journal of Human Resources,* 1977, *12* (3), 387–395.

McClelland, D. C., and Winter, D. *Motivation and Economic Achievement.* New York: Free Press, 1971.

Maccoby, M. *The Gamesman, The New Corporate Leaders.* New York: Simon & Schuster, 1977.

McGee, J. P. "Job Design Technology in DuPont to Improve Productivity and Job Satisfaction." *AIIE Proceedings,* Spring 1981.

McGeveran, E. D. "Mediation at the Telephone Company." *Wharton Magazine,* 1981, *6* (1).

McGregor, D. *The Human Side of Enterprise.* New York: McGraw-Hill, 1961.

Machlup, F. *The Production and Distribution of Knowledge in the U.S.* Princeton, N.J.: Princeton University Press, 1962.

McKenzie, R. B. *The Political Economy of the Educational Process.* Studies in Public Choice, Vol. 2. Boston: Martinus Nijoff, 1979.

McNamara, W. "Retraining of Industrial Personnel." *Personnel Psychology,* 1963, *16* (3).

Mager, R. *Defining Educational Objectives.* Belmont, Calif.: Fearon-Pitman, 1972.

Makin, A., and Psacharopoulos, G. "Schooling and Income Distribution." *The Review of Economics and Statistics,* 1976, *58* (2), 332–338.

Mangum, G. *The Emergence of Manpower Policy.* New York: Holt, Rinehart and Winston, 1969.

Mangum, G., and Glenn, L. *Employing the Disadvantaged in the Federal Civil Service.* Ann Arbor: Institute of Industrial and Labor Relations, University of Michigan and Wayne State, 1969.

Mansfield, B. "The Supervisor's Share of Job Enrichment." *Personnel Management,* 1980, 12 (4).

Markowitz, H. "Portfolio Selection." *Journal of Finance,* March 1952, *12.*

Maslow, A. *Motivation and Personality.* New York: Harper and Row, 1954.

Mason, E. S. (Ed.). *The Corporation in Modern Society.* Cambridge: Harvard University Press, 1960.

Mennemeyer, S. T. "Really Great Returns to Medical Education." *Journal of Human Resources,* 1978, *13* (1), 75–90.

Merton, R. *Social Theory and Social Structure.* New York: Free Press, 1957.

Messinger, C. "My Managers Are Buying Me Out." *Inc.,* 1981, *3* (4), 61–62.

Meyer, W. G. *Vocational Education and the Nation's Economy.* Washington, D.C.: American Vocational Association, 1980.

Milbourn, G. "A Primer on Implementing Job Redesigns." *Supervisory Management,* 1981, *26* (1), 10.

Mills, C. W. *The Power Elite.* New York: Oxford University Press, 1956.

Miner, J. B. *The Management of Ineffective Performance.* New York: McGraw-Hill, 1963.

Moberg, D. J. "Job Enrichment Through Symbol Management." *California Management Review,* 1981, *24* (2).

Molz, R. "Managing Underground Executives." *Business Horizons,* 1984.

Moore, G. A. "Equity Effects of Higher Education Finance and Tuition Grants in New York State." *Journal of Human Resources,* 1978, *13* (4), 482–501.

Morse, W. J. "Estimating the Human Capital Associated with an Organization." *Accounting and Business Research,* 1975, *5* (21), 48–56.

Morton, S. D., Gustafson, D. P., and Foster, C. E. "Assessment for Management Potential: Scale Design and Development, Training Effects and Rater/Ratee Sex Effects." *Academy of Management Journal,* 1977, *20* (1), 117–131.

Mundale, S. "New Work Systems." *Training,* 1981, *18* (4), 27.

Nadler, L., and Nadler, Z. "China: An HRD Study Tour." *Training and Development Journal,* 1982, *36* (3), 50–60.

National Academy of Education. *Economic Dimensions of Education.* Washington, D.C.: National Academy of Education, 1980.

National Center for Productivity and Quality of Working Life. *Productivity in the Changing World of the 1980's: Final Report.* Houston: National Center for Productivity and Quality of Working Life, 1979.

Neuman, S., and Segev, E. "Human Capital and Risk Management—A Proposal for a New Insurance Product." *Journal of Risk and Insurance,* 1978a, *45* (2), 344–352.

Neuman, S., and Segev, E. "Human Resources and Corporate Risk Management." *Personnel Journal,* 1978b, *57* (2), 76–79.

Newland, K. "International Migration: The Search for Work." Worldwatch Institute, Paper 33. Washington, D.C.: Worldwatch Institute, 1979.

Nichols, M. "Distinguishing Between Education and Training." *Training,* 1982, *14* (5).

Niehouse, D. L. "Breaking the Promotion Barrier with Flexible Leadership." *Business,* 1982, *32* (4), 22–26.

Niehouse, D. L. "How to Measure Your Leadership Potential." *Supervisory Management,* 1983, *28* (1), 2–7.

Nitzan, S., and Paroush, J. "Investment in Human Capital and Social Self-Protection Under Uncertainty." *International Economic Review,* 1980, *21* (3), 547–557.

Nollen, S. D. "What Is Happening to Flex-time?" *Across the Board,* 1980, *17* (4).

Norrblom, E. *An Assessment of the Available Evidence on the Returns to Military Training.* Santa Monica, Calif., and Washington, D.C.: Rand Corp. Advanced Research Projects Agency, 1977.

Norton, S. D., and Gustafson, D. P. "Assessment of Management Potential: Scale Design, Training Effects, and Rater/Ratee Sex Effects." *Proceedings of Academy of Management,* 1975, pp. 237–239.

Oaxaca, R. L. "On the Use of Occupational Statistics." Paper presented at Census Bureau Conference, April 1978.

O'Connor, E., and Barrett, G. V. "Informational Cues and Individual Differences as Determinants of Subjective Receptors of Task Enrichment." *Academy of Management Journal,* 1980, *23* (4), 250.

Odiorne, G. S. *Management Decisions by Objectives.* Englewood Cliffs, N.J.: Prentice-Hall, 1969.

Odiorne, G. S. *Personnel Administration by Objectives.* Homewood, Ill.: Irwin, 1972.

Odiorne, G. S. "Ten Technologies of Training." *Training and Development Journal,* May 1975.

Odiorne, G. S. "The Executive Under Siege." *Management Review,* May 1978.

Odiorne, G. S. "Clearing Corporate Deadwood." *Management Review,* June 1979.

Odiorne, G. S. "How to Avoid Being Fired." *Management,* June 1980a.

Odiorne, G. S. *The Portfolio Approach to Human Resources.* Westfield, Mass.: MBO, Inc., 1980b.

Odiorne, G. S. "Training to Be Ready for the Nineties." *Training and Development Journal,* December 1980c.

Odiorne, G. S. *MBO II: A System of Managerial Leadership for the Eighties.* Belmont, Calif.: Fearon-Pitman, 1981a.

Odiorne, G. S. "Strategic Planning: Challenging New Role for Corporate Staff." *Business*, May-June 1981b.

Odiorne, G. S. "Strategic Planning: New Product for Staff Departments." *Business*, May-June 1982.

Odiorne, G. S., and Haan, A. *Effective College Recruiting*. Ann Arbor: Bureau of Industrial Relations, University of Michigan, 1961.

Odiorne, G., Michael, S., and Carlisle, A. *Priorities of CEO's*. Unpublished manuscript, 1983.

Ouchi, W. *Theory Z*. New York: Avon, 1981.

Packard, V. *The Pyramid Climbers*. New York: McGraw-Hill, 1962.

Passmore, D. L., and others. "Economics of Training." *Journal of Industrial Teacher Education*, 1978, *15* (4), 66-77.

Peter, L., and Hull, R. *The Peter Principle*. New York: Morrow, 1969.

Peters, T., and Waterman, R. H. *In Search of Excellence.* New York: Harper & Row, 1982.

Philippon, D. J. "Monetary Returns to Nonuniversity Health Personnel Training in Saskatchewan." *Journal of Education Finance*, 1980, *6* (1), 77-93.

Polachek, S. W. "Sex Differences in College Major." *Industrial and Labor Relations Review*, 1978, *31* (4), 498-508.

Presthus, R. *The Organization Society*. New York: Knopf, 1962.

"Productivity: College and Universities." *The Review of Economics and Statistics*, 1976, *58* (3), 326-331.

Puett, J. F., Jr., and Roman, D. D. "The Human Resource Asset." *Management International Review*, 1976, *16* (2), 47-60.

Pye, G. "Gauging the Default Premium." *Financial Analysis Journal*, Jan.-Feb. 1974, p. 31.

Pyle, R. "Corporate Fitness Programs: How Do They Shape Up?" *Personnel*, 1979, *56*, 58-67.

Pyle, W. C. "Accounting for Your People." *Innovation*, October 1970a, p. 40.

Pyle, W. C. "Human Resources Accounting." *Financial Analysis Journal*, Sept.-Oct. 1970b.

Quattrociocchi, S. M. "Education, Employment and Income: The Financial Rewards of General Education and Vocational Education." *Lifelong Learning: The Adult Years*, 1980, *3* (10), 8-9, 26-27.

Quible, Z. K. "Solutions to the Productivity Problem." *Management World*, 1981, *10* (12).

Quintero, R. G., and Shaw, J. C. "What Is Vital to Learn About an Acquisition Candidate." *Management Focus*, 1981, *28* (6), 28-34.

Rank, O. *Will Therapy*. New York: Knopf, 1945.

Raymond, R. D., and Sensowitz, M. "Physicians' Assistants: Is There a Return to Training?" *Industrial Relations*, 1976, *15* (3), 357-358.

Read, W. "Job Enrichment." *Cost and Management*, 1983, *57* (2).

Richard, S. F. "Optimal Consumption, Portfolio and Life Insurance Rules for an Uncertain Lived Individual in a Continuous Time Model." *Journal of Financial Economics*, 1975, *2* (2), 187-203.

Ricker, E. W. "Economic Thought and Educational Policy Making: An Historical Perspective." *Journal of Educational Thought*, 1980, *14* (3), 68-86.

Ritzen, J. M., and Winkler, D. R. *On the Optimal Allocation of Resources in the Production of Human Capital*. Unpublished paper, 1979.

Roethlisberger, F. J., and Dickson, W. J. *Management and the Worker*. Cambridge: Harvard University Press, 1939.

Roham, T. M. "A Job Enrichment Experiment Backfires," *Industry Week*, 1980, *204* (2).

Romano, M. B. "Goodwill . . . A Dilemma," *Management Accounting*, 1975, *57* (1), 39-44.

Roos, P. A. *Sexual Stratification in the Workplace: Male-Female Differences in Economic Returns to Occupation*. Rockville, Md.: National Institute of Mental Health, 1979.

Rorke, C. H. "On the Portfolio Effects of Nonmarketable Assets: Government Transfers and Human Capital Payments." *Journal of Financial and Quantitative Analysis*, 1979, *14* (2), 167-177.

Rosen, E. "The Executive Personality," *Personnel*, Jan.-Feb. 1959.

Roy, A., Falomir, E. E., and Lasdon, L. "An Optimization-Based Decision Support System for a Product Mix." *Interfaces*, 1982, *12* (2), 26-33.

Rummler, G. "Seek Hidden Sources of Poor Performance." *Impact,* June 22, 1983.

Sager, L. B., and Kipling, R. L. "Alchemy of Career Changes." *Business Horizons,* 1980, *23* (4).

Sandell, S. H., and Shapiro, D. "Work Expectation, Human Capital Accumulation, and the Wages of Young Women." *Journal of Human Resources,* 1980, *15* (3), 335–353.

Schacter, B., and Walker, B. "Refurbishing the Workhouse." *Executive,* 1980, *22* (10).

Scheffler, R. M. "Reply to Professors Raymond and Sensowitz: Physicians' Assistant: Is There a Return to Training?" *Industrial Relations,* 1976, *15* (3), 359.

Scheman, L. R. "Management in International Organization: Is There Order in World Order?" *International Review of Administrative Sciences,* 1981, *47* (1), 15–26.

Schmookler, J. *Invention and Economic Growth.* Cambridge: Harvard University Press, 1966.

Schneir, C., and Beatty, R. "Developing Behaviorally Anchored Rating Scales." *Personnel Administrator,* Aug. 1979.

Schoeffler, S. *Nine Basic Findings on Business Strategy.* Cambridge, Mass.: Strategic Planning Institute, 1977.

Schultz, T. W. *Economic Analysis of Investment in Education.* Washington, D.C.: National Institute of Education, 1978.

Schultz, T. W. "Knowledge Is Power in Agriculture." *Challenge,* 1981, *24,* (4), 4–12.

Schumpeter, J. *Capitalism, Socialism and Democracy.* New York: Harper & Row, 1937.

Sharpe, W. "A Simplified Model for Portfolio Analysis." *Management Science,* Jan. 1963.

Sharpe, W. *Investments.* Englewood Cliffs, N.J.: Prentice-Hall, 1978.

Shaw, J. B. "An Information Processing Approach to the Study of Job Design." *Academy of Management Review,* 1980, *5* (1).

Sinclair, M. D. "Introducing Work Experience Programs in Third World Schools." *Prospects: Quarterly Review of Education,* 1977, *7* (3), 362–378.

Skinner, B. F. *Beyond Freedom and Dignity.* New York: Knopf, 1971.

Sloan, A. *My Years with General Motors*. New York: Doubleday, 1964.

Sloan, F. A. "Real Returns to Medical Education: A Comment." *Journal of Human Resources*, 1976, *11* (1).

Smith, H. R. "The Uphill Struggle for Job Enrichment." *California Management Review*, 1981, *23* (4).

Sobel, R. *The Entrepreneurs*. New York: Weybright and Talley, 1974.

Sorensen, E. "The Application of OD Techniques." *Armed Forces Controller*, 1982, *27* (1).

Sotherden, S., and others. "The Economic Impact of Mohawk Valley Community College upon Oneida County." Utica, N.Y.: Mohawk Valley Community College, 1979.

Stone, D. C. "Innovative Organizations Require Innovative Managers." *Public Administration Review*, 1981, *41* (5), 507–513.

Striner, H. E. "The Reindustrialization of the United States: Implications For Vocational Education Research and Development." National Center for Research in Vocational Education, Paper No. 71. Columbus, Ohio: National Center for Research in Vocational Education, Ohio State University, 1981.

Sufrin, S. "How Moral Can a Business Be?" *The Christian Century*, March 2, 1983.

Sullivan, D. J. "Improving Productivity in the Work Force: Implications for Research." National Center for Research in Vocational Education, Paper No. 72. Columbus, Ohio: National Center for Research in Vocational Education, Ohio State University, 1981.

Suzuki, N. "Transfer of American Business Education: International Business Educational Product Life Cycle." *American Association of Collegiate Schools of Business Bulletin*, 1980, *15* (3), 24–41.

Tavernier, G. "Getting Employees to Analyze Their Ambitions." *International Management*, 1980, *35* (6).

Taylor, F. W. *The Principles of Scientific Management*. New York: Harper & Row, 1911.

Thackray, J. "The New Organization Man." *Management Today*, Sept. 1981.

Tinbergen, J. *Econometric Models of Education*. Paris: OECD, 1965.

Tobias, A. *Fire and Ice.* New York: Morrow, 1976.

Treese, M. "Know Your Organization." *Supervisory Management,* 1982, *27* (11), 19-22.

Tregoe, B., and Zimmerman, J. *Top Management Strategy.* New York: Simon & Schuster, 1980.

Trussell, P., and Dobbins, R. "Human Resource Accounting." *Managerial Finance,* 1976, *2* (1), 60-72.

Tusheman, M. L., and Scanlan, T. S. "Boundary Spanning Individuals: Their Role in Information Transfer." *Academy of Management Journal,* 1981, *24* (2).

Veblen, T. *The Theory of the Leisure Class.* New York: Macmillan, 1899.

Vecchio, R. P., and Sussman, M. "Staffing Sufficiency and Job Enrichment: Support for an Optimal Level Theory." *Journal of Occupational Behavior,* 1981, *2* (3).

Vetter, E. *Manpower Planning for High-Talent Personnel.* Ann Arbor, Bureau of Industrial Relations, University of Michigan, 1968.

Von Recum, H. "Education in the Affluent Society: Problems and Conflict." *International Review of Education,* 1981, *27* (1), 3-14.

Wachtel, P. "The Effect on Earnings of School and College Investment Expenditures." Unpublished manuscript, 1976.

Wacker, J. B., and Teas, R. K. "Starting Salaries of the College or Business Graduate: An Empirical Examination of the Static and Dynamic Effects of an Explanatory Model." *Review of Business and Economic Research,* 1979, *15* (1), 70-81.

Wall, T. D., and Clegg, C. W. "A Longitudinal Field Study of Group Work." *Journal of Occupational Behavior,* 1981, *2* (1).

Warner, W. L. "The Corporation Man." In E. S. Mason (Ed.), *The Corporation in Modern Society.* Cambridge: Harvard University Press, 1960.

Waters, M. "The Dilemma of the University in Jamaica." *New Universities Quarterly,* 1979, *33* (2), 232-236.

Weber, M. *The Protestant Ethic and the Spirit of Capitalism.* New York: Scribner's, 1958.

Weinshall, T. D. "Help for Chief Executives: The Outside Consultant." *California Management Review,* 1982, *24* (4), 47-58.

Weisbrod, M. R. "Some Reflections on OD's Identity Crisis." *Group and Organization Studies,* 1981, *6* (2).

Weiss, M. "Human Capital: Asset or Liability." *Financial Executive,* 1975, *43* (9), 30–39.

Welch, F. "Human Capital Theory: Education, Discrimination, and Life Cycles." *The American Economic Review,* 1975, *65* (2),63–73.

Weldon, D. J. "MBO: Success or Failure?" *Leadership and Organization Development Journal,* 1982, *3* (4), 2–8.

Wellar, B. S. "The Future of Small and Medium Sized Communities in the Prairie Region." Regina, Saskatchewan: Canadian Association of Geographers, 1977.

Wente, M. A. "Remaking the Management Mind." *Canadian Business,* 1983, *56* (1), 23–24, 82.

Westcott, R. "A Slide Rule to Assess the Personnel Position." *Personnel Journal,* 1982, *61* (5), 366–369.

Westrum, R., and others. "Technology and Social Change." In *Sociology.* Lafayette, Ind.: Purdue University Press, 1977.

Wharton, C. R., Jr. "Reflections on Black Intellectual Power." *Journal of Black Studies,* 1980, *10* (3), 279–294.

Whyte, W. F. (Ed.). *Money and Motivation.* New York: Harper & Row, 1955.

Whyte, W. H. *The Organization Man.* New York: Simon & Schuster, 1956.

Williams, J. M. "Risk, Human Capital, and the Investor's Portfolio." *Journal of Business,* 1978, *51* (1), 65–89.

Williams, J. M. "Uncertainty and the Accumulation of Human Capital over the Life Cycle." *Journal of Business,* 1979, *52* (4), 521–547.

Williamson, J. *Investments: New Analytic Techniques.* New York: Praeger, 1971.

Witmer, D. R. "Has the Golden Age of Higher Education Come to an Abrupt End?" Houston, Texas: Association for Institutional Research, 1978.

Wojtyla, H. L. "Bringing in the Sheaves: The Next Stock Market Cycle." *Financial Analysts Journal,* 1979, *35* (2), 49–52.

Wood, S. "The Study of Management in British Industrial Relations." *Industrial Relations Journal,* 1982, *13* (2), 51–61.

Woodward, N. "The Economic Evaluation of Apprentice Training." *Industrial Relations Journal,* 1975, *6* (1), 31–41.

World Bank. "Basic Education and Income Inequality in Brazil: The Long-term View." Paper No. 268. Washington, D.C.: World Bank, 1977.

Young, J. J. *Discrimination, Income, Human Capital Investment, and Asian-Americans.* San Francisco: R. and E. Research Associates, 1977.

Zemke, R. "Using Assessment Centers to Measure Management Potential." *Training,* 1980, *17* (3), 23–24.

Name Index